La Strada Bianca

Tuscany, the artist's story

Nino MacDonald

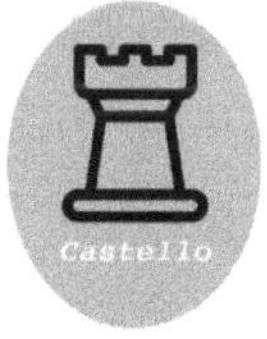

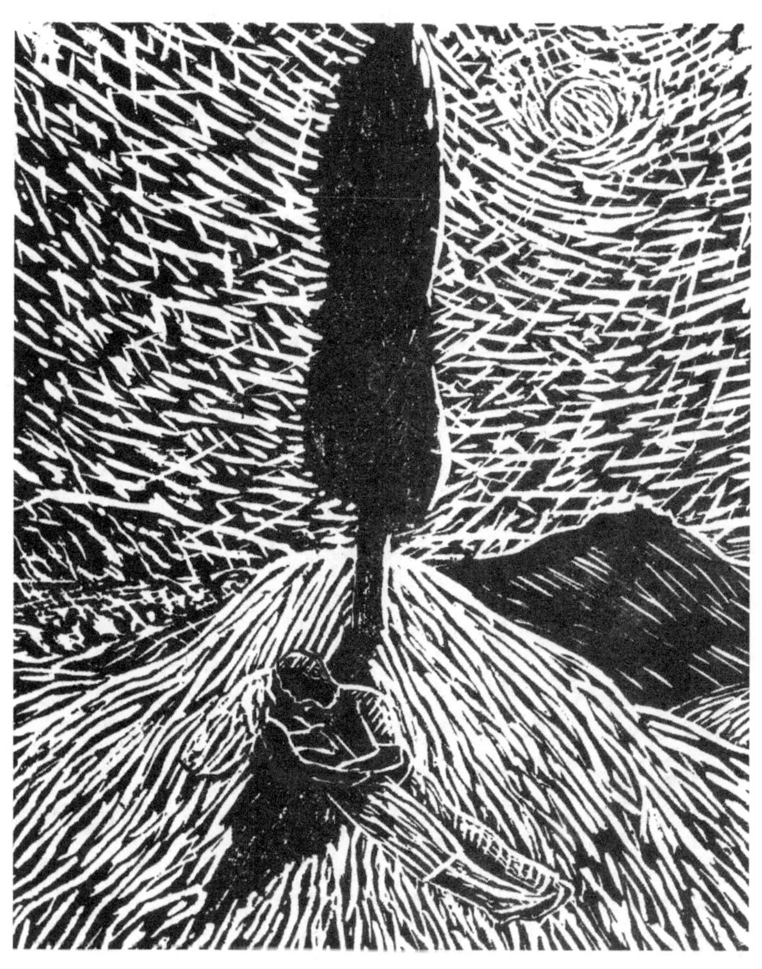

La Strada Bianca

Revised Second Edition. 2023

ISBN: 978-0-646-87793-8

Above the Lake

First Edition. 2012

Dedicated to

Judy D'Abbs, Carolyn Edwards

and my mother

Alexandra.

Prologue 1999

When I inform Olivero we are leaving Tuscany and moving back to Australia "for the new millennium" he looks at me and just laughs.

"Really? Is there anywhere in the world better than Tuscany?"

"I'll send you a postcard if I ever get there," I reply limply, equally unconvinced.

"Bravo. I'll still be waiting for you here then—in paradise!" Still chuckling, he guns his Vespa once more and shoots off down the white road (*la strada bianca*); a plump figure with a boyish, over-heated face, doubled up across the handlebars, parting the wheat fields like an Evel Knievel surging up the further rise and disappearing again over the brow of the hill, leaving behind a flowering cloud of thickening white dust and the sweet smell of two-stroke.

I stand stock still for a long while after, staring defiantly at the sun until my vision blackens and the landscape fills with tiny swirling green and orange orbs, then finally turn back towards the house disconsolate: Judy's bombshell has taken me completely by surprise. She told me she had an epiphany sitting at our kitchen table and after fifteen years living here she wants to move back to Australia with the boys. An epiphany! Judy! It is so unlike her that I have to take note but it hurts all the same that she is giving us no choice!

Part 1: Cortona 1980

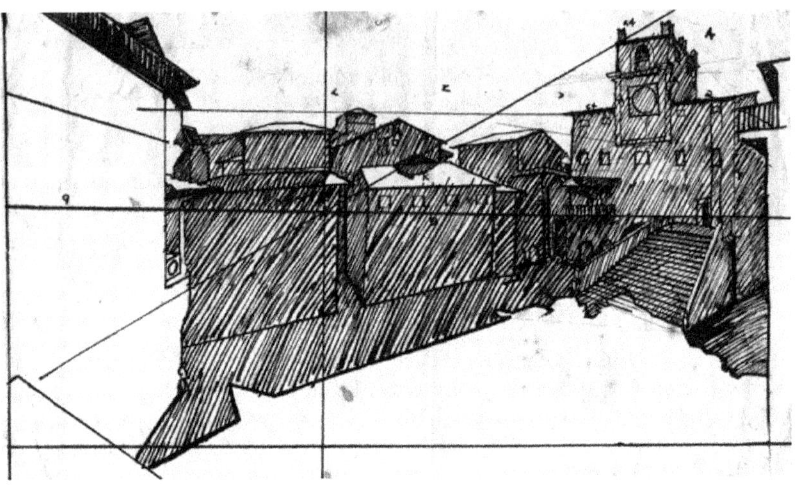

Chapter 1.

The spirit of the sixties has finally come to rest in the seventies, buried under a Thatcher landslide and a Reagan sleight of hand: from Blow Up to A Clockwork Orange to Star Wars all in the blink of an eye; high-jacked by market forces and advertising agencies, rushing us headlong into tyranny and greed. A whole army of Hooray Henries driving open-topped BMWs are populating my streets, and Arab princes in Rolls Royce's and Ferraris are cruising the London West End. Can you believe it? These days, the punk rockers on the Kings Road are a bigger tourist attraction than Horse Guards Parade, with busloads of Japanese tourists merrily snapping photos from the safety of their tour buses. To cap it off; Willie Whitelaw our new Home Secretary is offering the public "short sharp shocks" and more policing instead of more: love love love.

I share a flat in Queensgate Terrace in London's SW7, with Tish, the receptionist at Annie Russell's trendy World's End hairdressing salon. Tish looks more like an exotic pixie with her pyramid cut of shocking red hair (temporarily, I look like a skinhead), and although we share a bed we don't claim to be in a relationship. Tish is doing me a favour letting me into her bed so I can use the spare room as a studio to paint in. We are both typical Pisceans, swimming in all directions, hard to tie down and emotionally confused with addictive personalities; she drinks like a fish rolling around the flat button holing me, I float towards the ceiling, euphoric on a cloud of hashish, but we are also empaths, sensitive, highly attuned and importantly, good friends.

Officially neither of us is supposed to be living in the flat; Tish has been subletting the apartment ever since her oldest friends Alain and Gerard split up and moved back to France. A pity, them leaving; no more heaving dance parties in the flat, dropping acid or snapping poppers and having group heart attacks; no more bearded ladies in lurid wigs and lime coloured tutus opening the door to police officers and unabashedly inviting them in, with the elderly neighbours downstairs still complaining about the noise.

Lately the landlord has been knocking on the door too, looking for Alain and asking me awkward questions about who I am and why I'm here. I'm beginning to ask myself the same questions, feeling trapped on the third floor, flat-lined on a London skyline and probably feeling paranoid, smoking way too much dope. London; the only place I've ever wanted to be but at 25 I can feel the change a coming; being an artist, it's not as if I'm tied down to any particular place and commercial galleries are not exactly beating down my door to get my work, not yet anyway; early days I say!

My fledgling artistic career to date comprises of a private exhibition at a friend's house in Fulham, and selected for the Kensington and Chelsea Art Show, from which I was fortunate enough to be singled out in the local press review:

"… *Two large canvasses by Nino MacDonald dominate one gallery: Before the Flood, in which a dummy figure gives a surrealist impression of a corpse, and Heaven's rush, another surrealist painting of a pair of male nudes. Both extremely well painted, obviously have an allegorical meaning. But what is the good of allegory when it is unintelligible*?"

My aunt Tante Eliette, my mother's sister, also like a second mother to me, knows which way the wind is blowing and has been encouraging me to get out of town for a while.

"Ninotschki. I have been speaking to my friend Nella about you and she has agreed to rent out her place in Cortona if you want it. She says you could have it for six months."

I find the idea very appealing, just to get out of the city and be able to concentrate entirely on my painting for a change. To date I have had a few odd jobs, mostly part time, but even so find them very distracting; dividing my energy and time makes me schizophrenic.

My father doesn't pretend to understand much about art, nevertheless is very supportive of my efforts to establish myself as an artist and has offered to pay the rent. At 50 years of age, he retains a rebellious streak even though he is part of the stuffy Edinburgh business establishment, and I suspect deep down he gets off on the idea of living his freedoms vicariously through me.

More than anything else, it's the notion of living in a tower that is firing up my imagination. I can just picture it: a beacon appearing on the side of a hill, jutting out above the surrounding woodlands, the upper floors bathed in an intense golden sunlight. I idly fantasise about being an explorer, a Livingstone figure, discovering distant Tuscan hill towns deep in the interior, never set foot in before by foreigners! Even so I hesitate before making a final decision; mentally, I need to prepare myself before propelling myself into an uncertain future; so I consult the I Ching, the book of changes, several times before I am given an answer I can understand clearly and just to be absolutely sure, visit a trusted clairvoyant in Sloane Square; then one month later I am on the train to Florence with my head stuck out of the window, glimpsing three doves flying over the carriage, which I take to be an excellent sign, musing: "Love, maybe family."

Chapter 2.

I'm en route to Sabine's place high in the mountains north of Prato from where we plan to drive down to Cortona together. Sabine and her boyfriend Roby are the only other people I know in Italy, although currently Roby is away in Aberdeen, working as a deep-sea diver on a North Sea oil rig. Roby comes from Frascati near Rome and is equally at home diving for sponges in the Aegean sea. Sabine is a Parisian and works in Prato as a freelance stylist, designing yarns for the textile industry. She is one of those people of indefinite age, old enough to want to keep her age secret, yet possessing enough youthful energy to put anyone younger to shame.

She has a chequered history of younger lovers too but Roby (who is my age) seems to be enduring. Before she moved to Prato they lived in Paris where Roby, early on in their relationship, confronted her ex-lover, a Glaswegian called Tommy, vowing if he ever attempted so much as to put his foot inside the door of her apartment, he would be leaving by the third floor window. Long live the new King!

Sabine, Roby and I often go on holidays together, an arrangement that suits her well because she gets a break while I keep Roby busy playing chess. They are lovers but he and I are dedicated chess partners; I taught him the moves originally but these days he topples my king more often than not, fuelling a furious rivalry between us that drives us on to play endless games wherever and whenever we find ourselves occupying the same space; usually accompanied by a couple of bottles of his dad's fantastic Frascati wine. Frascati wine was always my favourite tipple in London; coloured an anaemic white, I was dismayed to discover that the genuine article is actually amber in colour.

It is a chilly, damp May morning when Sabine and I set off on the two-hour drive south to Cortona. Bleak when it starts to bucket down but not as dreary as London would be or as cold, I remind myself. The wipers are smearing the spray from the autostrada into greasy long streaks of silver grey, turning the landscape into a blubbery graveyard. By the time we exit at Arezzo, following the rim of the Valdichiana towards Cortona, alarm bells start ringing. Is that it? Is this what I have come for?

Glimpses of Cortona up on her hill flicker in negative space between the constant stream of buildings. And I thought Cortona was going to be remote! Not approached by housing estates and industrial parks all along the way.

I shouldn't have fretted though as any doubts quickly evaporate on the winding road up to Cortona from Camucia; a big bird soaring above us as we are magically transported into a timeless, Rip Van Winkle zone through what I can only surmise is a wormhole.

"Bloody hell! Can you believe this?!!"

Sabine parks her white Fiat Uno in front of the chemists under the town hall, and by the look on her face—yes, she is as gob smacked as I am, staring up at the palazzos, stacked ten storeys high, creaking into clouds. Finally the storm that carried us here has abated and there are people scuttling across the glistening flagstones of the sloping piazza; calling out to each other, bouncing unfamiliar words off the stone walls before disappearing off stage, trailing their voices behind them; like words breaking on the ground with the tinkle-tinkle-tinkling of splintering ice.

To reach the tower, we leave the well of the piazza and grapple up the spine of Cortona, negotiating such a treacherous ascent that I am genuinely concerned Sabine won't make it to the top without stalling her car (which would be epic: Sabine only passed her driving test a few years ago and is probably the worst driver I have ever had to endure as a passenger. She is the kind of driver who likes to brake as she is overtaking!).

Thankfully we make it without incident and, turning down a narrow-gravelled lane, she cries out, "La voilà, *chou-fleur*! La Tour!" *Chou-fleur,* meaning cauliflower, is her pet name for me, after I mistakenly started calling her that instead of the intended French endearment—mon chou, i.e. my cupcake!

The tower is square with a pitched roof and not round and flat as I had expected it to be. More like an elongated house, standing out from the surrounding stone buildings and walled gardens cascading breathlessly down the hill towards the valley floor. The caretaker, Bettina lives next door: a stout, peasant woman with dyed black hair, who has the keys for me and gives us a brief tour, offering her services cleaning, which I politely decline, much to her annoyance.

Sabine and I climb out onto the tiny balcony at the top of the three flights of stairs and open the bottle of Lambrusco to celebrate and get tipsy in the afternoon just for the sheer joy of it all.

"Look out for the view over paradise when you get there," the stranger at the next table in the Picasso Café on the Kings Road had enthused when I told him where I was going. And now I understand exactly what he meant. Sabine and I have ringside seats with all the plain spread out in full glory below us: a great western arc, stretching from the edge of this world seemingly into another dimension; a flat earth dropping over the horizon with shafts of light like spears of steel stabbing sober-looking clouds, stroboscoping the Valdichiana from dark into light, light into dark.

Stained red rooftops huddle together in the bleachers all around us like a thousand hastily raised umbrellas; pigeons of stone plummet down to Earth, then lazily flap their way back up to stone loggias and window ledges. The view is hypnotic. Ecstatic, for once, I can actually say the reality supersedes the fantasy I had of this place before coming here.

Sabine is on her usual busy work schedule and ready to leave early next morning. She has recently been voted as one of France's top ten stylists and is in high demand across Europe. Running on empty, she's not above washing down her vitamin pills with a bottle of cough medicine as a pick me up or fainting in the Paris metro with exhaustion.

Living on my own and answerable only to myself for perhaps the first time in my life is a very novel and powerful experience. Like being parachuted behind enemy lines: a fifth columnist, where nobody knows me or even that I exist, where I have lost contact with the outside world altogether. The dial on the telephone by the front door is padlocked and the only indication of human presence is a tin letterbox wired to the wrought iron entrance gate by the lane.

Bettina, in her drab olive housecoat, drops in occasionally to check up on me and points to the cobwebs on the ceiling or runs a fat finger over the dust on the mantelpiece, hinting. I can safely say: "spider" is my first word of Italian: *ragno*, followed by *ragnatela*, cobweb and *polvere*-dust. Not that you can build much of a conversation on the strength of those. It's frightening not speaking the language, like being in a parallel universe. However, I do appreciate Bettina's efforts to understand me, scrunching up her eyes and knitting her eyebrows together in an attempt to fathom my words. Language divides us but can also act as a bridge.

The master bedroom on the second floor has wall-to-wall windows and the view at eye level, lying down on the Queen size bed, which is raised on a wooden platform, is definitely Cinemascope. At night, the Valdichiana is a pulsating universe of light. What appear to be empty tracts of farmland in the daytime blaze into life in the dark with farmhouses, villages and factories mashed into the landscape and the autostrada slicing down the middle. I can hear the distant hollow toot of the train and the rocking on the tracks as it approaches Camucia station; the tracks a dark slash on the plain.

Really, I am in the mission control of a spaceship cleverly disguised as a mediaeval tower. The only hint of a landing is the calling card I have now wedged into the tin letterbox on the gate: raised on sumptuous, thick card in Garamond are printed the sole words Nino MacDonald. Painter. London. My idea of a joke at the time, having them printed without my address or contact number; or perhaps a conceit, that obviously being so well known, anyone could find me! Whatever the original reason the joke soon backfired as I quickly found myself obliged to hand write my details on each card, every time I handed one out.

I venture down the hill each morning with a sketchbook tucked into my canvas army bag and settle at a table outside Bar Signorelli on the corner of the central piazza. Tea, I have discovered, comes as a pot of boiled water with a slice of lemon and a tea bag draped off to the side of the saucer. You have to order the milk separately, so I drink cappuccino instead and smoke in between mouthfuls of sticky sweet *bomboloni*: custard-stuffed, sugared doughnuts the size of a cricket ball. High up on the wall opposite the bar is a circular plaque with the familiar hammer and sickle sign emblazoned in gold and red on a green ground and PCI-Partito Comunista Italiano painted in bold letters around the circumference. The old lady from the bar explains in broken English that Cortona has been run by the communists since the Second World War. What does communism have to recommend itself with, I ponder, but this is no gulag and I can only smile at the thought of socialism being a dirty word in America; or my mum, the year I reached voting age, declaring not voting in the general election, as I had intended, was the same as a vote for communism! Reds under the bed! It is entertainment enough watching the ebb and flow of the morning crowd from my table vantage point, spilling out like high and low tides from the Corso, the main street, into the piazza and back again. Listening to the breezy, chattering hum of people going about their daily business.

It takes time for the eye to acclimatise, before patterns begin to emerge along with form and colour, homing in on details in the crowd: the old men loitering on the corner by the hat shop, or the two misfits in beige work frocks at the top end of the piazza, delivering crates of bottled drinks to the CRAI supermarket. They roar in every morning, bundled together in the tiny cab of their three-wheeler Ape van (pronounced "ah-pay" and meaning "bee"). The younger is hunchbacked; slouching, his hands almost reach the ground. He has a mop of razor-sharp black hair, heavy-set eyebrows that give him a permanently snarling look and a classic nose that breaches from the forehead like Roby's. His partner, an older man, has a flabby, pasty face, and frequently whipping off his red and white brickie's cloth cap, pauses to wipe his brow. He looks like he is drunk most of the time and regularly breaks out into a ditty and a jig, haranguing or kidding the passers-by who are obviously immune to his charms and ignore his aggressively loud voice booming out across the piazza.

I shop at the CRAI: euphemistically called a *supermercato* but it is really a family shop run by the Molesinis'. As a "tourist" I am forced to assert myself more than the others and stand my ground: there are no queues, just huddles that form in front of the counter. You have to catch someone's eye to be served and I find the young matronly woman with short blond hair behind the counter, intimidating. "Lei?" she snaps like a grim reaper, reluctantly indicating my turn with a short jerk of her head, hardly looking up, and perhaps carrying on a conversation with someone else over the counter. Her father, Sig. Molesini, is the baker. He is a short, frail, elderly gentleman with a ghostly pallor (or a permanent dusting of flour), and I watch him limping across the piazza in his white baker's hat and coat. He holds court behind the counter of the shop and has a genuine smile and a welcoming open face, bending over backwards to accommodate the fussiest of his customers, expertly picking out a loaf from the jumbled pile in the bread bin and more than happy to pinch the crust of each loaf in turn to demonstrate how well baked it is, just to accomodate individual tastes.

Struggling up the hill with my plastic shopping bag filled with fruit, rolls, cheese, prosciutto and mortadella: coffee and wine (salted butter and fresh milk don't seem to exist, or cream, only UHT or long lasting milk), I might catch a glimpse of Bettina sitting like a siren at the window above her front door. She hardly acknowledges me, or nods briefly raising her eyebrows as I trundle past. Sometimes from the tower I hear her calling over to the neighbour across the lane. They communicate in shouts from first-floor kitchen windows, even though they could practically shake hands if they reached out far enough. I look over this neighbour's walled back yard from my bedroom and note that the son, who works in the barber's shop on the Corso, has a bald patch on his crown, something he can hide at ground level. They keep a hunting dog, a *Segugio* that looks vaguely like a cocker spaniel, permanently caged in a compound at the back of their yard; a desperate-looking animal with matted hair that often simpers, then howls all night long, driving me to distraction and to plotting its unfortunate demise; the only note of discord so far in my new-found paradise.

I did wonder if I would ever see my old school trunk again with my mother's painting easel strapped to the side, watching it shrink into the bowels of the luggage office at London's Victoria Station. Ma likes to claim the time I appropriated her easel from home in Scotland was the time she stopped painting, but how serious can she be? While it's true she stopped using brushes, she started using finger paints instead, exhibiting them in the Royal Academy's summer show, a feat I have yet to emulate. The silver tin trunk contains a Bang & Olufsen hi-fi and my collection of LPs (Marvin Gaye, Neil Young, Lonnie Liston Smith, Stan Getz, Eno, Satie, Debussy, Delius etc…I am catholic in my music taste); packed are painting materials, unprimed canvas, some clothes and a few paperbacks—in short, all I need to survive for six months.

When the telegram is delivered notifying me the trunk has arrived, I go to Bettina and ask her for directions to the station.

"Tur-on-toe-ler station?"

She looks at me with that puzzled expression on her face.

"Tur-on-toe-ler,"

I have to repeat several times before she gets it, unfurling her brows and throwing up her hands. "Ayee! Tay-ron-tu-la!" Rising on the second syllable and sighing in relief, as if she's just won the bingo.

I should consider Bettina my first Italian teacher, not that she gives me lessons but she has made me aware how crucial hand gestures are to any conversation and, importantly, knowing the right words count for very little if you can't pronounce them properly with the correct cadence. I'm pronouncing Italian words as they are written in English and dutifully practice gestures and cadence in front of the bathroom mirror:

"Ahhh, Teron-tula!" Waving my shaving brush in the air and feeling pleased with my progress.

Chapter 3.

The tower has three bedrooms, one to each floor; the carpeted bathroom is on a half landing; the main room is on the ground floor, a step up next to the front door, and there is a generous kitchen and pantry in the basement below street level. Old terracotta pavings and wood panelling, combined with a collection of neglected antique furniture, give the place a patina of stately decadence, exactly how I like it. If there is a heaven then surely the afterlife will provide everyone with a stately home to live in?

The tiny room on the top landing serves as my studio, the last stop before heaven. A pair of house martins offers company, nesting under the eaves directly outside the window. Sitting behind my easel, so high above the earth, feels like being strapped into a rocket and launched into orbit. As far as the eye can see the Valdichiana is a patchwork of Naples yellow, mauve and viridian. In the morning, the horizon is a thick, soupy blur, only progressively burnt off by the sun towards midday. The view gives me vertigo and I feel over-exposed, so I have decided to decamp downstairs onto firmer ground as soon as I finish my first painting: the view, that view over paradise.

I explore my immediate surroundings on foot. Everywhere there is elevation and distance from the hurly-burly. The massive Etruscan wall, with its three-thousand-year-old foundation stones, coils around Cortona like a giant sleeping serpent, protecting its denizens from the modern sprawls of the plain below. Porta Montanina, the top gate, is only a stone's throw from my tower and from there I can follow the ancient wall all the way up the outside to the Fortezza Girifalco (The Hawk), an elevation of 3,500 feet. No brooding mass the fort, or curlicued fancy but angular and Norman in aspect. On my first visit I was caught right at the top in a violent thunderstorm; black clouds, dammed behind Cortona, suddenly burst through the barricade of mountains piled up behind, invading the plain and driving me down to seek the nearest shelter in the Basilica of Santa Margherita, Cortona's patron saint. Encountering the embalmed body of the saint herself in the church is a shock, mounted under the altar in a glass sarcophagus, sailing in a field of brightly coloured plastic flowers. Her brittle, parchment-like mustard grey skin barely covers the bony frame, and her face looks distinctly skeletal, a stomach-wrenching apparition that seems almost sacrilegious to my protestant eyes.

I have discovered a small, abandoned garden on a bluff behind the Fortezza, carpeted by wild purple flowers and shaded by young pine trees that are impregnating the first stirrings of summer with their intoxicating resin scent, the silence broken only by the white-hot buzz of the cicadas. I lie in the long grass and spy on the fluffy white clouds overhead or roll over and watch Hannibal's army routing the Roman legions in the bloody fields of Ossaia (the Field of Bones) far away below. With my camera I make films of the sunset one frame at a time. From the garden it is possible to clamber back up onto the fort's thick ramparts and easy to imagine standing on the bridge of a great ocean liner, slipping smoothly through the milky waters of the Valdichiana, heading out to sea.

Taking the train to Arezzo and Florence, I've been discovering first-hand the frescoes I had previously only seen in illustrated books: the Giottos, Uccello's and Piero Della Francesca's. The scale is electrifying after the picture books, and how the acres of cracked and crumbling plaster fresco grounds are casually shorn up and smoothed over with buckets of cement, marooning landscapes, decapitating heads or dismembering bodies in their wake. Plaster is all around us, the stuccoed buildings, painted in those creamy yellow and apricot colours, even cobalt blue farmhouses spotted from the train. And where the plaster has fallen, revealing the mishmash of masonry beneath, offering saucy snapshots of civilisation's petticoats. I love the way the plaster sparkles in sunlight and how it bristles when I run my hands across the surface, razor-sharp like sandpaper.

I paint from life mainly, people and objects posed in my studio, views from the window, anything conveniently close at hand because I am not the kind of artist who enjoys lugging his painting gear into the field if I can help it, preferring the comfort of a studio. I have real respect for Turner who lashed himself to the mast of a ship to study at first hand the sea squalls but my preference would rather to be ensconced in a glass box protected from the weather.

There are two giant terracotta pots opposite the front door with a dry stonewall behind them that are conveniently close and make a suitable subject for a painting. An olive tree with a mosaic of cerulean sky through the pointy, two-tone olive leaves is diffusing a buttery light over the somber, mossy flagstones in front. The passageway from the broad flight of stone steps that open onto a central garden. Bettina's house is diagonally across with my landlady's house, Nella, opposite in the other corner of the walled compound. I have only met my aunt's friend once briefly in London, and according to Bettina she hardly ever visits here. They both have separate entrances, so I retain my privacy. After a morning painting, I usually lunch under the shade of the *tiglio* tree at the top of the garden stairs; under its honeyed fragrance, sipping or guzzling- depending, the cooled, slightly

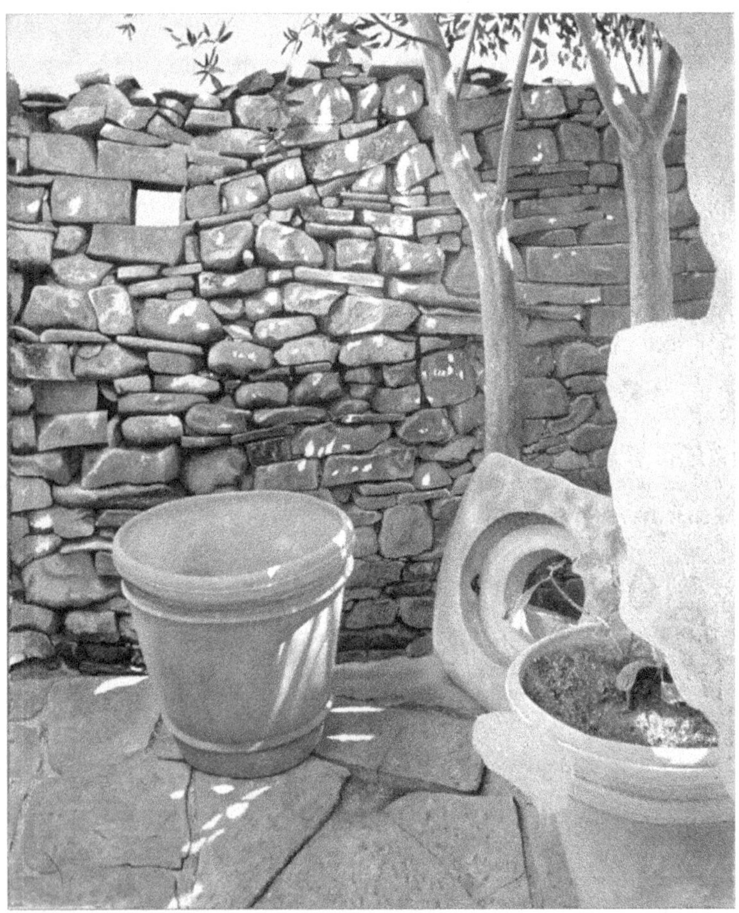

Alfresco.1980

frizzante Vergine white wine of the Valdichiana; and ripping through the Alexandria Quartet with the lingering salty taste of mortadella and moist crumbs of *rosetta* bread on my lips. It's incredible really, like a dream: here I am alone, knowing no one, but already feeling at home as if I belong here, a fuzzy warm feeling invading my solar plexus.

Every evening the Cortonesi gather for their *passeggiata*: lovers and family groups, teenagers and mothers pushing strollers, men arm in arm, walking at a leisurely pace up and down the Corso (also known as *ruga piana:* level street) to piazza della Repubblica, the central piazza dominated by the twelfth-century Comune or town hall whose giant clock chimes every quarter hour). Ranks of tired shoppers and people-gazers settle on the Comune steps to watch the elegantly dressed Cortonese collect into larger groups before them. I like to think of the promenaders as discussing Michelangelo or the merits of the Golden Mean, but more likely than not their animated discussions revolve around the teething problems of their babies, or football or about the evening meal. At dusk, a solitary bell tolls out from the top of Cortona, a reminder of the curfew in the Middle Ages, when the city gates—massive, heavy oak doors reinforced with heavy iron studs—were shut for the night. Rip Van Winkle town. Serene.

Chapter 4.

"Are you the painter Nino MacDonald?" A stranger with an English accent asks tentatively, approaching me near the *Comune* (Council chambers) steps.

"Yes, I am," I reply, taken off guard not recognising him and simultaneously chuffed that evidently somebody has heard of me.

"How did you know?"

"I was only guessing," he replies. "And I've seen you around lately sketching in the *piazza*. Then out walking one day I noticed the unusual calling card on the gate up at Poggio."

"The only hint of my landing you mean."

"Pardon?"

"Just my private joke. I'm on a mission and the tower is my cleverly disguised space ship."

"A UFO? I know," lowering his voice: "I hope you're not here to abduct people! Actually there have been plenty of sightings so you wouldn't surprise me if you were. By the way I'm Rupert."

"You're English?" I say, extending a hand. "Nino himself!"

"Pleased to meet you. I'm originally from East Sussex but have been here for a few years, so nothing to get too excited about."

"And I thought I was going to be the only foreigner here!"

"You mean the only alien? Haha. Actually, I'm quite interested in esoteric subjects, but sorry to disappoint you, there are quite a few foreigners living around Cortona. You can't miss them, you know, the *stranieri* (foreigners) are always the badly dressed ones you see in Bar Signorelli every Saturday morning during the market!"

An old Mercedes station wagon rolls into the piazza towards us with the driver impatiently sounding the horn.

"I have to go, that's my lift for lunch, but come and visit me," as he scribbles down his address in the back of my sketchbook before jumping into the car, me fervently hoping to be given an invitation to lunch as they disappear. It's fine being on my own, so much freedom with nobody telling me what to do and no expectations, but you can get a little crazy talking to yourself all day long.

A few days later I decide to take a walk and see if Rupert is at home. He lives just outside the wall on the eastern edge of Cortona. His abandoned-looking farmhouse is situated below the gravel road lined by cypress trees and precariously wedged onto a terrace with bramble thickets covering the banks behind. Calling out, I find him collecting wood on the far side of the house.

"Hello again," Rupert greets me, looking up. "How's the mission progressing?"

"Good thanks, I've been lying low. Looks like you're on a mission too," pointing to the pile of branches he has bundled together.

"It's for the bonfire later, a couple of friends are coming over. We're having a barbecue so why not join us?" An invitation I readily accept.

Rupert has a brooding eagle face; aquamarine also comes to mind because it is fluid, high cheek bones that pinch the skin as he smiles, an arched nose, fine shoulder-length light hair and deep-set pale eyes that have a way of collecting you in two directions. He offers to show me around the place, pointing out the date: 1312, carved into the lintel of the cantina cellar door and inside, the back wall has been chiselled out of the live rock; the foundations must be solid enough, I think, although upstairs, parts of the terracotta floors are warping badly, rising up in waves and seeing my hesitation, Rupert has to reassure me:

"It's old, I know but quite safe. I've fixed up the kitchen, see, and in there, the bathroom," proudly showing me. "There's even electricity and hot and cold running water."

When I look dubious, he explains:

"Only a stopgap while I find a better place, somewhere more permanent, so to speak."

"So what are you doing out here?" I ask as he picks up a steel string guitar, briefly strumming it before putting it down again.

"I was signed to April records in London as a singer/songwriter with Leo Sayer as a stable mate."

I am immediately impressed.

"In fact, we're having a jam session tonight."

"What with Leo Sayer?"

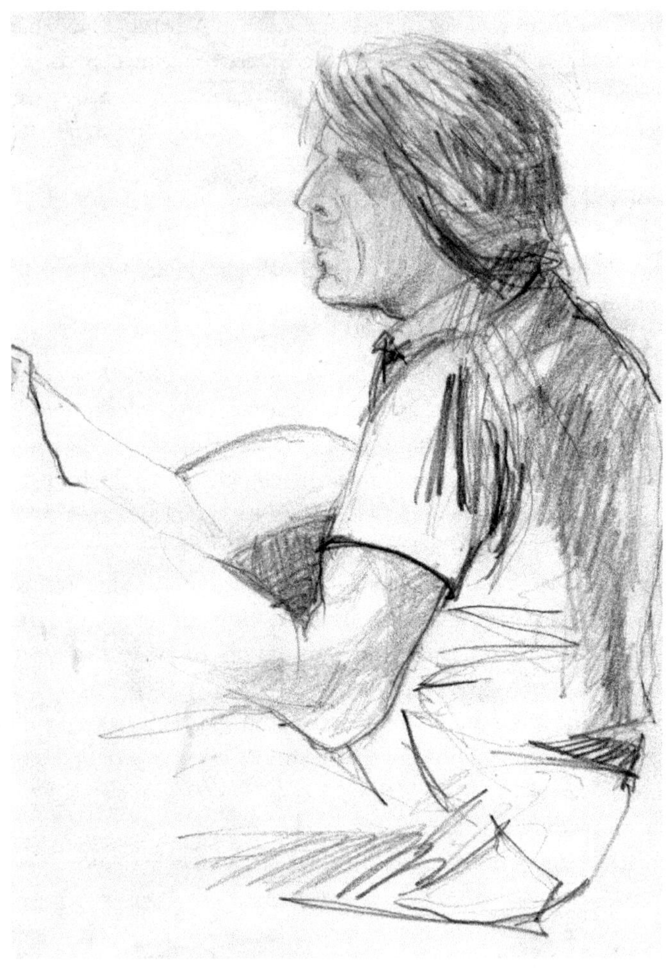

Rupert.1980

"Ha ha! No, I left all that behind, that's why I came here. In fact I'm a million miles away from that world now, translating technical manuals into English for a company that makes textile machinery in Arezzo."

"Well, that explains everything!"

Rupert doesn't offer to elaborate further and I detect a reticence in him so I don't push it although I am very curious to know why someone would give up a budding career in music already signed to a record company, to come out here and translate technical manuals.

Evenings can still hold a chill in June and by the time Ron, a young American painter and Roberto, a local musician, arrive, the fire is blazing on the terrace to the side of the house. Raking out a bed of coals, Roberto lays out the spicy Tuscan sausages he has brought on an iron griddle, while Ron pokes the jacket potatoes wrapped in tin foil with a stick and Rupert decants more of the delicious dark local red wine (known as *nero* or black) from a demijohn. Roberto speaks English reasonably well, which is a relief because as I point out to him nobody else in Cortona seems to bother. "My girlfriend is English," Roberto explains, "so I learnt to speak, and then I had a brief spell in New York City," continuing, "but you can blame our lack of English on Napoleon, Nino; for invading Tuscany because only French is taught in our schools as a result. Besides, us Tuscans, we are proud of our language and wish to preserve it. No need for English or French. Our Florentine is the language of Dante, the purest form of Italian—like your Oxford English."

"The Senesi might dispute you on that Roberto," chips in Ron.

"No way," Roberto replies, offended by the suggestion.

"Have you ever heard the Senesi speak, Nino? They can't even pronounce casa or Coca Cola, they must go *hasa* and *hoca hola*!"

And we all laugh.

Rupert starts tuning his guitar, and Roberto follows suit, lovingly taking his acoustic guitar out of its red plush-lined case. Ron, a diminutive figure, sitting cross-legged by the fire, leans forward with his elbows resting on his knees and cocks his head over to one side as if listening for a cue from the spheres. A purple-cloaked night has settled around the fire with a gushing fountain of red-hot sparks lighting up our faces and throwing shadows across the terrace. I feel the hairs stand up on my arms when Ron starts singing. His voice quivers on high, almost a castrato, gathering intensity in perfect pitch. He sounds like an Indian snake charmer or the Pied Piper calling his whole kingdom in, and I lie back, cupping my head and gaze starward, relishing the moment and realising with only a fleeting nostalgia that my undercover days have been blown: that the brief spell I had to reinvent myself is now over and from this day on my face will have a name.

Ron has offered to introduce me to some of the *stranieri* this Saturday morning when the market is on and we have arranged to meet in Bar Signorelli.

"Once you've met one, you've met the lot," Rupert snorts. "The domino effect." He prefers to stay away.

Under the grandfatherly eye of the town clock, groups of *contadini* (farmers), older men mainly sporting fedoras, huddle around displays of highly polished and expensive agricultural machinery, deep in discussion. Stalls and lorries that fold-out from the side magically transforming themselves into mobile shops, fill piazza Signorelli behind the Comune, and line the way down to the Duomo. Here you can buy kitchenware, shoes, cheap clothes, bolts of cloth and rolls of plastic covers, carpets and doormats, cassettes, plants, cheeses, fruit and veg, rabbits and chickens as well as a *porchetta* van with a rapidly shrinking roasted whole pig carved off the counter top and stuffed directly into oversized panini; a tempting mid-morning snack.

By eleven, Bar Signorelli is seething with the morning coffee and midday aperitivo crowds, either overlapping or one and the same. Judging by the dress, it's mainly the *stranieri* occupying the new shiny metal tables and matching chrome chairs. Ron, grinning (he looks permanently stoned but I know he doesn't smoke), is standing in the corner by the counter fingering his clipped moustache. He has the easy, clean-cut good looks of an American preppy although I hadn't noticed before the kohl eye makeup. A bright red, artist's beret caps his head and he is in tight-fitting, stonewashed denim shorts and sneakers.

"Try Benito's famous cocktail, *La Bicicletta*," he says in greeting, lifting up a champagne flute filled with a red bubbling liquid and a slice of lemon, then pointing to a New York Times clipping taped to the wall above the espresso machine with a picture of a smiling barman shaking a cocktail mixer.

"That's Benito, our new barista. Hey, Benito! Meet Nino, the new boy in town. Another painter!"

Benito takes a quick drag on his cigarette before stubbing it out under the counter and leans over to shake my hand.

"I see you in here before."

His thinning curly black hair looks oiled or it might just be the stress of work.

"Welcome to Cortona," he says displaying a genial smile.

Marsiglia, his wife, dyed blond hair with black roots, slides a bowl of assorted nuts along the polished marble top towards us, arching her dark pencil thin eye brows in greeting but saying nothing, and Benito disappears with the tray of drinks she has prepared for him.

"The bar has undergone a radical makeover since I arrived in Cortona." I mention to Ron, surveying the crisp new layout. "It's amazing really how it's been transformed almost overnight into a palace of mirrors, chrome and glass, although personally I liked the way it was before—you know, a bit dowdy but presenting character."

Benito returns and, looking at Ron but tilting his head in my direction, asks "Bicicletta?"

"What's in it?" I gesture to him lifting my hands palms upward with a shrug of the shoulder, and he places a forefinger to puckered lips.

"Campari e Prosecco, my *segreto*!" Demonstrating the shake in his cocktail mixer and pouring it with a final flourish.

I raise my glass to him. It's hardly eleven, but what the hell; looking about, everyone else seems to be on their second round.

"Is only one rule," says Benito confidentially, still smiling and tearing off the receipt from the till before handing it to me: "not leave my bar without your receipt. *Grazie*."

"He's terrified of getting fined by the *Guardia di Finanza* if they catch you without one" Ron explains. "Recently there was this kid who they prosecuted in Sardinia because he couldn't produce the receipt for his 300-lira ice cream when plainclothes policemen apprehended the lad outside the *gelateria*. Can you believe it? I think the kid was only about eight or nine and it caused uproar in the country when the Finanza refused to drop the case." Adding: "Benito's forever calling you back when you're trying to rush out of the door without it."

"*Maledetto*! You always the first to forget!" calls Benito over his shoulder.

"I know what you mean about the décor though," continues Ron. "The bar recently changed hands and it's called progress! Yi ha!" He slaps his thigh with his beret then pretends to throw it back in the air.

"Soon we'll have shopping malls here just like the U S of A. To think I came here to get away from the American dream!"

"Don't, um, be silly Ron," says an earnest looking woman in her thirties, sidling over to the bar with a glass of red wine in her hand, a ruby twinkle starring her eyes.

"The Italians love everything American but the Belle Arti would never allow such a thing!"

"What about the Romanesque church they pulled down to build that monstrosity to Santa Margherita?" insists Ron. "That's no better than a Disney theme park. All smoke and mirrors."

"I was shocked to see Santa Margherita right there on the altar," I interject.

"What!" Jane smacks her lips in mock exaggeration. "This is Catholic country," and, flicking back her straight auburn hair, "where they worship mothers, um, and saints, as much as they um worship whores!" Lowering her voice a little "And in the thirteenth century, Margherita had a reputation for being all three."

Ron, grinning. "Nino, this is Jane, meet Nino. Jane's English like you."

"I'm Scottish," I reply defensively.

"Makes sense with a name like MacDonald," Ron replies, back tracking. "Sorry, didn't mean to offend, it's the same story with the Canadians and Americans, but you do have an English accent."

"Or Sicilians," adds Jane, "if you call them Italian."

I am actually confused about where I came from, or more to the point, where I belong and usually cut the subject short. It always starts with Nino and you must be Italian moving on to MacDonald so you must be Scottish, or English with that accent of yours; yet truth be known I am German as are both my parents: I was born in Düsseldorf and christened Hermann Leonard Pöhling. However, whenever I am asked I say I am Scottish and I have a kilt to prove it.

"Did anyone ever tell you you look a bit like Mick Jagger?" continues Ron.

"Yes, it's the lips, I know! In London I was once stopped in the street for an autograph. So, I signed my name and they were so disappointed. Now I get Italians who think they are being so funny asking me if I am related to the McDonalds hamburger chain. Ha ha! At least, if I'm lucky I'll be spared the chorus of "old MacDonald had a farm" while I'm here."

"Surely with a name like Nino" Insists Jane " You have some Italian blood in you?"

"No, I don't have any Italian blood, Jane, but with a name like Nino I was probably destined to be here. How long have you been here?"
I ask, changing the subject again.

"I came with my two brothers a few years ago. That's them sitting over there—John! Martin!" She calls out and I nod in their direction as they turn their heads.

"We bought an abandoned farm house together up in the hills behind Cortona."

"Jane leaves the farm over winter" adds Ron "and moves into my apartment, which is just down from the *Corso*. Needing your creature comforts, don't you, Jane?"

"Nonsense! Um, actually Nino, I teach English in Cortona and when the roads ices over it's impossible to get to work and I can't afford to miss any days! Money is tight, so it's convenient to stay with Ron and I help out with the rent, don't I!"

"I've been thinking about renting out a room in the tower I'm renting up in Poggio, if you hear of anyone?" I say. "It's too big for me alone and I could do with the extra cash, plus I wouldn't mind the company if I'm being honest."

"Well, actually, I know someone looking for a place: an English writer who's just come back from America. Jane knows him and he's a friend of Rupert's. I'll bring him over if you like? His name's Jef."

Chapter 5.

Ron has become a regular visitor to the tower. He enjoys talking as much as I enjoy listening so we make a good match especially as I have taken this opportunity to pose him for a portrait as he reclines in a comfortable green baize chair in the middle of the room. I have decamped from the top floor and now use the living room on the ground floor as my studio, which is convenient because I can still paint while receiving visitors, not that there are many of them. I have had a few letters from friends in England wishing to come out, which I have conveniently delayed answering.

Ron's pet topic of conversation is the provinciality of the Cortonesi. "You know, Cortona might be communist but it's not like you can trip down the *Corso* dispensing comrades or *ciaos* left, right and centre to everyone you meet." He warns. "You can easily give offence; the Cortonesi are petit-bourgeoisie at heart."

"Rupert warned me to address people by their proper title." I say.

"Ah Professore-come sta? Signora, va bene?" Ron mimics. "Avvocato! Ingeniere! What about Maestro for us artists! Anyone called you maestro yet?"

"No," I mumble, busy behind the canvas. "Keep looking ahead like you were. Yes, there you are."

"Me neither, and have you noticed how Tuscans never introduce themselves, they simply presume you know their names?

"You know what? I love sashaying down the Corso in my denim hot pants just to freak them out and also wear makeup; they are so easily scandalised but I can see the men looking at me, pretending not." "You don't say Ron. Surprised you don't follow up."

"I met a guy once in the bar, he sidled over to me and asked if he could sit down. I thought here we go but then he asked me if I would teach him some English. He said he wanted to be able to chat up the American girls when they come to town; you know, the students on the Georgia University program and invited me to meet up at his place one afternoon. He was youngish, not very good looking, a lorry driver he told me who had a bit of a wild look in his eyes. "

"And did you go?"

"Not after he told me about the woman who jumped into the back of the cab with him only to discover she was really a guy, then decided what the hell and carried on anyway. Probably the type who parks up at night in those lay-bys on the Siena Road; where you see the scantily dressed girls at night, hanging out on the road side or the fat mammas during the day, squatting on milk crates, Kleenex strewn around them.

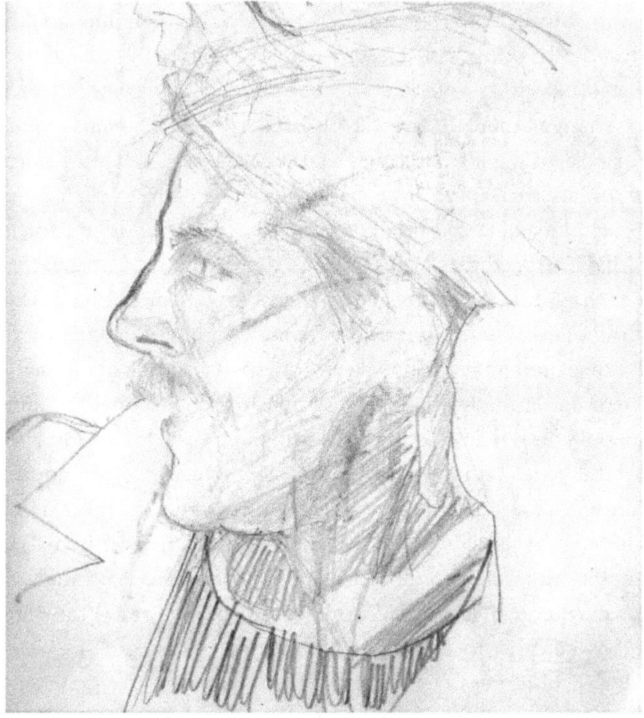

Ron.1980

Ron's a romantic at heart, a sensitive soul for all his braggadocio and at the end of the day only looking for his soul mate, not an Italian macho.

We are planning to visit Jane on the farm; her brother Martin is organising a picnic to celebrate the arrival of his seven-year-old daughter Holly, over from England on her summer holidays. They live out of town up in the hills so transport is a problem, Ron doesn't drive, but Sabine will be here for the weekend, so the three of us can drive up together. I have come across Martin selling cauliflowers out of the back of his truck outside *Porta Colonia* on weekdays, apparently doing a roaring trade.

The farm is about twenty kilometres from Cortona, over passes and through tapering valleys, along good but winding roads cut into the sides of hills, an ocean swell of mountains eventually crashing down on the *Valdichiana.* Martin hitches a trailer to a tractor and we all jump in for a tour of the farm, a perilous journey zigzagging along terraces of olive trees interspersed with his vegetable patches on the side of a steep hill, Martin pointing out some of the features like the huge dam lined with plastic sheeting that he has dug with his brother John. Sabine is full of praise and charms everyone with her French accent and the power older women can exert over younger men. Roby will be back from Aberdeen soon and I'm looking forward to a game of chess and a bottle of his dad's Frascati wine. He never forgets to bring a little hash with him either, which is an added bonus. So far I have resisted the temptation to go out and look for it myself although I have noticed that Martin has a crop drying in the barn.

There are two houses on the farm—the *padronale* or master house where Jane and John live, a huge three-storey stone building in a state of disrepair. Jane is a horse person and she agists horses to supplement her income, stabling them under the house. She says her dream is to open a riding school and take people on horse trekking expeditions into the hills. John is the more practical of the three and a builder and is slowly restoring the house. Martin lives by himself in a small workers cottage fifty yards away. "The challenge of being here is surviving winter." Martin warns as the two of us settle into his kitchen while he rolls a joint. Holly is busy drawing on the kitchen table.

"Holly's mother went back to London; she couldn't stand the winter even though it was her idea to come out here in the first place." He says glumly with an edge of bitterness.

"The thing is, you don't need much to keep you going in the summer, you can live the idyl, but winter can be brutal: you freeze your balls off and it's damp to boot."

I haven't smoked a joint since leaving London and home grown is a treat, appreciatively, languidly drawing the smoke deep into my lungs, evincing an immediate feeling of well-being and goodwill edged with a little paranoia. I am still smoking tobacco and have discovered the pleasures of the Tuscan cheroot: Toscanelli.

"We spent all our money buying the farm and life was unbelievably basic for our first few years. Did Jane show you the cast-iron hand pump outside the big house? It was our only water source and often froze solid in winter. We had to cut wood, drag it up from the bottom of the valley with a donkey and sell it as a means to survive." Martin, wiry framed, has a rugged, good-looking, blue-eyed, Michael York type of English face; framed by sun-red curly hair that tumbles down over his shoulders. His flattened boxer's nose doesn't detract, either, but adds character.

"No, I didn't get it in a boxing ring." Martin says noticing me staring at his nose. "A cricket ball at school."

"Same here," I say pointing to my chipped front tooth.

"I keep a daily record of the weather conditions and temperatures," Martin continues, as Jane walks in and strides towards the fridge.

"Got any UHT? Martin's a fanatic about the weather, see!" She points to a calendar stuck on the fridge door with entries religiously penciled in for each day of the week. "Keeping records helps me to compare from year to year. Have you noticed how the seasons are changing? Spring and autumn are no longer so distinct? The *contadini* around here never stop talking about it."

"I know, there has been a lot of talk about depleting the ozone layer and the greenhouse effect." I offer.

"If you do decide to stay for longer, beware! We all fall in love with Tuscany in the summer but the honeymoon ends with the winter!"

"Come on you two, John's already got the sausages on the barbecue." Orders Jane.

Before 1 leave, Holly presents me with her drawing of a house or a tent and an apple tree in a field: **To Nin♡ from Holly** written in bold headlines along the top, and which way to the ball, written down one side.

Chapter 6.

My front door bell rings. It is a small brass bell on a string with a wrought iron figure of a stooping man next to it, the frame bolted to the wall above the door.

"Hi ther! You Nino?" Says a man with an American accent in an easy rider t-shirt and jeans and ankle boots as I open the door.

"Yes, that's me."

"Ron said I should come over and introduce myself, I'm Jef."

"Yes: Ron mentioned you, said you were looking for a place to live?"

"Good to meet y'all then." Jef sticks his hand out and we shake. Fortunately, he doesn't go for the high five which always confuses me. "Come in. Would you like a coffee?"

"Yea, with brandy if you have it."

"It's a bit early for me but yes can do that."

"*Caffe corretto.* I need one after that climb."

"In Paris, I worked in a factory and every morning before clocking in we would go to the bar next door and drink an express with a glass of calvados." I add.

"Set you up nicely for the day!"

"This is like eight in the morning!"

"Convenient!"

Once settled in the studio, coffee made, rolling tobacco out, we fall into easy conversation. Jef is in his mid-thirties at a guess, shoulder length shaggy dark hair parted down the middle, piercing piebald eyes of green and grey and a Sergeant Pepper's moustache, showing no trace of self-consciousness about his accent explaining he has just got back from America.

"I took off for the States at New Year to rejoin my girlfriend Caroline, only to discover when I got there, she had fallen in love with someone else and had been two timing me."

"Ouch! That must have hurt How long had she been away?"

"Not that long, she was here last summer on the Georgia University summer arts program and left in the fall. By then we were living together; we had a house just below the *parterra*: she was painting and I was finishing up my book."

"Ron told me you had a novel published. That's quite an achievement."

"Yep, but I wouldn't claim to be a writer; I only wrote *Black Jack* to raise some funds for us to be together."

"A bit of a long shot as a money maker?"

"I got real lucky and scored a big advance on a two-book deal with a publisher! After the break up, I decided to stick around for a while. So I was licking my wounds in a bar in Athens, Georgia one afternoon too many, when the phone rings and as a joke I told the barman I was only in if it was my agent, Peter. And it was! Can you believe it! Took him two days to track me down. He just sold the American rights to *Black Jack* and wanted to give me some good news."

"Not bad for a first-time author!"

"Yeah, only it's kinda gone belly up since because my publisher turned my second manuscript down. Damned if I'm giving back the advance though, I'm still living off it!"

"Are you still friends with her?"

"Nah. Not after that. The love of my life, laid it right out on the line for me as soon as I stepped off the plane."

"She could have saved you the fare and let you know before hand?"

"Yeah right. Doesn't matter anymore. At least I got to hang out with some old pals in Georgia and found a place to write that second book. But now I'm back."

"Ron said you've been in Cortona for quite a while."

"Too long! I came to Cortona eight years ago with my wife Ylva. She's German. That's where we were living before, but we're now divorced and she's still here: the lady with the henna hair and the Alsatian dog if you ever run into her."

"Yes, I've seen her around. So, you know Rupert too?"

"Hell yes. He's an old friend, been here as long as me. I used to live in that old decrepit house below the road where he lives. But that was long before Rupert got there. I put in the bathroom, although I know he likes to claim he did.

"We once worked together in a friend's business in Cortona, manufacturing leather handbags. Have you met Michele yet? The German expat cum entrepreneur? I was his office factotum and Rupert, can you imagine, he was the quality control."

"He'd have been better off becoming a pop star alongside Leo Sayer."

"Same stable right? Yeah. If only! Problem Rupert has is he's a dreamer and sometimes dreamers prefer to keep it that way."

"He told me it's because he's lazy." I say. "Too hard being an artist, you need perseverance as much as talent."

"And money don't forget! So you're a painter?"

"That's what it says on my business card!"

Stubbing out my rollie, I pick one up off the glass coffee table in front of us and hand it over. Just don't ask me for my address."

Jumping up he moves across the room to where Ron's painting is sitting on my mother's easel.

"I love your portrait of Ron; you've really captured him well."

"Yes, I'm pleased with the way it's turned out."

"Is that a Klu Klux Klan figure lurking in the Tuscan landscape?"

"Haha! Well spotted. It's a bit weird I know, but I've been listening to Neil Young's Southern man too much recently."

"You've gotta love Neil! What art school did you go to?"

"I didn't. After school I was thinking about the Chelsea Art School, but by then I'd had enough of institutions. I was in Rome for three months two years ago though and applied to enroll at the French Academy; Balthus was the director at the time and I love his work. Do you know him?"

"I know his work, a little risqué if you ask me. And what happened?"

"They said I wasn't French!"

"You're obviously talented. I'm impressed. Look at the way you've painted the chair, like you could actually touch it."

"You know, being self-taught I sometimes feel the need to prove I can paint."

"I would never call myself an artist and that's not being modest."

"Having a novel published is quite an achievement."

"Still doesn't make me an artist. How about that room, is it still up for grabs?"

Chapter 7.

Jef's arrival at the tower has heralded a major shift in my social life. He speaks Italian fluently and knows just about everyone in town. With Jef to hold my hand, congregating in Bar Signorelli on Saturday mornings has now become a weekly ritual; probably the only time the *stranieri* become discernible as a group per se: a veritable League of Nations: English, Americans, Germans, Swiss: a disparate group of all ages, often with little in common except the Tuscan factor. Generally, the *stranieri* seem to blend in well, absorbed into a jelly wobble of time like castaways on a faraway planet.

"The sun must be over the yardarm by now," says Jef, impatient, half-heartedly looking at his watch because he knows it is hardly reached eleven.

The atmosphere in the bar is festive, people are genuinely pleased to see each other: the big relax signaling the start of the weekend knocking back Benito's *biciclettas.* A fog of tobacco smoke and pitched conversations fills the air with people racing in and out, cramming round tables or crowding the bar; pushing through the Italians to catch Benito's attention for a refill, rushing out for last-minute market shopping: plastic bags overflowing with vegetables strewn around the back wall or abandoned under tables, awaiting retrieval later.

The frenzy is all over by two o'clock, the piazzas emptied of the market lorries and farm machinery and ruga piana the Corso re-opens to through traffic. Sleepy Rip Van Winkle siesta town in the grip of a hot summer's afternoon with no one around except the odd tourist looking for somewhere to shelter!

For over a week before the University of Georgia's much anticipated arrival, crossed miniature American and Italian paper flags on wooden stands have been appearing in the shop windows and bars along the Corso.

"The Georgia students, on their annual summer arts program, are about to hit town, is what all the fuss is about," Jef eagerly informs me. "Should keep you happy with a town full of artists. That's how I met Caroline, she was on the program a couple of years back, best thing is most of the students are girls."

"Ah! A town full of girls! Now I understand why you look so happy."

Jef is not somebody capable of keeping his own company for too long.

On the appointed day a big crowd turns out to greet the group in Piazza Garibaldi. A bedraggled bunch of students climb down from the bus and retrieve their luggage from the hold. The town band has assembled in the piazza and strikes up with a spirited rendition of the Star-Spangled Banner before we all troop back into town along the Corso to the Comune, students and faculty members carrying backpacks and humping suitcases. The only part missing is the ticker tape. The *Sindaco,* microphone in hand, the tricolor sash of office splashed across his chest and a cast of dignitaries lined up behind him, is standing at the top of the Comune steps waiting to give the official welcoming address.

The news of the arrival of this large contingent of predominantly female students has attracted a large influx of Italian youths as well; riding into town from the district every evening on their Vespas or in souped-up Apes, (wasps and bees) the cabs decorated with bumper stickers and colourful streamers plugged into the handlebar ends. The ensuing tumult is contagious; rumours are still rife about the "cheerleader" incident last year in the changing rooms of the local football team and testosterone levels are rising in a feeding frenzy of summer romance and sexual promise. A new nightclub has opened in Piazza Garibaldi called Tuculca: named after a mythical Etruscan monster, and a Pizzeria in the Park with an outside dance floor "under the stars" is open in the parterre (the public gardens). The bars along the *Corso* are doing a roaring trade late into the night and Tonino's restaurant opposite the new nightclub will become the university's *mensa* for the next two months. Tonino, the town's 'top dog' according to Jef, must be minting it in.

That the American university is made welcome in Cortona is obvious by all the hoop-la surrounding their arrival and besides the fillip to the local economy there seems to be a genuine mutual affection between the two nations. Rupert recalls a conversation he had on the *Comune* steps with two US Air Force veterans of the second World War, staying in Cortona for the first time. They were reminiscing about the time they flew a mission to bomb then German occupied Cortona but knowing it was an Etruscan hill town, decided unilaterally to abort and instead dropped the bombs out of harm's way on Monte Sant'Egidio, the mountain behind the town.

"They saved Cortona!" Rupert marvels. (Jane gave me a different version of the story: according to local lore, it was Santa Margherita who played the pivotal role, conjuring up a thick mist to hide Cortona just as the plane was making its final bombing approach).

Up at the tower, Bettina the caretaker, is showing concern with the increasing levels of activity and hovers in peripheral vision, like a fox surveilling the coup. Jef holds court upstairs in his room and more and more I am playing the role of gatekeeper. He purrs when he has company, his head to one side resting on a palm, his two-tone mottled eyes innocently grazing, shaggy hair waiting to be patted. Long informal lunches with plenty of wine have become the norm, entertaining the students and teachers from Georgia. The old-fashioned wood-paneled kitchen in the basement is cooler than the rest of the tower during the swelter of July and August and the large oak kitchen table can easily accommodate the crowd. The casement windows are at street level with a blunted view of the stonewall opposite, occasionally dissected by a car passing or the truncated leg of a pedestrian or the scrawny tom cat rubbing up against the grill, mewling to come in and participate.

Jef enjoys cooking, which is just as well because I don't, although he is gently trying to encourage me to contribute. In London my cousin Gabriele nicknamed me Noodles or worse still, puckering my chin she would call out Nooodly! Just because all I ever ate were noodles topped with Monday to Friday packet sauces off the supermarket shelf. Pasta has been my comfort food since childhood, when as a special treat, my mother, then single and working for a fashion designer in London as an in-house model, would take me to the Kenya coffee house in Knightsbridge for a bowl of spaghetti bolognaise washed down with a bottle of Coke.

Cortona may be a honey pot but sex isn't the only buzz in the air: art too is suddenly on the agenda and equally contagious as Cortona becomes a hive of creativity and cultural activities. Dotted through the town and made available to the students are: studios, stonemasons' yards, kilns, printing presses, exhibition spaces, marble from Carrara, steel, and oxyacetylene. Right now, my studio is entertaining the hopes of a future generation of American artists, determined to stay true to their art and not sell out. A novel situation for me, as in London, having missed out on art school and not knowing that many artists in London, I was almost resigned to becoming the token artist at my friends' dinner parties.

I suspect Bettina has been reporting all our shenanigans back to Nella my landlady, including that riotous evening the students put on a performance in the garden, with music and projecting slides onto the side of the tower. In any case, something has precipitated my aunt's friend unexpected arrival in town because Nella is fulminating and what a reception, we gave her! Jef has been complaining about a bad back on and off ever since he arrived: he blames it on too much Vespa riding off the beaten track looking for secluded places to have sex and it finally decided to pack up on him last night. What timing! They had to stretcher him out in the middle of the night, hollering in pain as the two paramedics maneuvered him with all the grace of removalists down the corkscrew top landing stairwell to the waiting ambulance in the lane. Nella is at the door first thing this morning with Bettina in tow, demanding to know what the hell is going on and who on earth is Jef? I must look a sight, standing on the doorstep after such a disturbed night and Nella's brusqueness is an unexpected curve ball speeding in my direction. I fluster, vainly try for a sympathy vote, explaining how Jef is a guest and was in such pain before they rushed him off to hospital and hoping it's not too serious.

I never expected such a frosty reception and to my amazement, Nella turns up again in the afternoon, plants herself squarely at the front door then absolutely insists on coming inside to inspect the tower, brushing away my feeble protest, claiming she has the right and marching straight in. I wait outside, stepping back to let her pass when she re-emerges ten minutes later, glowering through her spectacles and dragging out a mattress from the spare bedroom which she claims has been soiled, pointing to a stain.

Jef has been lingering in a mosquito-infested ward for nearly two weeks now, his slow recovery aided by the hospital bar's red wine and the ministrations of Meryl, a friendly young blonde acolyte from Miami on the Georgia program. They should have taken Jef to the hospital in Cortona, only 300 metres away, but he insisted on Castiglion Fiorentino, twelve kilometers up the road, because "the wine is better here," he protests. Given the state he was in that night I wonder how he had the presence of mind to redirect the ambulance or why they even listened to him. It makes my life harder visiting him, as I have to risk my neck every time I jump on his Vespa – nose-diving down the hill on the unwieldy, heavy machine that I find almost impossible to control.

Meryl has delayed her departure for a week to be with Jef, after the rest of the Georgia program reluctantly picked up and left for home; our most enamoured visitors have flown, all fervently promising a return ASAP.

Testosterone levels around town are returning to normal levels and the intense atmosphere of cultural and social busyness that has pervaded Cortona over the last two month has evaporated into thin air. A reminder that summer is coming to a close, and Latin lovers are taking their repose.

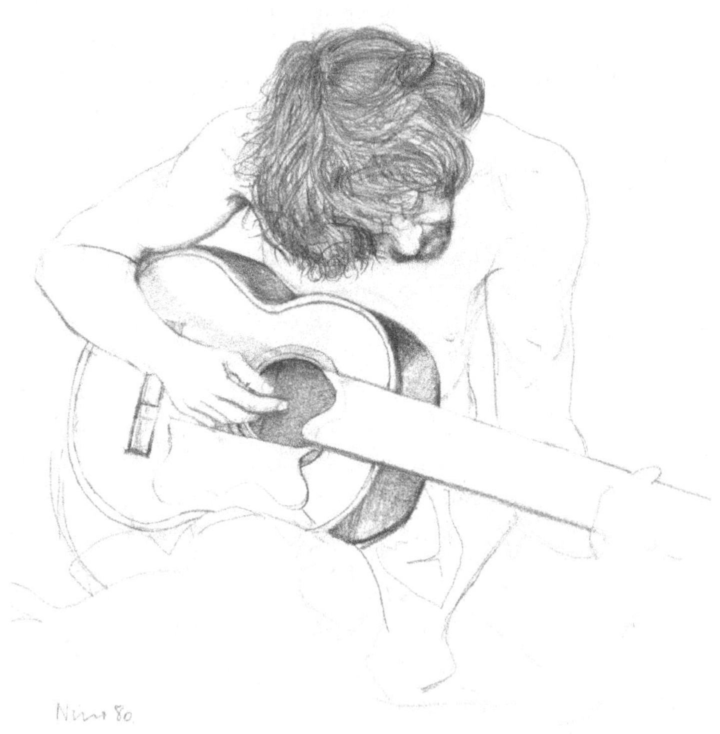

Jef.1980

Chapter 8.

Finally the doctors send Jef home to me; there is nothing more they can do for him, except prescribe painkillers and recommend he wears the orthopedic corset he has been issued. Meryl has returned to Miami and Jef, shuffling with an awkward old man's stooping gait is totally depressed. Making matters even worse, his release has coincided with bad news from his agent Peter at Curtis Brown in London; that no fewer than 18 publishers have now turned down his second novel *The Emirates File* and there is nothing more he can do with it. Retreating to his garret, Jef is a pale shadow of his former self, an apparition, and threatening to tear up the only surviving manuscript of his unpublished novel—a threat he has now duly carried out.

Holed up in his attic, one of his first requests is for me to get in touch with Carolyn, an Australian doctor he knows living in Valecchie near Cortona. Her house is buried halfway up a hillside along a dodgy track and without a phone, so he wants me to deliver a message to the shop in her valley. Dutifully I mount the Vespa and, now that I am getting the hang of it, swoop down out of Cortona, feeling the exhilaration of speed and the onrush of flat country rising up to greet me at sea level. The landscape is studded with olive trees, cypresses and majestic umbrella pines, burnt Sienna under forest green, dotted with villas painted bright yellow and ancient stone farmhouses with venetian red *coppe* tiled roofs.

Old ladies in black totter by the roadside, humping hessian sacks of foraged greens and old men with sun-hardened leather necks and cabbage hands are playing cards under the pergolas of the bars as I roar by.

The shop is easy to find located, on the road into the valley with its telephone sign hanging above the door, although in reality it is only the ground floor room of a contadino's house. A friendly, disheveled young man wearing a battered bandana, whose country clothes smell of sheep, assures me Carolyn will get the note and she duly arrives a few days later, bowling up to the tower in a blue Mini Minor with UK licence plates. A good looking, precocious white volpino dog introduced as Voss saunters in behind her, chattering in a bizarre raspy voice, like someone who has smoked too much and is drowning in catarrh. Carolyn adjusts her Alice band several times, pushing back her streaked silver hair as she walks in. She immediately qualifies as one of Rupert's badly dressed *stranieri,* in faded corduroys, a loosely knitted cream cardigan tied at the waist over a pale blue cheesecloth Indian shirt and desert boots. She is an attractive lady around Jef's age: the intelligent forehead and handsome nose more Germanic than Australian, cautious, with deep-set almond shaped eyes and finely chiseled, sensual lips. Did I really take all that in at a glance?

Jef is lying prone on his mattress placed on the floor. At night, lying on his stomach is the only position he is comfortable in and besides a minor crisis of scorpions dropping down from the rafters onto his back (Tuscan scorpions are small and rarely sting) he has hardly stirred out of his room. I had to rig up a special scratching stick for him so he could swipe the scorpions off.

Carolyn is not registered as a doctor in Italy and therefore can do little for Jef in the way of prescriptions, only offering sympathy and suggests he see a chiropractor: wear the corset and to exercise. She promises to drop in again soon. I waylay her downstairs before she leaves and we settle in the studio with a cup of tea, Voss still chattering over by the door is obviously keen to be on his way. She picks up my battered copy of the I Ching off the coffee table as if to weigh the contents (the Wilhelm edition with the foreword by Jung) and we quickly discover a mutual interest in Jung; Carolyn, besides being a GP is a trained psychotherapist and we have both visited his tower in Küsnacht on Lake Zurich. Normally I shy away from professionals like Carolyn, who in my mind, similar to psychics at drinks parties or customs officers, give me the uncomfortable impression that they can see right through me; but maybe she will prove to be the exception?

Jung believes in meaningful coincidences: a concept he labelled synchronicity, and so it shouldn't have come as a surprise that two days after meeting Carolyn a telegram arrives announcing that Joan and Alan, my old upstairs neighbours in Queensgate Terrace, London, are on their way to visit me, having left London by car. Both of them are Jungian psychotherapists, which makes me think this would be a good opportunity to invite Carolyn over to meet them.

I had completely forgotten about my invitation to them, which I must have extended in a moment of euphoria just before leaving London. We only met for the first-time last year when I was stripping the floorboards in my apartment, making a terrible racket, and left a bunch of roses on Joan's doorstep by way of apologising. Joan came down to thank me for being so thoughtful, a stocky woman in her early fifties with cropped greying hair and bright, girly eyes. The sanding machine I'd hired for the job was the size of a lawn mower and ploughed the floor in roars, shrieking every time it hit a loose nail. Tish was getting edgy "do we really need to do that?" And the neighbours downstairs -the retired couple, were already complaining about a crack in the plaster and damage to their ceiling rosette. Fortunately, they were moving out anyway and I was determined to finish the job, somehow believing the noise would disappear, entirely by symbiosis: having a pair of earmuffs clamped over my ears.

Casanova Jef, meanwhile, has revealed he hardly knows Carolyn and I presumed they were old friends: he just wanted an excuse to see her again and I do believe he is a little jealous when I mention my plans to invite her over. Jef can be gracious, he has charm, but not after a few weeks incarcerated in his room, me shuttling food up and down the stairs to him on a seemingly never-ending basis and my resentment is beginning to show. His only exercise is hunched up over his guitar or playing the flute. Admittedly he has difficulty walking, but that could equally be *rigor mortis* setting in.

Alan plants himself squarely on the couch in my studio every morning, chomping through a big bowl of muesli, while Joan paces the room like a forensic scientist enthusiastically unearthing the clues around her. In London, Joan would periodically borrow one of my surrealist paintings and present it for discussion at the workshops she held upstairs in her flat. She picks up a watercolour off the table, a study of a rock, and can't help herself, bursting out about princely transformations and how the rock is really a frog, showing me for confirmation. Alan, between mouthfuls, is as determined to engage me in earnest conversation, as I am to continue painting: a battle of wills.

The pressures of playing host are very new to me but once I've grown accustomed to their presence I'm beginning to relax and enjoy their company. Alan is measured, Joan is forthright: one of those people who like to talk but is also willing to listen.

The portrait of Ron is tailor-made for Joan's interpretative skills. Ron is reclining apparently naked in the club chair (actually he was wearing his ubiquitous shorts, hidden by the armrest), gazing dreamily straight ahead in a three-quarters profile, his body painted half black half white, the two sides held together by a blue bandana tied around his forehead.

"The integration of the conscious and the unconscious," Joan declares. "Bound together, you notice, by the blue bandana, representing the transcending force." Joan has an earnest doctor's voice with a sauntering Derbyshire lilt that is pleasant on the ear; it carries authority wrapped in a tissue of empathy. Ron's feet are firmly planted on the tiled floor of the studio.

"The tiles represent stability, a secure foundation," says Alan. "And look at the archetype, the Ku Klux Klan figure lurking in the background landscape." Whoops Joan with delight.

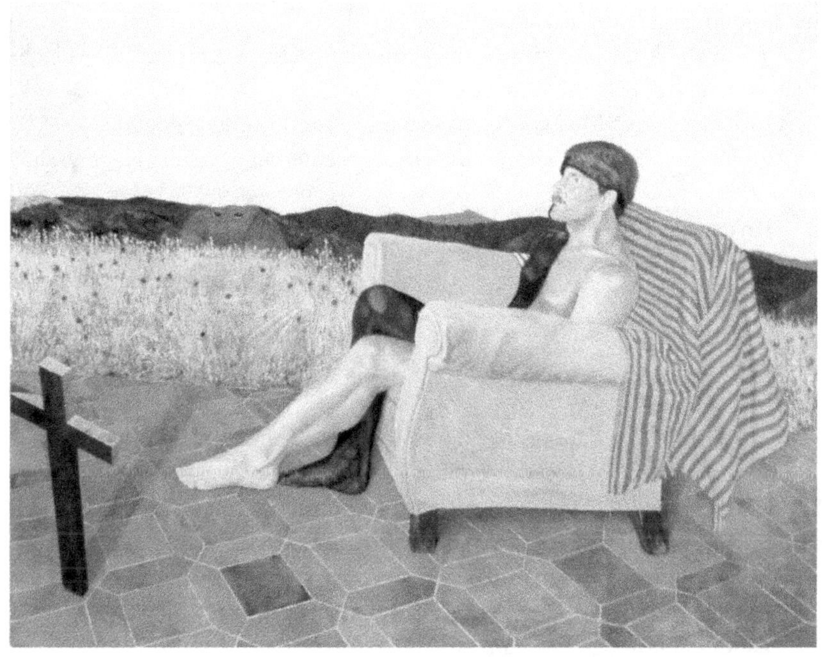

Southern man.1980

More than merely providing a pretext to see Carolyn again, Joan has been throwing us together at every available opportunity: dinner at the tower hosted by Joan, followed by lunch at Carolyn's place, a pizza at La Vallone, where Alan nearly killed us after turning the car onto the wrong side of the main road at a stop, and I am appreciative of Carolyn offering to take my guests on a guided tour of hill towns, allowing me to stay at home and paint.

I like Carolyn's humour and the coy flirtatiousness that occasionally breaks through her calm reserve: her laugh is contagious and so is her dog! Voss is the spitting image of that happy leaping white dog on the tarot card the Fool or Wanderer in the original A.E. Waite pack; one of my favourite Tarot cards: innocence fearlessly stepping into the abyss, so confident, not even considering the consequences.

Carolyn and I are alone in the basement one evening sitting at the kitchen table, Joan and Alan are in Rome and Jef is safely locked up in his room, out of sight.

"I prefer working as a psychotherapist; being in a surgery prescribing pills all daylong gives me a headache."

"You'd think delving into peoples' minds would be more of a headache than dishing out pills?" I surmise.

Carolyn laughs. "I bet you're someone who never visits a doctor?"

"Or shrinks for that matter—they make me nervous; I don't like revealing myself!"

"Isn't that the point?"

"Exactly. You know I sometimes duck down an alley way off the Corso just to avoid seeing anyone."

"The privacy of the confessional would be perfect for you! You need a priest."

"I have Joan!"

I'm starting to get butterflies in my stomach whenever I am near Carolyn.

Joan knows. She sees me coming from a mile away, and has already tackled me head on about any preconceived notions I might have about our age differences. Carolyn, I have discovered is thirteen years older than me, which is a little disconcerting. Calculating: 26-39/36-49/46-59… Does it really matter?

"I should know," states Joan.

"Look at us…

"A shining example," fills in Alan.

"Happily married (Alan concurs with a nod) and I could almost be twice his age!"

"Age no obstacle," Alan intones in his deep plodding voice, stroking his beard.

As Carolyn gets up from the table to go home, I slip my hands round her waist, touching her for the first time. Her reflex is to cup my head and so I pull her closer towards me:

"Why not stay tonight?" I say emboldened.

"Should I?"

The next morning, looking into her eyes I whisper:

"It feels so good to wake up with someone next to you and not wanting to be a million miles for a change!"

As a parting gift, Joan has waved her magic wand over Jef; she could see I have been getting nowhere fast with him and in her professional capacity suggested I stop taking him his meals. A bit extreme I thought, starving him out, but on doctor's orders, why not?

In retrospect I don't think he holds it against me, we are still on speaking terms and now here he is, wearing the corset underneath a long silk dressing gown, moving awkwardly I grant you, but heading straight down the stairs to the kitchen on his own two feet!

Chapter 9.

I did have high hopes of extending the lease to the tower past the October deadline, but after the kerfuffle with Jef, relations with Nella have taken a turn for the worse and she has made it very plain she isn't interested in prolonging my stay; instead, she has found a new tenant, a retired Admiral no less, the fucking pirate!

The Cortonesi are in winter preparation mode. The house martins, the swifts and swallows, the cuckoos, the nightingales and hoopoe birds have long since flown, along with the University of Georgia and the crowds of tourists who, at the height of summer, on Ferragosto in the middle of August, pack the Corso tighter than the rush-hour on the London Tube. The days themselves are drawing in, taking counter-measures against the unfamiliar chills. Woodpiles jam the deserted alleyways, waiting to be secreted away and neatly stacked in cantinas. A pleasant sweet scent of wood smoke gathers in palls above the narrow, ancient streets where an unfamiliar dankness also begins to lurk.

The question of returning to London has hardly crossed my mind; I feel at home in Cortona now and there is my developing romance with Carolyn to consider. Thankfully, finding a new place to live over winter has turned out to be relatively easy. I have been asking around about places to rent and old man Renato at the hardware store opposite Bar Signorelli, has introduced me to his son Paolo, who has a furnished house adjacent to Porta Montanina, only 50 yards further up from the tower, which as a favour to his father he is willing to rent to me over the winter months. The house is a duplex, Paolo's sister owns the other half but no one lives there. It wouldn't make any difference even if they did—the stonewalls are so thick you'd never hear them and the terraced garden is all on my side of the house. The garden is the most breathtaking part, almost overhanging the crumbling stone portico of Porta Montanina, just where the wall plunges headlong down the hillside, scything through the countryside, neatly demarcating town and country limits.

A narrow stone staircase zigzags left and right from the lane up to the front porch. Inside there are two open-plan floors with an inter-connecting staircase. It's not ideal but the rent is low. The windows are uniformly small, hinting at a gloominess ahead that is mirrored by Paolo's choice of dark, cumbersome furniture. The kitchen and bathroom are both tiny and the only splash of levity is Paolo's collection of brightly decorated ceramic vases sitting on the mantelpiece above the fireplace.

Jef was as reluctant to move out as I was and has found a hole in the wall near the Post Office: literally one poky room with a kitchenette with only the glass in the front door for light. The walls are damp and become coated with a black mould that is almost impossible to get rid of. Ron has the same problem in his kitchen: you can scrape off the spongy spores with an ice cream scoop, like a dollop of chocolate chip it's so thick, and within days it inevitably resurfaces. Welcome to winter, and I'm beginning to understand Martin's warning; the honeymoon is over.

Winter officially starts with the first tramontana in November, a biting north wind that crashes headlong across Europe all the way from Siberia, scouring the snow-topped peaks of the Apennines before descending into Cortona like a an avenging harpi from hell, whip-cracking along the Corso and penetrating every wall, window, door and bone. The only heating in my house is the fireplace and a small mobile electric radiator that follows me around like a lost puppy on a leash. Howling, I go to bed with a woolly hat on and leggings under my nightshirt or I rug up and paint all night just to avoid the icy bed sheets. Carolyn refuses almost point blank to stay overnight and who can blame her; although her house, without electricity, can get equally cold. Painting outside is a warmer option than staying inside and offers more light, propping my canvas against the side of the house with the garden behind me, and more of those spectacular views of the Valdichiana to my right. Or I sail down the hill to the central piazza gripping my canvas as I tack to the wind.

Setting up on the small terrace above the loggia, no one pays me much attention; in Cortona people are accustomed to seeing artists in the streets beavering away behind easels. I am painting my Livingstone story—more about Stanley now that I've discovered I'm not the first explorer to reach these shores. A self-portrait with the Comune as the backdrop, while I hover above the piazza with one hand extended in front, preparing to deliver Stanley's famous words.

Some mornings I see Jef below, with his Swiss army coat pulled over his pyjamas, hurrying across the piazza to Bar *Signorelli*, where he huddles up against the tall radiators on the central column with an espresso and grappa chaser.

Most days I venture out to scavenge for firewood; a new quest, and in part a measure of living, to augment the stack of wood Paolo very thoughtfully left for me in the small cantina under the house. Carrying a staff and wearing a floppy felt hat, a white scarf tightly wound around my neck and the tatty waterproof cape that Jane's brother John was throwing out before I bagged it, I imagine myself in a painting by Courbet ("Bonjour Monsieur Courbet") and take the timer shot with my camera positioned on a rocky ledge.

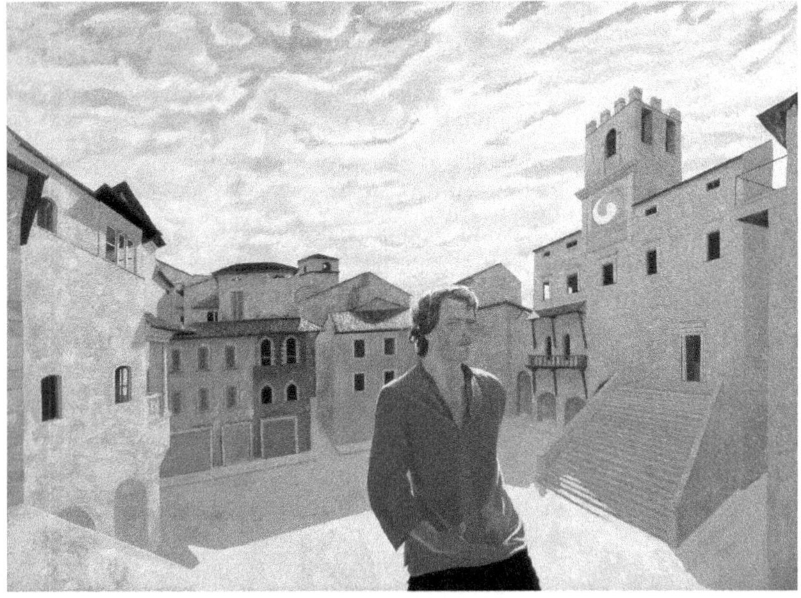

Dr.Livingston presume.1981

My route takes me along a half-buried paved track of Roman origin, into the wet, stinging mists that shroud the mountain, up past the chestnut and oak and through the pinewoods closer to the summit of Sant'Egidio. I carry a long leather strap with a buckle, to bundle up the faggots of wood I collect along the way and cart home later on my back like a *contadino*, I like to imagine. Dumping my load in the cantina, wet through and exhausted, it feels like an achievement nevertheless. The pity is not having a hot bath to wallow in after, only a feeble shower that delivers a stingy couple of litres of lukewarm water before running out, leaving me stranded on the cold, tiled bathroom floor. Carolyn at least does have a bath with almost unlimited piping hot water heated by a wood-boiler, *scaldibagno*. Such bliss.

Jef and I are like a couple of old codgers now when we meet in the piazza, hands in pockets, scarves and collars turned up, shivering whilst reminiscing about the good old days of summer wine.

"Ni, I can't take it anymore! I've decided I have to get out of *Cortona*. It's the only way."

Jef knows that people are losing patience with him after a protracted bout of depression lasting since he was hospitalised in *Castiglione*. I can empathise with him because I have been there myself and know just how damn hard it is to shake off the black dog. All the time, you know the remedy is as simple as doing something, anything! Just get off your butt; yet there is a vice like clamp on your body that paralyses and almost makes it impossible to act.

"It was probably a mistake coming back here." Jef confides. "I didn't count on there being so many memories of Caroline. I have to make a clean break, start over. So, I'm going to try my luck in Rome. At least I'll have a better chance of finding some work there."

It had not occurred to me that Jef was still pining for his ex but could explain the frenzy of activity over the summer and his ultimate collapse.

It must be the season, because no sooner has Jef departed when Ron announces he is leaving too.

"I've had enough and am going back to Philadelphia. After three years, anywhere is better than here; Cortona is just a stagnant backwater!" he says, emphasising his words, as if that will banish any lingering doubts he might be having.

We are in my place sitting in front of the fire roasting the chestnuts that I collect in the woods, using a special griddle pan that has a series of holes punched into the bottom. Rising off the couch to leave, Ron grabs hold of the mantel piece, an unsecured plank sitting on two rusty spikes driven into the wall underneath and it's already crashing down with three of Paolo's precious vases on top before I have the wit to warn him it isn't secured. Déjà vu: one time, in the tower, Ron went to open the window in my studio for a better look at the full moon and the entire window frame came off in his hand. Ron is an accident in waiting, but he can be poetry in motion too, spellbinding like his singing voice, a choreography that is worth watching to the end even if it spells a disaster.

Sweeping the shards on the floor into a pan after Ron departs mumbling his apologies, I wonder should I tell Paolo? I'm already feeling guilty about it, guilty for something I didn't do! So typical, and I make a brief mental inventory of all the pointless cover-ups I have involved myself in up until now: my first ever job in London working in the rag trade at a wholesaler, delivering racks of clothes to shops around town. One morning, driving my employer Bernie's brand-new van during rush hour, I badly scraped a parked car, not stopping, and got the sack because I didn't tell him, instead, parking the van in the garage that night with the damaged side squeezed tight against the wall so nobody would notice. Equally in Scotland, driving the tractor with a front loader through the barn wall, looking back over my shoulder thinking I was in reverse when I was in first and I shot forwards instead. Then shovelling grain in front of the gaping hole as if nobody would notice that either!

Postponing any decision concerning Paolo, I have stashed the broken pottery in a plastic bag under the bed, probably hoping he will never notice their disappearance.

Chapter 10.

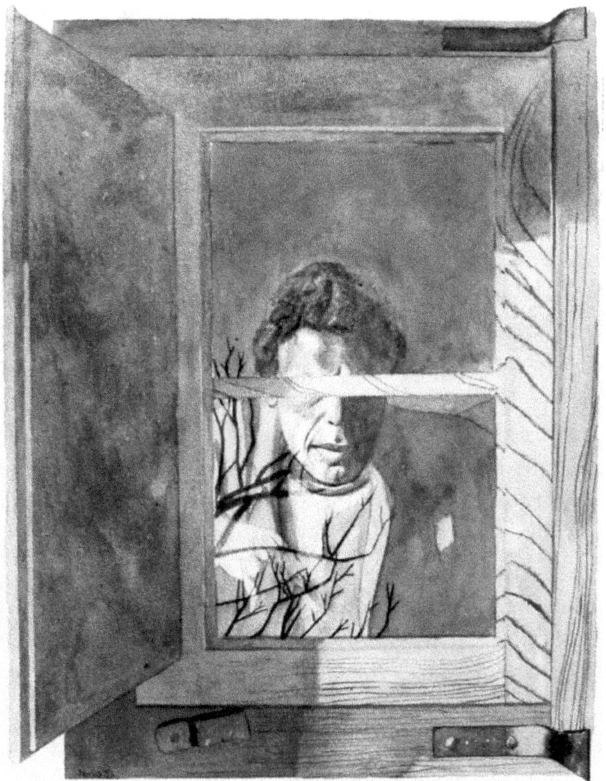

Through the Looking Glass.1981

Winter days spent on my own are a far cry from the euphoria of summer. With Jef and Ron now departed, I am even seeing less of Carolyn (and my new best friend Voss). I have discovered she is as private in nature as I am and hibernates in her garden flat in Rome for long periods, occasionally inviting me to stay. She came to Italy from Greece, fleeing the colonels with a mob of Australians in the early seventies and her flat in Trastevere is the same one she rented when she first arrived in Rome. Fortunately for her it is rent controlled and very cheap.

I sit upstairs in my bedroom at the long table, a woollen blanket draped round my shoulders, passing the time idly doodling or writing heartfelt poems; or I gaze vacantly out of the tiny window in a thought bubble of my own.

Directly opposite, the dirt road down to the centre is more like a country lane, wending its way between walled open spaces and terraces of olive trees with tall pine trees pushed up against the city wall. In winter, try walking down with ice underfoot and you're quickly upended. I feel cut off from the rest of town. Hardly a soul stirs up here except the postman on his morning round and he just shoots by on his Vespa, heading out of the gate to Tavernelle, his large leather mail pouch flapping off his belly, earmuffs clamped under his peaked blue cap. The old man from the camera shop in the Corso sets up his Hasselblad directly below my window one afternoon, a small man but he casts a giant Dracula shadow out in front of him, the way he is huddled over the camera in his long winter coat, taking picture postcards of Porta Montanina with a scoop of snow posted on the top. More treacherous still is via Berretini; thinking about the first time Sabine drove us up to the tower, the road is so steep that even negotiating it safely on foot you are forced to stem Christie your way down. Once, Voss, spying a cat lounging in the road half way down, took off at speed from Bettina's and found out the hard way: that once you've gained momentum there's no turning back and nothing to stop you from crashing into the wall at the bottom, he desperately back-pedaling, the cat meanwhile not even bothering to move out of the way as he shot past.

Cortona is dead after eight in winter, everyone is home having dinner in front of the TV. Benito is always impatient to close the bar and get home, or otherwise he gives the dead shift to his barmaid Carla and she's the same, grinning from ear to ear but eager to bundle you out of the door as soon she can. One evening, passing by the bar, rugged up against the Corso wind chill factor, I can see Bernardo through the glass doors, standing at the counter next to another man. Nine o'clock is late by Cortona's standards and Benito must be getting impatient.

"Heya! Nino! Can you spare a minute?"

Bernardo yells out catching sight of me. Bernardo is German, but nobody calls him Bernhard. Benito is polishing wine glasses and rolls his eyes as I enter, tut-tutting as if to say "You foreigners!"

"What's up Bernardo?"

I ask, seeing him struggle to keep the slumped figure from slipping down the bar, his head face pinned to the counter as if he is asleep.

"Do you mind giving me a hand, so I can get him to the taxi when it comes?"

"Sure, what happened to him?"

Bernardo smirks, looking flushed but triumphant and baring all his teeth.

"I drank him under the table."

"More like onto the table judging by where you are!" I point out.

I can imagine Bernardo in a Munich beer hall wiping the foaming froth from his moustache and leering at the waitress through the bottom of his giant glass.

Benito starts to wipe down the marble top and sensitively skirts the man's marooned head. I have to stop myself from apologising for him even though I don't even know the guy. You rarely see Italians blind drunk in public: it's more than likely that it will be the foreigner who will make fools of themselves.

"Who's your friend?" I ask Bernardo.

Like so many Germans he speaks an impeccable English.

"Meet Bob. An American artist. He's rented that place you were interested in, the one Jef lived in with his girlfriend, below the tennis courts at the end of the *parterra*."

"Really, that's interesting, I always did wonder what happened to that place. Shame too. It would have been perfect for me with the separate studio."

"Well at least it's an artist who took it." Bernardo says commiserating.

It was the first house I looked at this winter when was looking for a place to rent and I was fully expecting to be offered it but never heard back from the owner, an Australian lady.

We shovel a highly intoxicated Bob into the taxi when it arrives, giving the driver instructions on where to go and some notes to cover the fare. By now, Benito is staring daggers, turning off lights and locking the double doors immediately behind us, with only a curt goodnight.

Winter does have some compensations: for starters there is a great calm that settles over Cortona and as a *straniero*, you gain kudos with the locals for being more than just another fair-weather friend. The Cortonesi are flattered by the show of solidarity and our presence only serves to confirm their very high opinion that there's no better place in the world to be than Tuscany, even in winter.

For extended periods the town is completely severed from the plain below, when the Valdichiana is flooded by thick cloud so white, seen from above it dazzles like a vast field of freshly powdered snow. Driving up from Camucia is like take-off in a plane, bursting through the heavy cloud cover into the crystal-clear blue skies that reign above Cortona, that Camelot-like, rises out of the misty lake, one of a chain of island peaks sprinkled all the way down to Monte Cetona.

Cotton wool tides fraying at the edges gently bob and lap to and fro, pouring into every spur of the surrounding valleys, wispy hoary fingertips probing every nook and cranny. I am far above the lake out of harm's way, safely swaddled in sleepy Rip Van Winkle's petticoats.

Not surprisingly, Bob doesn't remember me a week later when out of curiosity I pay him a visit, but he is happy to invite me in, especially when he learns I'm also an artist. The small stone cottage is light and airy, quite the opposite to my place, surrounded by an olive grove and situated on the gentler slope below Cortona facing south, secluded but within easy walking distance of Cortona along the *Parterre.* I notice Jef's novel *Black Jack* lying open on the kitchen table as soon as I enter and, pointing it out, turn to him:

"How funny, did you know the author was living in this house when he wrote that book, probably right here on this table?"

"You don't say! It was the first book I picked off the bookshelf and I haven't put it down since. Quite a subject: Terrorists in the Valdichiana, huh!"

"Yeah, a hotbed. I've been driving my girlfriend's Mini around and there are police roadblocks everywhere! Have you noticed? We live in a police state."

"Hey not that surprising when you consider the past!"

"There's a police force for everything here, even one for the railways; all armed to the teeth!"

"Carolyn, my girlfriend says you can even be stopped for transporting more than five litres of your own olive oil in the back of your car and did you know artists can be fined for transporting their paintings in the car? It's a joke. But like everything else here, there is always a work around. In these case it's enough to write out on a piece of paper declaring they are your work and signing it."

"I don't drive, never have," says Bob, looking for the bottle opener.

"But I'm thinking of buying a second hand *motorino* if you hear of one?"

I settle on the couch while Bob uncaps a bottle of Co-op red: plonk, sold in all the grocery shops in that distinctive Chianti flask shape, only the covering is fake straw made out of plastic. Even cheap table wines taste good in Italy though. Bob would be in his forties, but it's hard to tell with his mop of thinning white hair and one-inch beard spiked ginger that curls under his chin. His teeth are stained as are his fingertips, he must be a heavy smoker and I notice the pack of Nazionale on the table, the same Government brand that I like to smoke. They are the cheapest and nastiest tobacco, dry as sawdust exuding a very distinctive aroma and delivering an almighty whack to the back of the throat. Carolyn is asthmatic and can't abide the smoke so on occasion I find myself hanging out of the bedroom window for a puff after we make love.

"You know, I looked at this place too when it was on the market and would have definitely rented it had it been offered to me, which obviously it wasn't." Picking up my glass.

"Gee, I'm sorry if I messed with your plans. I guess Belinda prefers the Yankee dollar to the British pound."

"Or maybe she thought you looked more responsible! I'm curious, how did you find out about it?"

"I was in Verona when I saw her ad in the Herald Tribune and caught the train down immediately. The only downside is my girlfriend Jane is in America still. Damn! I miss her."

"Isn't she coming over?"

"That's yet to be seen. We shared a loft in Chicago and I was going crazy working nights as a barman in an Irish pub and painting during the day. Let's just say I had to get out for my health's sake, but she wasn't ready to leave and didn't want to quit her teaching job. I still call her every week, hoping she will have a change of heart especially now I'm more settled, and you gotta say it, Cortona's just unreal." Waving his hand.

"Copy that." I say, trying to sound American.

We refill our glasses and move over to the studio, a demountable room off to the side of the house. I'm surprised: "You work fast! I thought you said you've only been here a few weeks?"

There are a dozen or so small oil paintings on the floor propped up against the skirting boards. I can count the number of paintings I've done since I've been here on the fingers of one hand. Bob's are mostly landscapes: the surrounding olive groves, views of the house, some with a sprinkle of snow. Not exactly my taste and, a little disappointed, I avoid making too many direct comments. (Dissembling hints for awkward moments in an artist's studio: say nothing but smile a lot or bury your head in the painting with your back to the artist and mumble. You can always ask about the title and how long the work took and hey, that's my favourite colour etc.; focusing on details you can usually find something positive to say. "Oh, what fun" is probably the standard English fare.

Bob is extremely passionate and verbose about his art, keen to show me everything with a child's delight, which is endearing, and I suspect anyway he is thick-skinned enough not to be too concerned about other peoples' opinions of his work. Artists need to find the confidence to back themselves. I was depressed for weeks in London after Erik, that "successful" artist, came to see my paintings and said point blank I should consider taking up another career! Ultimately, though, the experience rebounded as it served to steel my resolve to carry on.

"Another glass of wine?" Bob hangs a friendly arm on my shoulder and leads me back to the house where he pulls out a packet of photos from a bureau, keen to show me his previous work.

"Here take a look at these, my last works in Chicago," sliding them across the table one by one, offering a running commentary.

"From my last show downtown in the business district, just before coming here, see…we hung the paintings like banners off the first-floor balcony of the building's atrium."

"Great! This is so different from your new work." I genuinely enthuse.

"Yeah, I know, it's very different what I was doing before!"

The semi-abstract paintings look like large swirling galaxies with great plumes of black smoke.

"This one I built up using sand, hard to see in a photo, though." Raised sections like the rim of a volcano protrude out of the canvas and briefly connect me to my own experiments with the cement like impastos reflecting the fresco grounds I so admire.

I'm genuinely puzzled though by Bob's change of style; it's so incongruous and hardly feels like a step forward, but for once, Bob becomes taciturn, unwilling to delve any deeper into the subject except to say:

"Look I want to live here in Italy and I want Jane to be with me, so I've got to give it my best shot and sell paintings if it's going to work. Besides, I kinda like the challenge; I've never painted landscapes before."

Chapter 11.

Carolyn is currently rehearsing in an amateur production of The Pirates of Penzance, opening soon at the Anglican Church in Rome. Normally I wouldn't be seen dead at a Gilbert and Sullivan production, but she is in the chorus and I have promised to be there on opening night. Occasionally I babysit Voss at her place in Valecchie, so she can go to rehearsals in Rome without having to worry about him, and I drive her to the station at Terontola in the Mini. Staying at Carolyn's is a welcome break from the bleakness of Porta Montanina but Voss remains a fraught responsibility, considering how independent he is and a serial wanderer. In Rome he can disappear for days at a time, his nose eagerly sweeping the ground: then suddenly he's latched onto the right scent and is gone, driving Carolyn mad with worry searching for him, but he always finds his own way home: the prodigal. The rake! I am mindful. He is a charmer, innocently cocking his head sideways, looking up at you, pricked triangular ears, tongue draped casually out the side of his mouth and batting his long dark eyelashes at you; all a prelude to scarpering, a freedom I normally wouldn't begrudge him, but not on my watch thank you, not if I have to be answerable to Carolyn. I double the guards.

Carolyn's rustic hideaway is cosy; a small stone workers cottage on two levels that she has restored lovingly but simply, reflecting her nature and her desire for privacy. It is tucked into the side of the hill above the valley, with no electricity or telephone and the water is gravity fed from a spring at the top of the hill behind the house. Having a bathtub is a definite bonus. A bath has to be one of life's ultimate luxuries and I miss not having one at my place. Apart from the pure physical pleasure of immersion, soaking in a bath remains the best excuse I know for doing absolutely nothing and not having to feel guilty about it: a space nobody can reasonably invade or hold expectations of you undertaking anything for them. I rush up to Carolyn at the station on her return, kiss her and then proceed to make a show of breathing all over her face. Voss bounces in behind me, as happy as I am to see her again.

"Notice anything?" I ask her enthusiastically.

She looks at me in alarm and then twigs.

"You don't smell of tobacco!"

"Yes! I've stopped smoking!" I say jubilantly. "It's been over a week."

I'm hyper-ecstatic having made it this far without any serious signs of weakening. No more bulky cigarette packets to find pockets for in summer, or worrying about running out or kissing with a tobacco mouth. Now I don't have to look foolish with the other smokers huddled on the verandas of non-smokers' houses. Instead, I'm chewing matchsticks—which are soaked in paraffin, Bob points out.

"Whad'ya think keeps'em burning, dumbass?"

Turps anyway is an addiction I can live with, I breath it in every day in my studio sending me into a tail spin of addiction.

Finally, winter is on the retreat; a few almond trees tentatively blossom in February and the green-tipped shoots of winter wheat carpet the Valdichiana by March. Our fair-weather feathered friends return one by one: first the nightingales, tuning up deep within the bramble thickets, then the cuckoos, zeroing in like waves of stealth bombers, flying low across the fields and through the valleys into cover of the trees. I am certain I could be the first letter writer to The Times to announce their arrival and I play Delius's "On hearing the first cuckoo in Spring" in endless loops on my record player.

It will be a relief to see the back of winter and Porta Montanina. The two have become synonymous in my mind; cold and dark and depressing, huddled over the heater, painting in candlelight to all hours of the night just to avoid climbing into a freezing bed. Carolyn in her understated fashion has already suggested apropos of moving out of Porta Montanina, that "if all else fails" I can stay with her. Hedging her bets, she hasn't come right out and said why not move in with me? She is not so bold; and probably unsure herself, but then again, she isn't suggesting I move into the spare room either. She finds committing as hard as I do and my understanding to date is, except for that Greek tenor who only lasted a few months, she hasn't really been in a serious relationship before.

The approaching spring has also brought Bob the good news of Jane's imminent arrival; his perseverance has paid off, although he had better get his act together quickly and stop binging to all hours; it must be the Irish in him. Bob loves a good yarn too and is a marvel to hear speaking in Italian, already sounding fluent in his fashion although he has a tendency to garble.

He is garrulous to the point of hijacking conversations, which is putting some people off, but I find him amusing and underneath the bluster he can suddenly become astute, offering up something with genuine insight.

Bob has become something of a mentor to me, generously sharing his time and sharing his knowledge of painting and the more technical aspects, something I missed out on not going to art school: how to properly stretch a canvas, or wetting the stretched canvas on the back to achieve a better tension and iron out creases; how to mend a torn canvas or make frames, as we labour together with his new mitre saw. He is also encouraging me in my work, which I appreciate, even if I do feel embarrassed not to be able to fully return the compliment.

Early in the morning: it must be! I was up all night again, painting "Which way Jerusalem" a candle held to the night and the moon above the shadowy building opposite seen through my window, when Bob, bright as a button, appears on the doorstep with Jane. I've been half expecting them. Rupert had already alerted me to her arrival and that Bob's been busy racing all over town introducing his new bride to all and sundry as" *La mia Signora*". I can see how delighted he is, beaming all over his face but standing on the porch, having just gone to bed, sleepy and with only an oversized shirt on, I'm not inclined to invite them in, hoping not to appear too rude. Jane hangs back , hiding under her straw hat and glasses, her fine lips a hint of passion but her chestnut hair reined in tightly and she appears nervous; probably jet-lag, although she says it's her bio-rhythms that need time to adjust. She speaks softly but with a firm

voice, quite the opposite to Bob who is all over the place and yes, she is probably just what he needs right now, someone to take the rudder and steer him gently into harbour.

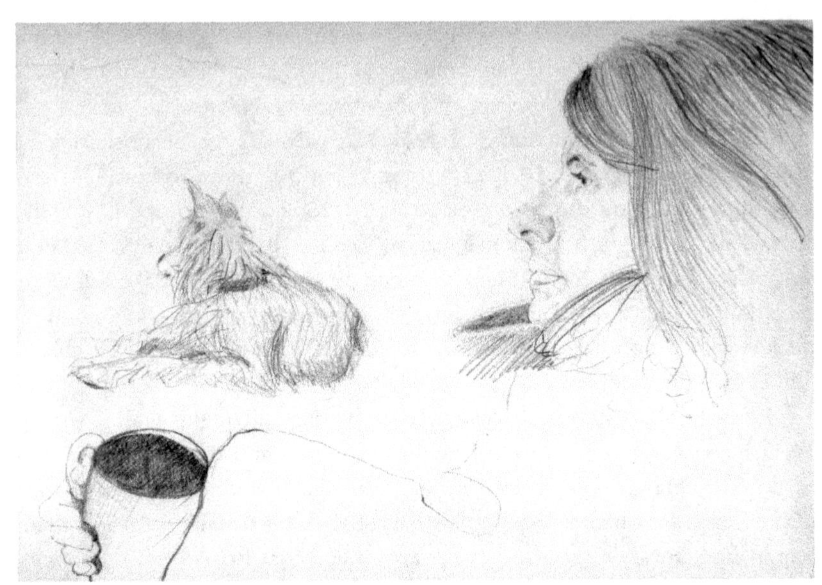

Carolyn with Voss.1982

Chapter 12.

Almost exactly to the day of my arrival in Cortona, May one year ago, Carolyn bowls up to Porta Montanina in the Mini (she drives with panache) leaving Voss at home, so we can fit my trunk and easel onto the back seat. Paolo turned up at the last minute to inventory the house and immediately noticed the three missing vases. He was annoyed and asked if I had kept the shards, which much to my embarrassment I had only recently disposed of in a last-minute fit of cleaning. I have promised to make amends. Paolo collects rare books; his father has a display in his shop, and if he gives me a list of what to look for, I have offered to visit the antiquarian bookshops in Charing Cross Road next time I am in London.

Carolyn reverses (for traction) at full throttle up her stony track, scrunching the gravel, scraping the Mini's bottom but deftly negotiating an awkward bend, some potholes and tree roots without slowing down to reach the top. She is impressive in full flight. Voss is eagerly awaiting our arrival at the top, barking and barking, rasping and rasping, his spiraling tail beating eggs, half crouching like a wolf with his snout pushed into the air. The gurgle-gargle of his bark catches in the back of his throat and explodes as a fart instead. There is hardly time to step over the threshold of the house and put my bags down on the rug when Carolyn bursts into tears. The dawning reality, we sit together on the couch in front of the fireplace not knowing whether to reach for the Kleenex or pop the champagne cork. Yes, we are both in uncharted waters now, so better reach for the champagne!

Carolyn speaks fluent Italian and is formally addressed as *Dottoressa*, or indirectly as *l'Australiana*, but having lived in the valley for a number of years, she is more affectionately known by the *contadini* as *La Carolina.* She has concerns now about what they might think about my moving in but I honestly don't think it matters to them, we are not Catholics or Italians and I suspect that *stranieri* are not expected to behave or are judged by the same high standards. Margherita, the spritely old *contadina* who runs the shop (*La bottega*) at the valley crossroads, smirks knowingly whenever we come in, as though we are newlyweds. Carolyn's neighbour Amelio, living by himself just down the hill, a veteran of the second world war, has up until now been taking care of her land but is now refusing to come and she thinks he might be jealous. He ploughs her terraces, helps with the olives and brings up the heavy gas cylinders and cut wood for the fire on his baby tractor and trailer. We cross paths occasionally, a lanky, rosy-cheeked *contadino*, his frayed Cossack hat always off at a jaunty angle although he is far from jaunty whenever he sees me out walking with Voss; stonewalling my attempts at friendliness. Carolyn says don't worry, he'll get over it, but the only reason he stops at all is because Voss is friends with his Chihuahua and we have to wait while they circle and sniff.

Spring is warmer this year and not as wet. A thick scent of jasmine and honeysuckle permeates the balcony by Carolyn's front door. She brings out her geranium pots from the under the house; the fragrance of hothouses in London, and places them along the broad slated shoulder of the balcony wall. Voss can comfortably snooze here, resting his head on crossed paws, leaving one eye open in alert.

The house was originally divided into two workers' cottages, but the other half has been let go with only the back wall left standing and a few broken stone steps at the front. Carolyn has restored this half in the traditional style with the living area on the first floor and the cantina underneath turned into a spare room, only adding a bedroom and bathroom above the main floor, reached by almost vertical galley stairs. The thick, flinty walls remain un rendered and the rustic floorboards have the odd colourful scatter rug thrown over them. The house embodies Carolyn perfectly: a spartan but comfortable retreat hidden in the profusion of nature, aesthetically pleasing with sunny aspects over much of the valley looking towards Lago Trasimeno. We eat from old wooden plates, and drink from Cortona ceramic goblets; those stylised sunflower blooms painted green over a yellow ochre ground. In winter Carolyn cooks on the open fire, but she has a gas stove and a gas fridge discreetly hidden under the kitchen bar behind the galley stairs.

For entertainment we mostly listen to the BBC World Service or the RAI on a transistor radio. My Bang & Olufsen record player languishes under the day-bed along with my records of Japan and The Police, Marvin Gaye, Neil Young and Stan Getz. Even Eric Satie or Delius languish or have they been banished too? Carolyn, I have discovered, is a woman of exclusively classical tastes that hardly go further than Mozart. She prefers Gregorian chants and the Baroque, plays the recorder and is teaching herself the viola da gamba.

There is no room in the house for a studio so I have decided to look for a somewhere in Cortona. It's become frustrating painting in makeshift corners. Smelling out the place with turpentine and dripping paint on the floor isn't really an option, and over by the entrance at the open French doors I have to deal with through traffic, when ideally, I need to be left alone and undisturbed in my own space. I admire Magritte dressed in a suit, serenely painting in his living room but that's not for me. I try painting outdoors but never really feel comfortable. Unlike Bob who has become a maniac on his new *motorino*, devouring the road in search of landscapes in all weathers: one time riding as far as Montalcino, a round trip of 120 kilometres to his house.

So instead of painting and as a way of introducing myself, I am bonding with the land and clearing the messy overgrown olive terraces below the house. Covered in blackberry brambles, their spiny, spidery tentacles are arching over the terraces, threading paths through the olive trees and threatening an advance on the house itself. Carolyn is quite content to live in this wildness but something deep down in me also seeks order. Wild roses with thorny stems as thick as rolling pins are climbing the trees behind the house and smothering the tall oleander, while ivy is creeping up the rear of the house. I see myself as a kind of swashbuckling hero, liberator of earth, Carolyn's white knight, cutting swathes through the thickets, single-handedly slaying the hydra-headed monsters and in the heat of battle freely shedding my blood. Also, equipped with a long-handled scythe, I have been slashing the long grass in the small meadow fanning out from the side of the house at the bottom of the stairs. Carolyn has ideas about digging a hole for a small pool on this side so I am preparing the ground.

She practices scales on her viola da gamba every morning, pulling a chair over to the French doors and gripping the instrument between her knees in the cleft of her loose Laura Ashley dress. She is self-conscious and asks me to go away, but I am fascinated by the delicate way she holds the bow with her hand upturned and the way her fingers trill the strings on the neck. Embarrassed, she lugs the viola up the galley stairs to the bedroom but remains within earshot.

"Why don't you take Voss out for a walk!"

I don't mind and can empathise; I was the same when I started painting, shy about showing my work to anyone, and I am not the only one. Rupert has introduced me to another Roberto, a local artist who has lives in Cortona and the first time I visited him he kept me waiting in the hall while he sped around his apartment turning all his paintings to the wall! Bob can get snarky too, if you start commenting on unfinished works. Carolyn's is a work in progress. I can wait and I can go for walks with Voss who, anyway, is keen to introduce me to his many special places.

Bob and Jane have moved from Cortona into the caretaker's lodge of the Belvedere hotel on Monte Sant'Egidio. The hotel used to be a popular summer hill resort but is closed now and up for sale, the second time in as many years. Bob gives painting lessons to the owner, a contessa aspiring to be an artist, but he won't divulge if this is in lieu of rent. The lodge is in a stunning position, cast adrift in a clearing at the end of the hotel drive, backing onto pine forests with elevated panoramas of the Valdichiana and Lago Trasimeno. His house though is cement-rendered and not very attractive, with two rooms plus a kitchen and bathroom. Jane has commandeered one room for her sewing machine. She comes from a farming family and is not a new comer to country life, already having planted a vegetable and herb garden around the house. Bob has "hunkered down for the duration" and is on his best behaviour these days. He has trimmed his beard and cut his hair and wears new slacks tailored by Jane. Safely on the wagon, he has even quit smoking and become a model of sobriety. The power of love. Every Sunday the two of them ride down to Cortona on their his-and-hers *motorinos* to join the throng of Cortonese after Mass, sipping cappuccino in the Corso and buying ice cream for lunch or cakes daintily wrapped in boxes tied by ribbons.

The lodge is fairly isolated, but being situated on the scenic route from Cortona to Sant'Egidio, there is a surprising amount of traffic with people often driving by on their way to visit the monastery, L'Eremo di Sant'Egidio, or to take picnics in the surrounding forests. Bob usually sets up his easel at the front of the lodge near the road and is guaranteed to attract passing motorists, curious to see what he is up to. He welcomes visitors with open arms and will inevitably invite them to hop over the chain straddling the drive and proceed to offer them a private viewing of his latest works; dashing into the cantina under the house and hauling out numerous canvases which he will line up against the wall. Surprising too, just how many paintings he sells in this manner.

Already this summer, he has had a sell-out show in Cortona at Palazzo Vagnotti. More than 500 people signed his visitors' book and with buyers lining up at the opening he had the temerity to turn them all away, saying he wanted to enjoy his big night and if they were serious to come back the next day. Amazingly, it worked.

Chapter 13.

Martin is putting on an exhibition of his photographs in Cortona, the result of a year spent in the woods documenting the work of the charcoal burners, a tradition that is fast dying out, as is *contadina* culture itself as successive generations move away from the land. Never the less their way of life has not been entirely extinguished and it remains one of the greatest surprises to me, coming from London and largely in ignorance, that right here in the heart of twentieth century Europe a peasant culture does still exist: living off the land in run-down farmhouses, dogs chained in the yard, millet hung out to dry on the walls of the house, later to be turned into brooms: gleaning for cobs in the fields after the harvest, foraging greens by the road side, collecting acorns for the pigs, planting by the phases of the moon. The culture of the land is iconic and deeply embedded in the Tuscan psyche and serves to enhance this sense of a land living beyond time.

Life is so amazing here; all those shooting stars filling the night sky with so many wishes to fulfil. A meteorite sailed right over the roof of Carolyn's house as we were sitting on the balcony. A huge chunk of sizzling rock the size of a marble if held out at arm's length to the horizon, it was so big, trailing a blazing tail of green fire behind it that sounded like burning cellophane before plunging over the hill. I eagerly scoured the newspapers in the bar the next day searching for reports of a sighting and was disappointed nothing was mentioned although Sabine, holidaying with Roby on Panarea, an island off the northern coast of Sicily, swears they saw something similar.

Jef has really landed on his feet in Rome and is working for the American Broadcasting Corporation. He claims he was only hired to make photocopies in the local newsroom but I don't believe him; he approached the office and was hired on the spot for his bilingual skills just when NATO General James Lee Dozier was kidnapped in 1981 by the Red Brigades and the American media was going ballistic.

We are once more in summer's languid phase and people in the valley are wilting. This is country life as opposed to the feeding frenzy of Cortona. When the heat brings everything to a standstill, Margherita in the *bottega* soldiers on, staying up to all hours in her kitchen and keeping an eye out on the shop in the adjacent room. Margherita only catnaps by the front door in the afternoon, her chair angled against the wall, feet swinging sweetly off the floor, her small, chafed hands folded in her lap clutching a handkerchief, but always ready to spring to attention if someone ventures in. In contrast her husband Nello, a goblin-like figure with silver hair and a purple nose, lies low; slouched in his favourite chair in the dimmer recess of the cavernous room over by the fireplace, often drinking his red wine the colour of blackberry juice, which he sells from under the counter in two-litre bottles.

Margherita keeps the street entrance to the shop shuttered and closed, obliging you enter through her kitchen; she is mindful of the carabinieri driving past because they will fine her if they find the shop open outside normal trading hours and people here come and go up to all hours, provided Margherita is still awake. The glass in the front door rattles like a bell when you enter the room with its vaulted brick ceilings and partitioning columns down the middle. Often Margherita will be standing over in the far corner by the stove, her grey hair tied up in a bun, strands falling loose around her shoulders. She is a small, compact woman with a kindly, malleable face and—wiping her hands on her pinafore, with a toothless grin if she has forgotten to pop her dentures in or is taking them out of her pocket—she will lead the way to the shop in the adjacent room. Most people, like Carolyn, keep an account with Margherita, who slipping her glasses on dutifully inscribes each grocery item into her ruled notebook, kept handy behind the small glass deli counter. She tots them up with a pencil later when you come back to settle up; there's never a rush or any pressure to pay your account.

Margherita's house is an imposing, fortress-like building with three storeys, almost buttressing the road, commanding a view of everything coming in or out of the valley. News travels fast via the shop, everyone knows everyone else's business almost immediately, with Margherita at the focal point of a wheel of spokes radiating gossip out into the valley. Margherita is also more than happy to take down messages over the phone and holds the post for the outlying areas. In fact it is not uncommon to see her leap out of the front door to flag you down as you drive past, if there is mail or a message has been left for you! I always check my rear-view mirror as I pass just in case Margherita's been slow off the mark. Often in the evening, four or five people or more will be gathered around the long kitchen table under the single circular neon light, with Margherita standing at the head by the stove cooking, good-naturedly orchestrating her pots and pans; Nello ensconced in his armchair at the far end. Whenever I walk in on this scene, Van Gogh's Potato eaters' springs to mind, although "bean-eaters" might be more apt for Tuscans.

Sometimes I see Hans, who is Dutch, and his Spanish girlfriend Dominique seated with the others. Nello has allowed them to build a small cabin on his land near the mill in return for helping him out on the farm. Like many of the *stranieri* they stumbled on this place by accident, likely down that wormhole and never returned home though at the time they were only intending to stop off in the valley for a couple of nights! They had just been to Assisi and were on their way home to Spain, traveling in a covered wagon drawn by a donkey. Hans was fore-filling a promise he had made to undertake a pilgrimage to Assisi if St Francis saved his ailing dog. Hans is now studying to become a vet. I often meet Dominique as she drives Nello's sheep around the valley. In summer you always know where she is by the tonking of the sheep bells. Hans is a burly cherub faced bloke while she looks more like a sprite with a halo of golden flax framing her weathered but attractive face. Their newly built cabin, is constructed out of the old wooden railway sleepers now being replaced by concrete ones and sold off cheaply at the railway yard in Terontola. The cabin has one room with a potbelly stove in the middle and a neat double bed that tapers at the foot like a wedge of cheese in order to optimise the space. I gave them a drawing as a house warming present when the cabin was completed but unfortunately, our relations have cooled recently; sitting by the swimming hole near the old mill one evening, I took umbrage when Hans declared in his booming voice that "artists don't know the meaning of work" and he meant it.

Carolyn's plans for a pool are taking shape. 'Pool' would be an exaggeration; a hole in the ground more like, as long as it can seat three or four people and holds the water, she will be content. Jane's brother John is in charge of the project. He has been around the valley lately, frequenting his new girlfriend Germaine, the Australian writer, who lives in an isolated almost inaccessible spot right at the top of the valley. Carolyn knows her and we visit occasionally, abandoning the Mini half way up and walking the rest of the way in although Germaine has an old battered Land rover that successfully completes the journey. The thrumming noise of a diesel generator announces the approach to her house like some ancient tug boat chugging through the long grass. John has erected a huge *serra* out front, a long black plastic tunnel, where Germaine dries the wild flowers, she collects in the surrounding hills; ingredients for the homeopathic herbal remedies that she plans to export to England. John and Germaine make the most unlikely couple: he is a country boy with straw thatched hair, a thick stilted voice and a laugh that winds itself up and up; the practical, slow to be roused, down to earth type, good natured and good with his hands, where as she is all intellect, an irrepressible force of nature who clashes like steel with her wit, a shark in a small pond who makes me tremble every time she fixes a stare on me, letting me know I am on her radar. They want to have a child, he confides, although she is in her forties; a last role of the dice. Carolyn doesn't want to have children; her mother died of an accidental overdose when she was a child and her father, who she worshipped died before she reached twelve. An unhappy childhood has coloured her thinking, although to be honest I think Voss is enough for her and they both treasure their independence.

John and I have dug the hole for the pool, situated on the edge of the terrace behind a screen of young oak saplings that tub-side offers a serrated view across the valley. The hole is about four feet deep, six feet by four feet across and is lined with heavy-duty plastic covered by stones cemented into place to form the wall of the tub. Filled by a garden hose there is also an outlet valve to drain the water down the bank when required. Strangely enough the pool has been the trigger of a dramatic improvement in relations between Amelio, Carolyn's incalcitrant *contadino*, and myself. A couple of Carolyn's girlfriends from Rome were staying so we were all in the pool and just happened to catch him; a peeping tom hiding behind the *ginestra* gorse bushes nearby.

"He does have history," Carolyn admits.

"Especially when my girlfriends are sun baking in the meadow by the house!"

Actually, it was Voss who busted him, innocently wandering over to where he was hiding to say hello. Amelio, blushing, shot up from his crouching position and tried to act normal, desperate to extricate himself with a plausible reason for being there; trying to make out he was just passing through. After he recovered himself sufficiently, to save face, he complimented me on my efforts clearing the land and offered to show me exactly how to use the long-handled scythe without wrecking my back, taking up the tool and deftly demonstrating how to swing the blade from the hips.

I am grateful his attitude has changed towards me and drop in on him from time to time, always calling up from the bottom of the stairs first, announcing my presence in advance, as etiquette requires. Amelio is a reserved man and doesn't necessarily respond, even if I know he's at home, but then as if he has changed his mind, he will suddenly appear on the porch, his gangly frame towering high above me: "Oh it's you," casually, as if he didn't already know, and then invites me up. Amelio's house is on the fringes of the hamlet just down the hill from Carolyn's. He lives there by himself but often walks down to his younger brother's house in the *borgo* for meals. Michelina his brother's wife also takes in his washing.

Amelio's place is small: two rooms with a cantina below where he keeps his tractor and his pride and joy, his car: a navy-blue Fiat 126. His house retains the iconic features of the case *coloniche*, the traditional contadino farmhouses: the outside staircase, the portico or loggia, a large fireplace inside, a *forno* (bread oven) outside, structurally solid unadorned stone buildings (brick in the province of Siena) built on two floors with the animals stabled underneath and according to Amelio, providing an extra source of heat in winter for the family living on the floor above. These days they are being snapped up and converted into holiday homes and residences; led by the foreigners and followed soon after by wealthy Italians.

Sitting in Amelio's small dusty kitchen, everything layered the colour of butter/grey in the dim light, I watch him decant the wine out of demijohns into two litre bottles then seal them by pouring a thin layer of oil over the top. Taking up a bottle he then shows me his trick of decanting, twisting the end of a wad of cotton wool down into the neck then dunking it carefully into the olive oil and adroitly removing the sop in one clean dramatic flick, explaining: "so you don't have globs of oil left in the wine when you drink it!'

Chapter 14.

Bernardo has found a studio for me in Cortona much to my relief because it's been a really frustrating period of a few months not having a space that I can call my own to paint in. I require a settled outer stillness in which to distil the inner turmoil of my art. Bernardo is in his fifties: he lived in Munich prior to arriving in Cortona at much the same time as I did, having ditched a successful career as a civil engineer and is now working as a builder, renovating houses mainly for foreigners. Luckily for me one of his clients, Peter, a German psychotherapist, has just bought two adjoining apartments in via Coppi below the Corso.

"When I get married," Peter informs me. "I will bring my Turkish bride to live here. My plan is to knock them into one big apartment but that is still a way off so meanwhile I am happy for you to use the space as you will."

Peter's lips are stretched in a permanent grin and he has a slightly off kilter feeling to him, a thousand-mile stare, as if he isn't quite here, but who am I to judge? He is being very generous considering he doesn't even know me and on top of everything else he is refusing to take any rent, even though I felt it incumbent to offer! I'm surprised Bernardo, a confirmed bachelor with a taste for younger women, hasn't taken it himself; although by choice he does seem to prefer the nomadic existence, living out of an old sea chest he carts around with him from job to job and bedding down wherever he is currently working.

I will have the run of both apartments, which occupy the top floor of a four-storey palazzo in spitting distance of the Corso. From the top landing I also have access to the roof, and climbing up a rickety wooden staircase, through the attic I can reach a small but spectacular terrace cut into the pitch of the roof, with more of those incredible views across the Valdichiana and Lago Trasimeno. I could sell tickets to the best show in town! Or give them away! But no, this is going to be my best kept secret ever.

I've already been down to see Dante, the local carpenter in Valecchie, about having some large stretchers made up. He made the doors and windows for Carolyn's house but was reluctant at first to touch the stretchers: not his kind of work, and only agreeing after some wheedling from me and showing him a doodle of what I required: a simple interlocking male-female mortise cut on alternate ends of the wood, so I can slot them together or pull them apart as needed, thus making transporting more convenient. Pointing me to a jumbled pile of seasoned pine, Dante suggests I run my eye down the length of a few and pick out the straightest. Endearingly unselfconscious, he makes no attempt to patch his one vacant eye socket shuttered by a drooping lid and is a sight to behold anyway with his black curly mop riddled in sawdust, a roguish grin and the tops of several of his fingers shaved off!

Dante is saving me a fortune on the stretchers. My mother also, by sending out two bolts of Belgian linen from Russell & Chapell in London, which still work out cheaper than buying the canvas in Italy. I am a moth to the flame when it comes to art supplies and can only envy Picasso's ability to sign cheques that were never cashed because his signature was deemed more valuable. Who can resist Zecchi & Sons in Florence? The large, glass apothecary jars behind the counter, filled with brightly ground pigments with exotic names like lapis lazuli, cinnabar red or ercolano orange? Lining an entire wall are stacked tubes of oil paint neatly displayed outside their boxes, the topmost rows only reached by a library roller on wheels hooked onto a rail under the ceiling. Or what about the Freschetti brothers in Arezzo? An Aladdin's cave of goodies run by two old-fashioned brothers: Ali Babas in tan work frocks, who bustle around the cramped shop space up and down step-ladders, fetching and carrying a treasure trove of dusty boxes begging to be opened, with the fat lady who never speaks, on her tall stool behind the counter ringing up the till.

If I need something urgently, I pop down to the *cartoleria* in the Corso, where I am greeted by my friend Giulio. Tall, bespectacled, keen eyed and always ready for conversation and always prepared to go out of his way to help.

"Why on earth would you want something so arcane?"

He asks me intrigued, peering over his glasses at me, as I attempt to explain about CFO's and holes in the ozone layer and the damage they are doing to our atmosphere.

"I am trying to cut down on my aerosol use." I explain "So if you stock atomisers then I won't have to use shellac spray to fix my pastel drawings anymore."

"You know, I used to stock something like that but it's been such a long time since anyone asked for one."

Obligingly though, Giulio gets down on one knee and starts rummaging through a large bottom draw and even surprises himself, coming up with a small bottle of fixative and an odd metal contraption that looks like a bent cocktail straw cut out at the elbow.

"I think this is how it is done, dip the straw in the bottle and blow through the other end."

And low and behold a fine mist appears out of the middle floating in an arc across space.

"Looks like you'll have your work cut out for you to save the atmosphere!"

He grins good natured but still not fully comprehending my purpose, and as usual offers me a generous discount when we finally arrive at the till.

Peter has warned me that he has given Noemi and Emilia, the pensioners living on the ground floor, permission to use the attic and that they have a key to the landing. The last flight of stairs to the top landing are enclosed by a door at the bottom and I occasionally hear them letting themselves in and rummaging around the attic, but they don't disturb me. I often go up there myself to sit on the terrace and gawp at the view while I'm eating my panino and can see how busy they are: the bunches of drying grapes festooning the rafters and the racks of drying tomatoes spread out on the floor, with jars of olives curing in brine sitting on top of an old fridge.

Sabine has commissioned me to do some artwork for her and bustles into the studio, ladened down with her samples, photos and colour charts, ready to supervise my painting small abstract watercolours for what she calls (throatily) "*l'atmosphère!*" that she uses in presentations to clients of her yarn colour ranges—*mes gammes de couleur*—or for decorating her clients stands at trade fairs. She is in the business of predicting fashion trends in colours two years in advance and in Prato much can rest on her clairvoyance. It's a mystery to me how she does it, also working on winter collections in summer, although she claims it's easy, no crystal ball required, and nothing delights her more than when other "fashion people" miss that particular boat and get it wrong:

"I am a naughty girl," she says smiling with mock innocence.

My new studio apartment has several bright rooms with odd sticks of furniture, terrazzo floors and large windows with views skimming roof tops and looking out towards Lago Trasimeno. The second apartment on the back side is darker but has a functioning bathroom and kitchen and a double bed if ever I am feeling tired.

One lunch time there is a knock at my studio door and I find Emilia, my downstair neighbour, standing outside on the landing, offering me a plate of pasta *al pomodoro* delicately balanced in one hand. She is a short, square-shouldered woman with cropped greying hair and is wearing a sleeveless floral housecoat over a drab shift. She introduces herself, smiling nervously and proffers me the plate:

"We thought you looked a bit thin," the enquiry in her eyes brimming with concern, and then hastily retreats down the stairs.

"Don't let it get cold!" She shouts up after her.

I do take a look at myself in the mirror after, just in case and when I return the washed plate later that afternoon, she invites me in and introduces me to her husband Noemi, an avuncular man, who orders her to fetch down the glasses and bring out his vin santo for a toast.

"You have seen my grapes drying in the attic. Do you know what they are for?" He asks playfully. (Actually I had no clue).

"This!" He booms with satisfied pride, pouring out two glasses of the deep amber liquid.

Voss is standing beside me, clacking his teeth and drooling his tongue, happy to be part of the scene and, saying goodbye in the small hallway after, Noemi pats my belly smirking. "Come down for lunch anytime, you're always welcome, we will feed you up, ha ha!"

Emilia concurs and so does Voss, grinning with the rest of them.

Chapter 15.

Carolyn and I have been down to Mario's service station on the Terontola road to see about buying a *motorino* for me, so I can commute from Valecchie to my new studio and rely less on the Mini. Mario keeps an odd assortment of secondhand bikes on his forecourt and at first glance I liked the look of the *motorino* tarted up to look just like a Grand Prix motorbike, with the flash fairings and logos down the sides like a suit of plastic armour; but Carolyn is more practical, pointing out the paper-thin tyres and I end up choosing one more suitable that looks like a trail bike. It's only a 50cc, no licence required, and not that powerful, but it certainly knows how to screech; the high-pitched whine of the engine ricochets off stone walls, searing my ears as I ride past, and to my dismay, trumpets my departure and heralds my arrival in the valley miles in advance. I would prefer to glide in and out silently with grace, unannounced.

Patrolman Gino, the vigili urbano, has already pulled me over and warned me to fit a silencer on the bikeor else! He has threatened to fine me, only, if I do as he requests, the bike will lose even more power and never make it all the way up Carolyn's hill without stalling; resulting in an awkward effort to push it up the rest of the way. It's tricky enough as it is, charging the gravelled rutted track at full throttle if I want to reach the top. The solution of course is to do nothing except keep a wary eye out for Gino, who beyond the swagger is accommodating enough. In Cortona you can witness his arrival in piazza Repubblica around lunchtimes; looking like Zip Nolan, he purrs into the piazza from via Guelfa on his massive blue and white Moto Guzzi. Parking by the gift shop, he kicks down the stand and rocks back on the saddle to settle the bike, then just sits there for ages having a smoke and holding court with people he knows, before finally dismounting then giving a couple of short shrill blasts on his whistle, signalling he is ready for business. News travels fast along the Corso followed by the sound of multiple car doors slamming and engines starting up and cars being spirited away to avoid getting ticketed.

Voss enjoys commuting to Cortona with me. He eagerly hops up in front of me, onto the petrol tank where I can wedge him in securely between my arms while I'm holding the handlebar. He loves zipping through the countryside his eyes streaming with pleasure, now and then turning his head to lick my face.

I regularly drop in for chats with Emilia on my way in or out of the palazzo; she leaves her front door keys dangling in the outside lock to announce when she is at home. They have two sons: Alfredo who works at the Comune and has left home and Silvio his younger brother who goes out to work but still lives there although he is hardly ever around. The flat is small and cramped; utilitarian rather than homely. The narrow dining room with white washed walls, a fireplace and the television, is almost filled by the long table and benches: two small bedrooms, one is windowless, and on the other side of the gloomy kitchen is one of those classical loos tacked onto the outside of the building and overhanging the street.

Emilia is more effusive on her own, and she can easily become emotional, shedding tears freely in front of me, despairing: Noemi's health—he has trouble with his legs—or Maria her niece, who has to be on a dialysis machine in Arezzo twice a week. She even blames herself for Silvio not tying the knot sooner; he has been engaged for several years to the girl in the *profumeria* shop in the piazza:

"*La fidanzata* (his fiancée) comes from a better family and I suspect I'm not good enough for them." She laments.

The household at lunchtime is a delight to experience and I have taken up their offer to join them as often as I dare without overdoing my welcome. Emilia shops in the morning and cooks lunch with the help of her niece Maria, a young single mum, whose brilliantly behaved toddler Giuseppe is usually placed under the dining room table at one end, amusing himself with his basket of Kinder egg figurines, Voss curled up beside him on the mat. Noemi scrubs up when he comes in, he used to work on the railways but now spends his days tending his *orto* (vegetable garden) down at his son Alfredo's place below Cortona. Alfredo and his brother Silvio, will make an appearance at lunch, always late, rushing in at the last moment, switching on the TV news then leaving the table as soon as they have finished eating. Alfredo is short in stature like his mother, with thick chestnut hair pulled down over his face and a dark bushy beard. He never leaves the house without his black beret on, à la Sartre. A member of the communist party, he works as the assistant to the cultural attaché, the *Assessore* and is married with a baby girl, but still comes home to his parents at lunch during weekdays because it is closer to his office.

The first time I saw him at the house came as a mild surprise to both of us because we have already met several times in the Comune. I have been going to see him in his official capacity about putting on an exhibition in Palazzo Casali, a Comune run exhibition space, but am beginning to suspect he is giving me the run around as he simply will not commit to a straight answer.

Emilia and Maria bustle between the kitchen and the dining room carrying and clearing plates under Noemi's directions. He sits at the head of the table by the glass-panelled door, his back parked against the wall, wearing his favoured black and white striped Juventus shirt and track bottoms. Between mouthfuls, Silvio, in a tweed sports coat over an immaculately pressed open blue shirt (he works as a sales rep for a pharmaceutical company) shoots me puzzled looks across the table as if to say, why are you here, what's the big deal, huh? As if I should be bored or surely this is somehow onerous, when in fact I really look forward to these occasions, always bringing Voss as well as Carolyn at times.

Noemi, pontificating between courses, broadcasts his score out of ten for each dish that Emilia places on the table. Beaming at me, he fondly recalls his days as a prisoner of war in northern England, working on a farm outside Newcastle, and he never tires of showing off his limited English or reading out his treasured postcards from the Georgia students he has befriended over the years with his genial, open manner. Emilia fretting, never sits down to eat, holding her plate in her lap, half standing half sitting on the tiled ledge of the fireplace, while Maria, who is pale and waif-like with long dark hair, but has a deep husky voice and a friendly, business-like manner, snatches a bite to eat in the kitchen between chores and leans in the doorway after as we drain our coffee and, if Noemi is feeling particularly expansive, he will offer us a glass of his vin santo. He proudly describes how he dries the grapes in the loft for up to three months, to raise the sugar content he says, then ferments them in small vats for a minimum of three years but could be as long as twelve years. Vin santo is similar to sherry but more succulent, and is fast becoming my favourite *aperitvo.*

Roberto, the artist Rupert introduced me to in Cortona, has told me Alfredo is actually the culture Tzar of Cortona and a member of the ruling communist party junta, something I hadn't fully appreciated before. His boss the Assessore is an elected position whereas his is a permanent managerial post within the administration.

When I tell Roberto about the difficulties I've been having with Comune he is hardly surprised.

"Don't hold your breath, nobody around here gets an exhibition with the Comune, not least of all us locals."

"Why does Alfredo bother to see me at all if that's the case and what about Martin?" I counter. "He had that exhibition of his photographs in Palazzo Casali sponsored by the Comune."

"That's not the point. Alfredo's just stringing you along and Martin's exhibition wasn't sponsored by the Comune, it was part of an educational program paid for by the Province of Arezzo." Roberto says scornfully, fiddling with his moustache.

"Alfredo should have told you but he probably feels too embarrassed and hopes you'll just go away in the end.

"No way! Now that I have Alfredo cornered across the dining room table.at his parent's house and armed with Roberto's intel I can finally tease it out of him, albeit he remains reluctant.

"Try to see it from our point of view, Nino." Alfredo talking through his beard in muffled tones: "If the Comune gave exhibitions to every artist requesting one, we wouldn't be able to cope with the demand and would be put in an untenable situation of having to choose one over another. Turning local artists down would only sow discontent and create further resentment."

Roberto claps his hands when I tell him this news and linking arms pulls me along the Corso a few paces. "What a load of rubbish! Doesn't he understand the resentment's already been caused?"

Chapter 16.

Friends who come and stay at Carolyn's inevitably wax lyrical about our rustic way of life. Most are Australians, raving about cooking on the open fire and candlelight, or no electricity or TV or a telephone for distraction. Of course, it is an idyl. Me as well, I can remember the very first time I came to Italy, bunking down in a half-abandoned mill of an artist living near Lucca; picking grapes, sweating under a glowering autumn sun, talking poetry and art with comrades as we walked in together from the vineyard to cups of wine and sumptuous meals laid out under pergolas on long trestle tables accompanied by the rasp of the cicadas and thrum of frogs.

Carolyn's friends mostly arrive in summer when the living is easy! They don't have to deal with washing sheets in cold water, or frozen water pipes; with candle wax and smelly paraffin lamps, humping wood or huddling around a fire for warmth, then often leaving the door half open just to stop the smoke from spewing out into the room and choking us.

We have new neighbours in the valley living in even more straightened circumstances. Christian a German and his wife Mary Jane, an American, and their new born baby girl, live down by the mill in a semi derelict ruin and Wilfred on the hill opposite is in a similar situation; buying run down properties on the cheap and hoping to restore them while living there. Mary Jane used to be a model, she has jet black hair and an olive complexion, strikingly beautiful but rounding out now and taking on a slightly trammelled look, even shell shocked as the harshness of her living conditions sinks in. Christian as well, an alarming figure: tall, stooping, with feral hair and an untamed beard, like a wild man out of the mountains, a Naga Baba all sack cloth and ashes bearing down on you, his speech lilted and full of exclamations: "Oooh reeeally!" As if everything I have to say, truly is worth saying.

We play chess at his place; he's fixed the roof now but the floor is still packed earth and Mary Jane sits quietly in a corner suckling the babe and keeps to herself. There are times when passing by on the lane I see her at the window and I will wave but she does not acknowledge me, just vacantly stares out into space. Carolyn has started counselling her in exchange for the unpasteurised milk they sell from the Jersey cow they keep, but she is not over confident she can be of much help. Wilfred, also German, is a retired teacher: now a refugee from a broken marriage and a damaged ego, holed up like some bandit on the run in his half of an abandoned *casa colonica* that has no running water! Take away his thick spectacles and he could be a Saxon with his pageboy-cut white hair, pale complexion and dark bushy, arched eyebrows. Wilfred scratches out a living growing millet whose fibres are used for brooms.

He was the subject of much gossip in the *bottega* (shop) after a recent visit from the carabinieri about a crop of marijuana and a suspected drug dealer who had parked his van on Wilfred's land. Wilfred had a hard time explaining it wasn't his crop but was thankful that the carabinieri managed to move the guy on because he was being intimidated by him and felt helpless to move him on himself. I was up there one evening and we were all sitting around a bonfire at night and this guy was there acting scary, with a hunting knife; making a big show of scraping out the dirt from underneath his finger nails with the long, hook pointed blade.

For a month now I have been delicately seeding the idea of putting on the electricity. Carolyn needs time to accept change but takes me by surprise in the end by how easily she acquiesces, not only to put the electricity on but to do the phone as well. I'm not fussed about the phone, I still go down to the *bottega* when I need to, but I I know Carolyn is eager because in Rome she is on the phone to her coterie of girlfriends all the time!

As soon as all the necessary bureaucratic arrangements are in place with ENEL and SIP, the state electricity and phone companies, Bernardo sets to work on the interior of the house chiselling out the channels in the stone walls for the cables, then sealing them in again with stone so everything is restored as it was before. Carolyn is incredibly particular; she has a highly developed sense of aesthetics and Bernardo has a reputation for meticulous, well-executed work. Even if he is slow and charges more than a Tuscan *muratore*, Carolyn considers the extra expense worth it; Bernardo is a perfectionist and pays attention to detail, unlike many of his Tuscan counterparts who can be slap-dash and haphazard, often needing restraint and above all constant supervision.

The electricity and phone cables are due to be laid underground from the last pole at the top of the track to the house, about thirty metres away. Carolyn is insistent that no pole will be spoiling the view in front of the house, and I agree. She is always sensitive to changes in her immediate environment: cursing Tranquillo for example, Amelio's brother, for erecting a 'supposed' 'tractor shed' half way up her track, especially now that his wife has hung curtains on the windows and the very modest edifice is sprouting a chimney stack. Or the day she screamed "*assassini*" out of the bedroom window when she heard the chain saws starting up and spied the Corpo Forestale rangers taking down a huge old oak tree.

Bernardo has brought along a labourer, Vigilio, to dig the trench for the underground cables from the last pole to the house and I can only describe him as chirpy, very chirpy. I have never seen anyone so happy to be digging a trench. He never stops whistling as he pick-axes and shovels his way through dirt and rock, progressing at a breakneck pace along the path towards the house. Wearing a pointy woollen hat, he looks like one of the seven dwarfs singing merrily, "Hi ho, hi ho, it's off to work we go!" with Carolyn skipping daintily at their head.

We have to laugh, Bernardo the Lothario! He has a young *mädchen* in tow who sits breathlessly on the sofa all day long not saying a word but gazing adoringly at him while he goes about his work; finishing with a final flourish of the paintbrush as he retouches the stonework with dabs of paint. Only the new light switches on the wall give the game away and when the work has been completed and the electricity turned on, Carolyn and I are like a couple of kids racing around the house flicking them on off on off. It's hard to imagine the thrill of arriving home at night and the instant gratification of electricity and just how quickly that escalates to the level of an addiction, judging by the anxiety attacks I experience whenever we experience the frequent power outages.

Ironically, one of the very first phone calls we receive is for me, from a Herr Kohl, a lawyer in Germany who has tracked me down via my mother, giving me the news that Bill Pöhling, my biological father has died and asking me if I would come to Düsseldorf to sort out some matters of the estate urgently. Apparently, under German law, as the first-born son I stand to inherit one sixth of his estate, even though I am not in his will. The news of his passing has not affected me at all, why would it? I have had no contact at all since my mother left him and took me to London nearly thirty years ago and the only real father I have ever known and loved is my step father. What has affected me though is the surprising news that I have three half-sisters by Bill's second marriage and I am excited to be meeting them.

Chapter 17.

A dull thump-thump, like the after-thuds of a series of detonations, reverberates across the valley. Clank clank clank goes the church bell below, making an awful racket. I step out onto the balcony wondering what's going on; Voss is sniffing the air at the bottom of the stairs, and high over the roof I am startled by a great arc of black smoke reaching up into the limp pale blue afternoon sky. Two helicopters with red, water sloshing, barrels swinging perilously off the end of creaking ropes, are flying up the valley. A fire, my god!

The sound of vehicles crunching up the track becomes evident soon after, then the hisses of walkie-talkies as a group of men in orange overalls, the *Pompieri*, emerges at a trot along the path immediately below the balcony. We are in a high-risk fire zone, and the *Corpo Forestale* must have raised the alarm earlier; during the summer months they maintain a round-the-clock fire watch from the Fortezza in Cortona. Some of the men are carrying absurdly small water spray packs on their backs as they disappear further up the hill warning me to be ready to evacuate.

Running around like a headless chook, I begin filling up buckets and cooking pots from the garden hose, but the water pressure is miserable and the job too slow, so I decide I would be better served gathering up our valuables; then decide rather than being on my own and panicking, I would be better off helping the others fighting the fire. I can hear the flames crackling and trees shrieking not that far away. Calling Voss, we scramble up the hill in the direction the men went. The fire front is moving down the hill towards us, towards Carolyn's house. Thank god she is in Rome because she would be freaking out right now. I can see flames squirting above the trees, roasting the air. and making our way round the hill I can hear the distinctive shrill voice of La Colomba above the din:

"Don't let the fire get past us, boys, hold the line or the church will be lost!"

Columba is the old spinster caretaker at the church; she would have been the one to raise the alarm earlier, sounding the bells. Amelio and his brother

Tranquillo, with Michelina his sister-in-law and Dante the carpenter, all wearing wet handkerchiefs over their mouths, and under a shower of red-hot embers, are working furiously damping the spot fires: Amelio is shovelling dirt and Tranquillo throws me a hessian sack indicating I need to start smothering the flames.

Fortunately, the lower reaches of the hill into the valley are terraces of olive trees mainly cleared and the hamlet below is not in any real danger, nor the church, but the fire almost reaches Carolyn's house, probably saved only by the small cleared terraced field that sits up just behind it. Come early evening the prevailing winds have changed direction, now driving the fire back up the hill towards the ridges and down the other sides moving towards Martin and John's place. Weary, Voss and I troop down to the shop and join the group of subdued onlookers already assembled outside in camping chairs placed on the road, hypnotised by the distant spectacle as night descends, an eerie glow of vermillion dancing across the whites of their eyes. Later, I call Carolyn to let her know and she hurries back in the mini the next morning from Rome, nearly having a heart attack driving into the valley and first witnessing the devastation behind her house.

The fire has left a big ugly, black stain behind the house and across the hillside up to the ridge, and after the rains it smells of fermenting apples. Our water supply has been cut off too. The poly pipe that runs from the spring at the top of the hill down to the house has melted in several places where it lay on top of the ground and much to my dismay after many futile efforts at repair, I have realised that the pipe also melted in places where it was still buried underground. The only solution has been to replace the whole length, all one kilometre and leave it sitting above the ground. I have no idea how Voss manages to keep his coat so white on our endless treks up and down the hill, because by the time we reach home I am inevitably smeared head to toe in dirty charcoal smudges.

Fire hasn't been the only threat to our water supply; we have had to deal with the hunters and also the quarrelsome, cantankerous Milanese neighbour who owns a holiday house close by and shares the same spring with us for his water supply. When the spring is low, Carolyn is convinced he deliberately pulls our pipe out at the source, thereby creating an air block and stopping the flow to our water tank behind the house. We have had words and accusations are still flying, neighbourly relations at an all-time low. The hunters are even worse, selfishly slicing the pipe open for a drink where they find over ground. They are such a pain, holding sway, swaggering up and down the hill with impunity, tearing up the vegetation to construct their stupid hides; and it's not so unusual to hear the ping pinging of hundreds of tiny lead pellet balls bouncing off Carolyn's slate tile roof, even though hunters are not supposed to discharge their guns within 150 metres of any habitation.

In Tuscany, hunting is traditionally the preserve of the common man and considered an inalienable right by him, unlike the UK where it is a rich man's sport. Here, hunting is one of the few issues that can divide locals and the *stranieri* communities and so entrenched are pro hunting attitudes that woe betide any landowner who tries to bar them from their land because trespass and private property is not part of the Tuscan lexicon; ask Paulo, who owns large tracts of terrain around Monte Sant'Egidio and whose woods have been torched twice over. Paulo's anti-hunting stance is unusual for a local, made doubly so because he says it is on environmental grounds and there is no environmental movement to speak of in these parts. (Yes, I know, I am a hypocrite! To my shame, we burn our domestic rubbish in a pit on the property and on the rare occasion shampoo and rinse Voss in the stream.)

The hunting season opens with great fanfare every year on the second Saturday of September. It's more like a Fourth of July event, when all hell breaks loose at the very crack of dawn, with Everyman and his dog invading the countryside, blasting off left and right indiscriminately. The pheasants that are so carefully released into the wild to breed in early spring barely scrape through the first two weeks of the season, and once they're gone it seems to be open slather for anything that can fly, crawl, hop or walk; reports of hunter fatalities appear in the press periodically and John's sister Jane claims she was shot at once while out walking in the woods. We have to be extra vigilant with Voss, but really the problem is the ignorance: nobody actually seems to know what they are shooting at or really cares, although the *contadini* claim those people are out-of-towners, most probably from Florence.

Carolyn and I are sitting on the balcony, eating breakfast and enjoying the last of the Indian summer, when a pack of gangly Tuscan bloodhounds appears on the path right below us, doleful mugs with big floppy ears, tiny bells strung around their collars tinging, followed by a single file of six men all shouldering arms, dressed in immaculate camouflage fatigues. Unfortunately, the track that goes from the top of the drive and past

Carolyn's house is designated a *strada vicinale*, or public right of way and the fact is, confronting a man holding a double-barrelled twelve-bore shotgun would be too unnerving. Not even Voss dares to venture down to confront them. His hair bristles, on his feet on the wall above them, beside himself with rage and farting furiously. Carolyn and I can only ignore their crisp *buongiornos* with daggered looks.

Dress code is an important aspect of hunting, as it is generally in Italian life. It goes hand in hand with the concept of *bella figura*, which embraces the idea of respectability as well as demonstrating status and wealth. Carolyn, for example, automatically qualifies for *bella figura* because she is a doctor, whereas she wouldn't do so if judged solely by her clothes.

The end of the hunting season is signalled by the wild boar hunts in February or March, when gangs of men organise large-scale hunting drives across the countryside, parading their trophies afterwards outside the bars, the limp, tusked wild boars unceremoniously strapped across the bonnets of cars. Only then can Carolyn and I relax, maybe even forgive them and join in with the fun at the *Sagra del Cinghiale*, the wild-boar festival in nearby Pergo.

Chapter 18.

I am gratefully sipping my first cup of coffee and mentally smoking my first cigarette of the day, feet up on the wall of the parapet, a crisp early morning full of the promises of an early spring.

I haven't had a cigarette for nearly three years and pat myself on the back, although it can still be a struggle and it's probably about time I weaned myself off the matchsticks. The worst thing is lighting up in a dream and waking up in the morning with that sinking feeling of feeling convinced I've started smoking again. A joint is the only concession I will allow myself as a non-smoker, especially when I'm with Roby, who rolls his with tobacco. Carolyn and I sometimes visit them in summer at Sabine's retreat in the hills above Prato. I refuse to go there in winter anymore, not even with the promise of a smoke; her house is basic, rendered brick with terrazzo floors and the roof leaks right over the guest room bed. Carolyn and Sabine have become friends so when we visit, I don't feel bad about sequestering Roby for the duration, playing marathon games of chess, drinking dad's Frascati and chain-smoking joints, much to Carolyn's mortification; she thinks I turn into a zombie when I'm stoned.

Nello's sheep are baaing and belling down in the valley and I can hear a shy hoopoe bird—hoo poo poo, hoo poo poo like a soft wind instrument—on the terrace below. Leaning over the parapet, I watch it skittering to and fro underneath the olive trees, opening and closing its delicate, fan-shaped crown of bronze. On spring days like these I wish I had a baritone's voice, powerful enough to pump up the whole valley with song, lift us all into grace.

Unexpectedly, the sound of car wheels spinning gravel breaks into the smoke of my reveries. Leaning over the parapet, I crane my neck further round to see who might be approaching and presently two men, both wearing aviator sunglasses, appear at a leisurely amble along the path; doubtless as rapt by the spring morning as I am.

"*Permesso? È permesso?*" one of them calls out from a distance, as Italians do, giving fair warning someone is approaching. Slightly irritated I trot down the stairs with Voss to see what I can do for them. "*Buongiorno*, what a beautiful day," one says cheerily.

"Bello, il cane, may I?" patting Voss gingerly at first.

"We have come to read your meter." He announces and noticing my hesitation, qualifies, "From ENEL, the electricity meter."

But really my mind is suddenly on flashback, dredging up a horrendous thought: have I left the telltale strip of film hanging in the meter? Did I forget to take it out last winter? Bloody hell! Yes, I did, is the answer! And now I'm totally screwed if these Guys see it in there.

"Can you show us where the meter is?" Says the other man, waiting.

My heart sinks at the realisation: me being my usual slack self; normally I leave it in the meter for a few days then take it out again, but somehow this time round I have completely overlooked it. The stupid thing is we are in May and I don't even need it. It is fairly well known in certain quarters how easy it is to jam up an electricity meter and save on electricity bills. All you need do is feed in a short strip of 35mm film under the lip of the front window until it snags the cog and stops the meter running! The trick is not to be greedy and leave it in for too long, but just a little bit at a time over the winter months and certainly never in spring when there is no point at all.

"I not speak any Italiano, I … I am …only guest here," I stammer, trying to dissemble and gather my thoughts.

The taller one of the two looks up at the house, and taking off his sunglasses he casually buffs them on a loose corner of his gingham shirt, checking the lenses against the sky before slipping them back on again.

"We *leggere* electric," he mimics in his brand of English.

"Where meter is pleeze?"

I squint back to communicate effort at trying to understand, and playing for time, invite them both upstairs. I need to come up with a plan so fast but my brain never works well under pressure, instead it tends to hit panic mode and freeze. Luckily Carolyn is in Rome, she has impeccable timing when it comes to avoiding crises! I don't even want to think about how she is going to react to this: better not go there, I have more pressing matters to deal with right here and number one is how do I get to the meter downstairs in the guest room, without these guys seeing me? So, I lead them off in the opposite direction upstairs and make a great show of looking in every corner: under the day bed, around the kitchen, under the galley stairs. Voss looks at me perplexed, his head to one side inquiring. Finally, grabbing a torch from under the sink I gesture for them to wait here while I go and check out downstairs. But heading outside, they simply tag along behind, still smiling.

What I don't know and should have guessed by now, given their nonchalant demeanour and that these two look more like Starsky and Hutch with their sunglasses, leather jackets, jeans and insouciant manners, is that they are not meter-readers at all but ENEL sleuths, here to bring a catastrophe upon my head. As I find out later they already know about the film dangling in the meter and are here following up on a report already lodged by the bona fide meter-reader. If by chance Carolyn and I are away when the meter man comes, he knows to go to Michelina, Amelio's sister-in-law, for the key to the house, which is exactly how this story will have unfolded. Starsky and Hutch are just playing with me and obviously thoroughly enjoying our little collective game of cat and mouse; but all the same won't let me out of their sight, as we traipse down the stairs together and enter the stable below. This room, converted into a guest room, is where Bernardo recessed the meter discreetly into the thick stone wall, and for good measure Carolyn placed a wardrobe in front of the hole to cover it up.

After another halfhearted look around the room and I realise there really is no point in carrying on with this charade. Full of dread I indicate the wardrobe on my left and stoop down to grab a corner by the foot to pull it away from the wall, suggesting we "might" find the meter behind it.

They are both standing behind me as a small wedge of space opens up in front of me and realising how dim it is in there, I decide one one last role of the dice, stepping forward two paces and pointing with one hand into the dark hole: "This must be it!" Whilst blindly grabbing for the piece of film and simultaneously swinging round to face them in one fluid move. A Zen moment if ever there was one! I can feel the film between my fingertips as my momentum slides the film out of the meter! Nobody has noticed! However, not daring to keep hold of the offending object, I let go and anxiously watch it flutter silently to the ground. Getting out his torch then pulling up a chair, Starsky hoists himself up to get a better look in at the meter, observing the telltale crack in the glass but missing the piece of film which he presumed he would find there. Irritated climbing back down he gives me the stare but then:

"Wait a moment, lift up your foot! Piero!" His partner barks. And there sure enough on the ground under his foot we can see the offending piece of film!

" Ah ha!" Crows Starsky. "What do we have here?"

Retrieving the strip from the floor he waves it in front of my nose, almost gloating, before sealing it into the clear plastic bag he has handy in his jacket pocket. We troop back up the stairs, everyone speaking in Italian now, a fact that elicits no further comment.

"We found a crack in the glass of the meter window which is already suspicious to us," says Hutch, taking over the proceedings. "And coupled with the discovery of a length of film, which on inspection revealed scratch marks, we are led to the conclusion that you, or at least someone, has interfered with the meter. That is to say property of the state. So," he continues officiously, "you will be hearing more from us in due course." He writes out a statement then asks me to sign the form.

As they are leaving, Starsky calls up from the bottom of the stairs asking permission to pick one of the cottage roses that are growing there in great profusion. He puts it to his nose and inhales deeply, then, as he walks away, I watch him slowly pulling each petal apart, tugging them loose and tossing them over his shoulder. I take this as a terrible omen. Plucked is exactly how I feel. Panic and dismay kick in almost immediately. What if I am sent to gaol? And how am I going to explain this to Carolyn when I pick her up at the station tomorrow? The best I can think of is that they will deport me.

Greeting Carolyn timidly off the train the next morning, I immediately blurt out the story. Carolyn explodes, which is so unlike her. She is as distraught as I am, two rabbits frozen in the headlights, not knowing which way to run.

"Oh my God! What? You left the strip in the meter and forgot it was there?
How fucking stupid is that! This could be the end for me."

"It's my mess, I'll deal with it, don't worry." I say hoping to calm her.

"What do you mean? It's my house, I'll be held responsible!"

"No, you won't, I can say I am renting it, that it has nothing to do with you."

"No one must know. Promise me you won't tell anybody about this," Carolyn insists.

I don't have the heart to remind her of Michelina, who has been coming to the house to clean for Carolyn for years and in all probability knows and undoubtedly will have broadcast the news right the way around the valley by by now. Michelina was a postal bride; a young bride from the South, darker in complexion than the locals, a stout woman with a slightly wooden demeanour that makes me feel ill at ease whenever I am in her company.

A week later, Carolyn and I are summoned to ENEL's regional office in Arezzo; they want their pound of flesh. Sitting outside the office I feel like that schoolboy again, waiting to be called into the headmaster's study to be caned for some nefarious deed! (In my case it was for starting a food fight in the dining room).

Indeed, ushered into the official's presence, he looks grim, no smile, no handshake just sit down and these are your options.

"We are satisfied," he says looking stern "that you have not paid in full the electricity you have consumed since we last read that meter. Therefore, we will be demanding reparation amounting to six hundred thousand Lira. If you agree to pay this fine then ENEL will agree to drop any future civil proceedings against you."

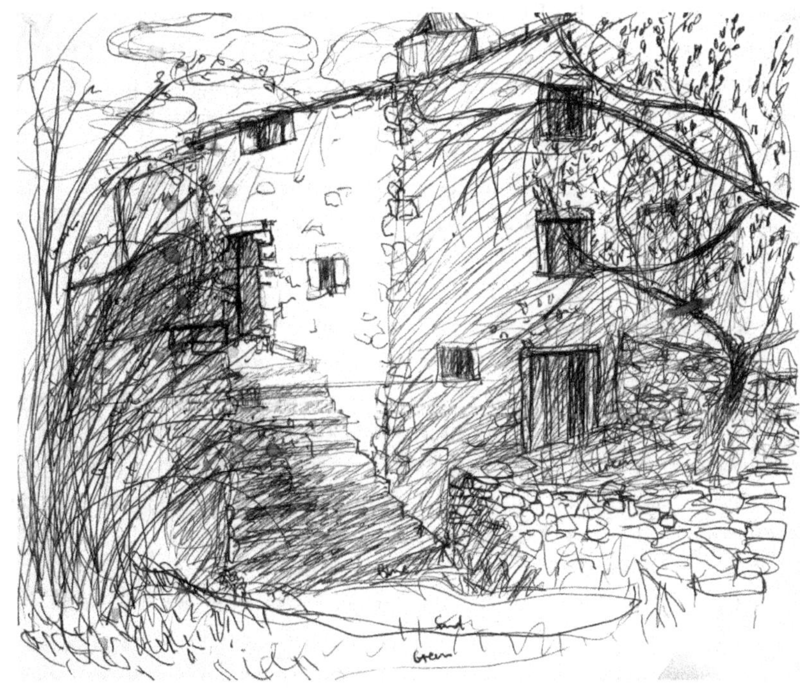

Carolyn's house

"Will that be the end of it then?" I ask hopefully.

"Not quite."

And I recall Starsky's parting words to me: "We are obliged to file a report with the Pretura, local court, but don't worry, it's only a question of a little letter slipped into someone's pigeon-hole, you understand, and then it will be up to a local magistrate to decide if you have a case to answer for, *capito*? Whether or not to proceed with criminal charges."

I am in awe every morning I step into in my studio and see Lago Trasimeno from the window, delicately poised like a seesaw on the fulcrum of the cupola of Santa Maria delle Grazie. I envisioned coming to Tuscany for only six months and here I am three years later: Nino in Wonderland. Perhaps that is what Cortona really represents—Wonderland. It must have been a rabbit hole that I stumbled down, not a portal. Sleepy Rip Van Winkle town all the same, a place out of time even if it does boast a judiciary!

It has been over two months since our visit to head office and I haven't heard a peep from ENEL or anybody else since. The silence is killing me, every waking moment is filled with angst even as I dare to hope the whole affair has simply blown over. Haven't I already paid a hefty price? I paid the fine promptly, didn't I? I am sorry ain't I? And I do promise, I promise never to do it again…EVER. What more would be gained by locking me up?
Or even deporting me?The self-recriminations with Carolyn have continued, which is probably the hardest part, the growing rift. I feel depressed and withdrawn. At the same time, Bob has been encouraging me to put on a solo exhibition, which could be a useful distraction.

"Keep the faith, bro, and show us what you've got, launch that boat."

Keeping my promise to Carolyn, I haven't uttered a word about my 'criminal' activity to Bob or anyone else, not even my parents, but keeping it pent up inside of me is a heavy burden to bare and it's not exactly a welcome topic of conversation with Carolyn either. We are arguing over stupid things now like: Voss is her dog and I have no right to tell her what to do with him! Occasionally I storm off down the path in a big huff:

"I'm leaving then!"

"Good! And don't come back!" Carolyn yells, sitting on the parapet, her long legs dangling over the ledge kicking furiously to and fro.

I will bunk down in the studio for one or two nights before we make up and I am in her arms again, breathing in her intoxicating scent.

Chapter 19.

Roberto together with his good friend and local artist Enzo, has finally managed to set up the artists' cooperative he has been talking about ever since I first met him. The space is in a prime location at the end of the *Corso* by Piazza Garibaldi; two rooms with vaulted ceilings in a converted cantina. The rent is low for members and, taking Bob's advice I have booked in for an exhibition for two weeks in September. This will be my first solo show in a gallery and the anticipation is only tempered by the fact that paying for a space iis not an accolade or affirmation of my work: anyone can rent a space and stick up their art works, although Roberto does insist, he wouldn't accept just anyone. Never the less, for the last couple of years people in Cortona have known me as an artist yet have never seen my work, so I regard this as a good opportunity to set the record straight.

I was nineteen and working in Paris for six months when I first seriously started considering becoming an artist; hanging out in the left bank studio of my distant German cousin Joachim, a painter. He encouraged me to go out into the streets and draw or paint and so I did, plucking up the courage to paint watercolours of the Seine in full view of the public; in Paris to boot, in awe of so many famous artists who came before me. Living in London four years later finally tipped me over the edge; I was working as a fashion photographer's assistant and we were on an assignment for Cosmopolitan magazine taking photos of an artist in his studio in trendy Chelsea. It was the intoxicating smell of turps and linseed oil and paint that did it! Soon after I quit my job and went home to Scotland just to find out if I really had it in me to paint and then coming back to London one year later with a stack of canvases under my arm honestly believing that would be enough to launch my career with recognition and galleries all falling into place thereafter. A bit naive I realise now, five years later, although that driving sense of mission is still strong; a belief that in some peculiar way following my path as an artist puts me in harmony with my fate; that the circumstances of my life are all conspiring towards that end.

Roberto and Enzo are both well known locally. In fact, Enzo by popular acclamation is regarded as the town's maestro. Not quite in the same league as Cortona's other painter sons: Signorelli or Severini but revered never the less. The word in Cortona is that everyone has an "Enzo" and I believe it; Noemi alone has two of his paintings, both hanging in the dining room (alongside the watercolour I gifted him). Noemi, beaming, never tires of telling me that he "commissioned" one of them: a picture of his *orto* at son Alfredo's, with Cortona silhouetted up on the hill behind.

Enzo's landscapes have a very distinctive painterly style suffused as they are in his trademark carmine ground, which radiates through the paint, between his green, blues and ochres. At first glance they are very appealing but given a room full, the novelty quickly rubs off as the effect can become a little too overwhelming.

Enzo doesn't know what to make of me; he is old school and suspects I have arty, city ideas, which makes us both slightly ill at ease when we meet. He can be incredibly funny at times but also very abrasive in manner, a salty sailor's tongue lashing is never far away especially with a belly full of wine as he trawls the bars along the Corso with his best mate Roberto.

Roberto is milder mannered and more considered. A poet as well as an artist; he's a sensitive and reserved man who is difficult to fathom, but also someone very open to experimentation: his paintings incorporating sculptural elements for example, unlike Enzo who remains rooted in populist traditions.

My parents are here for the opening of my exhibition and staying with us for three or four days. It is mushrooming season and we have been out picking chanterelles along the terraces behind the house. According to Roberto it is illegal to pick mushrooms in Tuscany unless you have taken an exam and paid for a licence, but I am not sure whether to believe him. Voss is showing us the way; Pa still looking trim in his early fifties but hairline receding, wearing gumboots and a sleeveless knitted jumper, his shirt outside his jeans, and in an uncharacteristically muted mood. Ma is starting to put on weight and her hair is thinning; she also looks glum. We have put them in the converted cantina downstairs where the errant meter is located and still mindful of Carolyn's wishes, not a word has been spoken even though my parents would normally be the first to hear about my woes. Carolyn and I were in Scotland last year for Christmas so I don't have to worry as much about them meeting for the first time. My parents seemed to approve of her even though my father did question the age differences and mother was suggesting that cultural differences can create difficulties in a relationship. For some peculiar reason she substituted my old double bed in my bedroom with two single beds instead, which subsequently Carolyn and I had to push together.

My big night: the evening *passagiata* along *ruga piana* is in full swing and there is a buzz in the air. I sent out specially printed invitations, with a picture from a linocut of two lovers under a cypress tree, Cortona in the distance, to everyone I know or have ever heard of in Cortona and there has been an enthusiastic response. People holding glasses of wine are spilling out of the gallery into the Corso, which in turn is enticing more people in and I am feeling naked to their eyes with my paintings hanging on the walls of the gallery all around us.

Carolyn is definitely not a fashionista, although I know she has been making an effort for my sake; no more duffle coats! Tonight, she is wearing one of those frilly Beefeater Diana collars and Sabine has been teasing her about it. Carolyn has prepared her signature dish for the opening, coarse liver-pâté crostini and bruschetta canapés and visitors are hoeing into a wheel of fresh pecorino from Margherita's shop. Earlier in the week I collected a couple of ten litre demijohns from a local vineyard, which I hope will be enough. Margherita only scoffed when I invited her to my opening, cackling it was too far for her to go (only five kilometres) and mischievously pointing out that the only journey she'll ever be undertaking is up the road to the cemetery, revelling in her gloominess.

This is the first time I have had the pleasure of putting red dots on the wall and feel the adrenalin rush of selling a painting; in particular that moment of suspense immediately prior to knowing for sure that you've closed the deal. Several watercolours have sold and a couple of oil paintings, mostly to friends but also to a couple of strangers. Bob, beforehand, was banging on about smaller paintings if I wanted a commercial success and I have really made an effort in the last few months to get out of the studio into the great Tuscan landscape and paint in watercolours: much easier than lugging around an easel with oil paints and canvases a la Bob.

Only one thing has slightly marred the evening: a comment Rupert's mother made about the painting of Carolyn playing a flute, sitting naked astride a horse (I make a cameo appearance as a groom leading the horse, in the bottom right corner). Ma happened to be standing next to the painting when Rupert's mother turned to me and innocently asked if my mother was the lady in the painting! The inference struck a raw nerve, notwithstanding comments from my father, the latest of which he delivered yesterday: that I was more like a glorified factotum than Carolyn's partner! Actually, he did preface that comment with 'I can see the love she has for you in her eyes but...'

I do catch myself wishing Carolyn wasn't 13 years older than me, especially when I see photos of her at my age; she is even more stunning in a tank top and beret, standing on the steps of the Parthenon in Athens, looking like a revolutionary Patty Hearst!

After the opening, Pa invites a group of fifteen of us to celebrate at the Trattoria Dell'Amico in via Dardano. (Named by the owner for the friend who gave him the money to start the restaurant up after World War 11). Pa loves giving after-dinner speeches, which can be very entertaining, but he also tends to over-sentimentalise and can become maudlin if he drinks (by that point Ma and I are usually shrinking down in our seats). He stands to make a toast:

"To my son the artist"

This time only a proud father and nothing to worry about at all. Martin comes up to me afterwards to tell me what a great dad I have and I agree. I feel a sense of deep gratitude to this man who adopted me and full heartedly has taken me on as his own son: unlike my biological father Bill, who disappeared without a trace when I was only one. Bill did gift me three half-sisters from his second marriage though, who I finally had the opportunity to meet on my trip to Dusseldorf. Being an only son, I went there with such high hopes: the eldest Patricia, only a couple of years younger than me even has my looks! Unfortunately for reasons unknown to me, ever since my return I have had no further contact, notwithstanding invitations to visit Carolyn and I in Tuscany;

other than a letter from my "step" mother, informing me what a fine young man I have turned out to be but that it would be better for all concerned if there was no further communication.

Roberto handed me the large iron key to the gallery and left me to get on with iit for the next two weeks. Sitting in the gallery from morning to night can get boring, with nothing to do in the morning except watch the old man opposite wheeling bicycles in and out of his repair shop. The Corso picks up gradually towards midday and then around one thirty everything abruptly shuts down again until late afternoon. I go back to the studio or stroll up to the Fortezza with my panino, taking in Severini's Stations of the Cross, and reacquainting myself with my secret garden. The weather is fantastic: summer dipping into autumn, grape harvesting, warm September days. The Corso is busiest between five and eight in the evening, gathering momentum with the *passeggiata*, when people breeze in and out of the gallery in gaggles and everything is go-go-go in Italian fashion. Don Bruno, priest, noted local historian and art critic for L'Etruria, a fortnightly Cortona rag, has requested an interview. We haven't met but his mercurial reputation as a crusher of spirits, and chronic imbiber, precedes him, making me nervous when I greet him at the gallery door. He is an imposing figure in his black cassock: built like a Picasso minotaur, breathing fire and brimstone, all bullish, stamping the ground, hooves sparking, and a thick butcher's neck with fine purple veins cross-hatching a moon-shaped face; but turns out to be a cultured man and surprisingly mild-mannered once I can get him to stop fidgeting and sit down.

Chapter 20.

One morning, an elegantly dressed, slightly plump but curvaceous young lady with dark, silky hair of a thousand strokes and glossy makeup on, breezes into the gallery. She is wearing a waist-length grey herringbone jacket over a tightly fitting matching skirt tailored to the knees and is carrying a leather briefcase under her arm, very sexy businesslike. Showing no interest in the paintings, she bustles over to me sitting behind my desk and asks if I am Nino MacDonald? Then hands me a large envelope, smiling disarmingly. We have not met but I do recall seeing her around town before and, intrigued, I open the letter and start reading it with her still there standing in front of me. It takes a moment for the penny to drop: this is the scene where the guy dives out the back door and disappears before the wily bailiff has time to serve the warrant. No!

"You have been served!"

Oh no! Carolyn and I have been summoned to appear at the local magistrate's court two weeks hence and the nightmare I had so fervently and hopefully buried comes flooding back in all its frightening detail. The lady harbinger of doom is not unsympathetic, perhaps thinking this is too easy, and seeing my crestfallen face, tries to soften the blow, offering me the name of a good lawyer, whom she urges me to contact if I don't already have one, before bidding me farewell with a "*buona fortuna*," no doubt off in search of another hapless victim.

I have had a few minor run-ins with the law in Tuscany but nothing like this before. One time I was on the *motorino* with Carolyn illegally riding pillion and we were stopped by a Carabinieri patrol in the middle of nowhere. I was fined on the spot, which was unusual enough for me to ask for a receipt. Was this a shake down? No, receipt given. Business over, I ventured to enquire how Carolyn was now supposed to get home? And fully understanding the dilemma we were in, the policeman told us both to remount and obligingly looked the other way while we took off down the road!

Driving Carolyn's Mini on UK plates is not legal either, nor is driving with a UK driving licence but the local police don't seem to be too concerned and quite a few *stranieri* prefer it, driving on foreign plates. Bernardo did have his German plated Golf impounded but that was mainly because he was blind drunk and crashed it over the edge of the road down into town from Portole. Legally speaking you can't actually buy an Italian car unless you are a resident but the main advantage of driving with foreign plates is that you don't have to pay road taxes and never pay parking tickets; in theory at least, as I was about to find out after the carabinieri flagged me down for driving the wrong way up the one way street just below the parterre. (A short cut into town taken by all the locals I should add). There must be some arcane system of accountability, some brilliance of detection by the police because when, as requested, I presented myself to the office of the municipal police on the following day, the sergeant, rummaging around in the top draw of his desk, fished out a small bundle of parking tickets for the Mini and dropping them in front of me, suggesting it was high time I pay! One of the tickets I noticed later was from Siena. How efficient is that! There was no mention at all of the original infringement, the one I thought I had been called in for in the first place or about driving a car with foreign plates.

The I Ching urges us "to be prepared in advance, in order to avoid misfortune later", but I don't see the point of throwing good money away on a lawyer when this is obviously an open and shut case. Carolyn slumps into a chair when I tell her, her face turns ghostly pale but she tells me not to be so stupid and to go and see the lawyer that the girl recommended and so I duly make an appointment with Avvocato Vialli.

His first-floor office is on the Corso and he greets me at the door, an older, portly dishevelled looking man in shirtsleeves with sleeve garters, damp patches under the arms, his trousers held up by green braces and smoking a Toscanelli cheroot. His hawkish eyes are hooded for the moment as we face each other across his desk and he peruses the summons.

"Carolyn is your wife?" He asks.

"No but we live together."

"And I see here the house is hers?"

"Yes that's right but I would like to keep her out of it, she has nothing to do with this, she wasn't even there when it happened." And I recount the bare facts of the case, concluding:

"Avvocato, they practically caught me red-handed, so what else can I do but plead guilty?"

"Wait a moment!"

Suddenly awake, flicking open his eyelids and flapping his arms up and down, then seeing my alarm, leans forward on the table bringing his wrists together in the universal sign for handcuffs.

"My dear young friend, defrauding the state of its electricity supply is a criminal offence."

He picks up a hefty tome anchored to a corner of his desk and thumbing through it:

"Ah, here we are: the maximum penalty is five years imprisonment! How do you feel about that?" He looks at me pointedly, I shrink back. "Tell me young man, what choice do you leave the magistrate if you go in there and say: I am guilty?"

I stare back at him uncomprehending.

"None! Is what I say." He answers for me.

"You need to appreciate the seriousness of the situation you and your good lady are in."

Triumphantly hefting closed the book with a thump.

"What choice are you giving him but to say yes! Okay! Go straight to gaol! Thank you and see you in a few years!"

He starts patting his brow with a handkerchief.

"And anyway, my friend, that is not how we do things here in Italy. What we really need are options." He says in a kindlier voice:

"Five years' gaol time with one year off for good behaviour. Is that what you want? Of course not!"

I can see his point, renew my hope.

"So let's not jump to any hasty conclusions or get carried away."

He waves the summons in front of me.

"This is only for a preliminary hearing, you understand, *capito*? This is not a trial we are heading into, just the investigating magistrate, who will look at the evidence and then decide if you have a case to answer."

"I see, so do you think there might be a chance?" I venture.

"That will depend on what evidence they have, but don't despair, in Italy there is always room for negotiation and as far as your friend is concerned, we will try to keep her out of it but she will still have to come along with us to see the magistrate."

We arrange to meet in the Corso outside the Pretura at the time of the hearing one week hence and I thank him as he opens the door for me to leave. Justice is swift in the land outside time, once the wheels start turning: from the gallery to the lawyer's office and now to the magistrate's court, all within fifty yards along the Corso.

Only the distraction of the exhibition has saved me from becoming a complete looney case this past week. Carolyn too: more conciliatory, she has been keeping me company as I sit it out in the gallery, but nothing can dispel the gloom as we rendezvous with Avvocato Vialli outside the Pretura at the appointed time. I feel like a dead man walking. Vialli however remains upbeat, he can't keep still on his toes, bouncing up and down, ready to give us a pep talk before we go in.

"Don't worry, my young friend, Signora. Let's see what the magistrate has to say. You just let me do all the talking, *capito*? Pretend you don't speak Italian and I'll take it from there. We will enter together and leave your lady out in the hall for the meanwhile, then see if she is needed after. OK?"

My apparent secondary role comes as something of a relief but then as soon as we walk into the magistrate's office my heart misses a beat because I recognise the magistrate! Surely not! I know the man standing behind the oval table; he walked in off the street into the gallery to see my exhibition, not two weeks ago, although I had no idea who he was then. An elegantly dressed man, with a coif of neatly brushed silver hair toppling back from the forehead, dressed in a shiny grey worsted suite; obviously a cultured man, we spent a pleasant if polite half hour together chatting in Italian about my work and painting in general.

We all sit down around the table and my lawyer, unaware of this development, immediately launches forth on my behalf. The magistrate in turn doesn't miss a beat and the two of them lock heads, ignoring my presence entirely. Statements are read over, the plastic bag with the offending piece of film is placed on the table, pushed to and fro and closely inspected. They are speaking so fast it is hard to follow anyway, and my mind drifts out of the window into the overcast sky above to plea bargain with a higher authority, only coming back down to earth when I become aware of my lawyer excusing himself from the room to go and talk to Carolyn. I am not sure how to react, now that the two of us have been left alone together in the room. I am spellbound, but the magistrate quite naturally turns to me and inquires pleasantly how the exhibition is going, have I sold any more paintings? And naturally I reply in Italian. The dumb show then resumes as soon as my lawyer re-enters the room, but this time it almost feels like the magistrate and I are the ones in cahoots not my lawyer and I, who is now leaning full-tilt across the table in more earnest discussion. Finally, he drops back into his seat, winking at me as he does and inexplicably starts kicking my shins under the table. The audience, it appears, is over and we get up to leave, everyone shaking hands and I none the wiser.

Carolyn has been waiting with baited breath on a bench in the hallway and as we emerge again together on the Corso, Avvocato Vialli excitedly explains: "The magistrate in his wisdom has come to the conclusion that the evidence is only circumstantial, *capito*?" He claps me on the shoulder.

"They found the film on the floor and not in the meter, so it cannot be regarded as a definitive proof, capito? He isn't going to take it any further."

"But what about the meter-man, surely he was a key witness and could corroborate the evidence?"

"Look, like I said before, this was not a trial, no witnesses are called and as far as the reports go, ENEL the electricity company were satisfied with the result; that you paid the fine. Case closed. Now go home and get some sleep—you look like you need some—and take better care of your charming wife!"

"Thank you Avvocato I won't forget this."

"No! And don't forget Monday morning to bring the three hundred in cash to my office." He concludes before dashing off.

I love Italian justice! Well why wouldn't I! It can be exasperating; self-serving or decided on the toss of a coin or even on a whim but in the end it is never just black and white or straightforward, contradictions abound yet resolution is never far away because there is always room for negotiation. Anglos are so rigid, so determined to have justice whatever the cost, too easily losing sight of the human face.

Unfortunately, when Don Bruno's review finally appeared, it was too late for the exhibition, which had already closed.

L'ETRURIA.

SCOTTISH PAINTER EXHIBITS IN CORTONA

"... *The interior harmony [of his paintings] coincides with a geometric construction, expressionism and objective reality fuse to create a new unity...All together this exhibition offers us an interesting new perspective and it is up to us to understand its significance... The artist will remain among us and his smile reveals his immense pleasure at being here in Cortona.*" Don Bruno Frescucci

Chapter 21.

"Will you take a look at this," I say to Carolyn, pointing at the menu on the wall as we enter the Osteria La Tufa in Ossaia.

"A tourist menu in four languages no less!"

We haven't eaten here in quite a while.

"Remember when the menu was chalked up on the blackboard or Serafino came to the table to let us know what the specials were?" Carolyn says disappointed.

"Ha! This is a good one: see how they've put carne translated into English as "flesh!".

"Not very appealing is it, hope it's not a sign of things to come?"

Nevertheless, looking around as we enter the main dining room, the Osteria is packed for the traditional Sunday set course lunch, and no sign of any tourists in the room.

Tuscany is certainly becoming ever more popular. Cheekily, the English press has started calling it "Chiantishire" as if Tuscany is just another English County. Since I have been here most of the shops and bars along the Corso have undergone major makeovers or disappeared altogether like Renato's *mesticheria* turned into a shoe shop or the barber shop now a *profumeria.* The Bars, in addition, are busy staking out new territory for themselves, laying on extra tables and chairs outside their doors, some consolidating the space with boxed oleander hedgerows. Benito in Bar Signorelli looks permanently under siege, exhausted, bags under his eyes, and he rarely flashes his trademark smile these days or shakes his cocktail mixer with quite such verve, but that could equally be down to him giving up smoking.

Germans too are homing in, zooming down the autobahn in their Mercedes, throwing fist-fulls of marks at farm houses that are basically ruins and helping to fuel a property boom. Amelio just frowns and guffaws at talk of the large sums of money being paid for the *case coloniche*, now that the canny *contadini* have been alerted to the pearl in the sow's ear and cottoned on to their potential worth. The irony is that after the post-war rush off the land and into the cities, what was once considered homes for the poor, are fast becoming the dwellings of the rich.

"At least they are no longer abandoned and are being lovingly restored." I venture in reply to Amelio's obvious disdain.

From the moment I stepped onto these shores, this island of castaways, I have fantasised about owning a *casa colonica*. Building a studio in one of those old ruins, like so many beached whales stranded in the landscape. I roam the countryside in search of them, stumbling across abandoned farmhouses covered in dense thickets of brambles, hidden in secret valleys, or deep in the woods or perched high up on escarpments with mouth-watering views; only a stained picture of the Virgin Mary hanging off a cracked wall or a rusty ladle lying in a broken grate offering evidence of a past life now reduced to souvenirs for house hunters. These places are empty spaces you can pour yourself into, and I do, pacing out the square metres, sketching out rough floor plans, dreaming.

Three years ago, my father gave me a modest lump sum of money, ostensibly to buy a house. He told me he was giving me my inheritance in advance in order to avoid paying death duties, so my fantasies at least have gained a ring of truth as I go exploring. I have even suggested fixing up the ruined half of Carolyn's place, maybe turning it into a studio; spending hours out front, sitting on the broken stone steps next door, fantasising on how it might look; cathedral windows and a minstrel gallery where Carolyn could serenade me on the viola while I am busy painting below, Voss skipping in and out.

When Carolyn bought her attached workers' cottage ten years ago, she neglected to buy the other half, which was then on a separate title. She never dreamed anybody would ever want to buy it, only then, a few years later word reached her via Margherita at the shop, of an impending sale. Distraught, what ensued was a frantic week for Carolyn, desperately seeking out the owner, who lived in Rome and then making a counter offer, effectively gazumping the unwitting buyer and her peace of mind restored. It would have spelt a complete disaster had someone moved in next door to her; this house is her sanctuary, her refuge and God forbid should anyone interfere! I should have known better too, that even after having entertained my ideas to build a studio next door, Carolyn would not be able to see it through and consequently my plans have been quietly shelved. She is thinking: what if we broke up and she was stuck with me living next door?!!

Taking another tack, I have even suggested selling her place and buying somewhere together, but she doesn't see the point of that or understand my concerns. I am thinking what about compromise, how much is she willing to sacrifice, especially given that she does not want to have children, but find it impossible to articulate these thoughts to her. My father's comment about being a glorified steward burnt deeply but even so, at times I think I am only ticking the boxes so that in the end I can justify to myself that I tried everything to make our relationship work.

Bernardo is happy with the extra work the Germans are bringing him, so are the *contadini,* with house prices sky rocketing as they are. Tuscans can be pragmatic and this second wave of Germans invading the countryside within forty years hasn't stirred up any great emotions either; for which I am grateful, too; even as I tend to bury any traces of my own German ancestry with proclamations of being Scottish! Atrocities were committed during the war in the Valdichiana, most terribly at Civitella where 244 people were rounded up and executed in reprisal for a firefight in a bar that saw three German soldiers killed. Amelio, who was forced to walk home barefoot from Albania after the war, talks about the priest in our valley who was hailed as a hero for sheltering *partigiani* in the church and Amelio took me to see the iron cross in Pergo, marking the spot an escaped Russian PoW, fighting with the partisans, was re-captured and hanged.

The tried and tested method of finding properties for sale is through a local *muratore*; there are no for sale hoardings planted outside houses and judging by the low profile kept by Cortona's two real estate agents, you could be forgiven for thinking that the property boom is just a myth. You need sharp eyes to see the two dilapidated display cases tacked up onto the walls of the *Corso*; each one filled with poor snapshots of houses for sale, accompanied by smudged, hand-written notes on ruled cards.

Rupert is now studying for his exams at the Chamber of Commerce in Arezzo to become a *libero professionista,* a self-employed professional. He wants to set up his own real-estate business, mainly renting out and managing luxury holiday villas. He reckons there is a good business opportunity in the market especially as he will be the first with no local competitors and also with the new possibilities opening up for bookings over the internet. Rupert is also a keen photographer and likes the idea of using his creativity taking photos of Tuscan villas and as an added bonus, Donatella, his wife, has the administrative skills required.

The manufacturing company Rupert worked for in Arezzo, translating technical manuals, has folded after its principal export market collapsed due to a NATO-led embargo on Iran over the issue of torturing dissidents. Ironically, Rupert has also been involved with a group of lawyers in Rome who are helping Iranian refugees who have fled from "the Ayatollah's revolutionary guard killer squads" as Rupert puts it and is currently employed writing for a business journal.

Martin and John have set up a business manufacturing a new wood stove that Martin had the idea for and designed after a trip he made to Norway. Martin ever mindful of winter's discomforts, and John, have been tinkering for years up on the farm with different ideas for heating these cold stone houses that foreigners are so keen on these days. In one experiment, radiators were fed by water heated in pipes placed immediately behind the fire grate but the "Attwoodstove" is probably their most commercially viable idea to date. It is an elegant cast-iron stove on four legs, painted in forest green or venetian red, you have the choice of colours, with a black-slab cooking top and a finely calibrated baffle plate making it economical on wood yet still capable of blasting out the heat. Most importantly, when properly fed last thing at night it will still be alight in the morning. There's nothing worse waking up to a cold stove on a miserable winter morning, then having to fiddle about in the grate, raking the ashes and blackening your fingers to rekindle the fire. Carolyn and I are both over that and have been on the waiting list for an Attwoodstove for some time.

Originally, they were building the stove up at the farm but production could not keep up wth the demand and Martin has since persuaded Michaeli to partner them. Michaeli's leather handbag manufacturing business, where Jef and Rupert used to work, is in the process of being wound up, and Michaeli was on the lookout for a new business venture. Apparently, his mother has pots of money and has been keeping her son afloat. Production of the stove has been moved into his more spacious workshop in Cortona, which is located in the same street as my studio. Occasionally on my way to work, I will see John at the canted window on the first floor, winching a new stove ready for delivery, straight down onto the back seat of his open topped Deux Chevaux car.

"That one for us John?" I might call up hopefully.

Rupert is engaged to marry Michaeli's long-suffering assistant Donatella, and Carolyn and I have been invited to the wedding. Jef is in town too for the wedding, with his new girlfriend Marina, who we have not met before. He must be serious this time because he can't stop calling her "Amore" and has already moved in with her, into her flat in Rome.

"Donatella is a brilliant administrator and such a hard worker." Jef declares, as we sit in the piazza sipping cappuccinos. "And he is not exactly known for his business acumen. I feel sorry for her. The stress is beginning to tell on her face."

"Hell!" Jef laughs, warming to his subject. "He is better known in Cortona for driving his jeep up the Comune steps blind drunk and falling asleep at the wheel at the top; then being arrested by the carabinieri. You can still see the damage he caused."

Jef offers to show us and leads the way across the piazza, pointing to the patches on the steps where they have been repaired.

"At Michaeli's expense!"

I can't wait to take part in one of those extravagant Saturday morning wedding motorcades that you often see coursing through village and countryside, hands glued to the horn, Italian style. The long-suffering, faithful Mini has finally carked it and we are taking our new Diane out for a spin. She's not as tenacious as the Mini was and only makes it half way up the track to Carolyn's house, alas! We park her next to Tranquillo's 'tractor' hut and walk the rest of the way up. However she is a joy to drive; bouncing along on a cushion of air, the gear shift stuck onto the dashboard, the soft top rolled back, still with English licence plates.

Rupert's wedding is being held in a chapel out on the flats of the Valdichiana near Donatella's family home, and a large crowd of guests is already spilling out of the tiny rural church by the time Carolyn and I arrive. There are no pews in the church and bedlam reigns with everyone standing, babies howling, children darting in and out of the crowd, friends calling out to each other across the way.

The arrival of the priest, walking ahead the bridal couple, clearing the way through the throng, accompanied by his young frocked attendant dispensing great clouds of incense, only quells the crowd to a susurrus. Rupert is smiling nervously, flashing white teeth, looking smart in a brown suit, his silvering straight hair neatly parted, and Donatella looks radiant in a white satin bolero and matching skirt, her lustrous chestnut hair braided and intertwined with wild flowers under a simple lace veil. She looks a Latin beauty, revitalised.

After the ceremony we drive in the noisy cavalcade across country to the reception at a popular local motel. Rupert warned me beforehand:

"It won't be the usual heavy wedding meal, but my father-in-law's own fatted calf, slaughtered specially for the occasion, and a super cake!"

All the same, the wedding meal carries on late into the afternoon with frequent and fervent interruptions of guests bursting to their feet to toast the newly-weds, roaring out "*Evviva gli sposi*! *Viva*! *Viva*!" Accompanied by thunderous applause and much cutlery banging. Rupert duly takes his leave with Donatella for their appointment with destiny as the guests are left to wind down at a leisurely pace over coffee and vin santo with the traditional *cantucci* biscuits for dunking, plus a drinks trolley is rolled in at the kill with home-made rose, lemon and pear-flavoured grappas. I can drive the Diane home, secure in the knowledge that if the carabinieri do pull us over, they will be infinitely more interested in my identity papers than checking my blood alcohol levels.

Chapter 22.

The completely shattering news that my parents are separating, ending their twenty five year old marriage, is shocking because it is so unexpected. I must have been blind when they were here not so long ago for my exhibition, not to have noticed something was obviously wrong, or too pre-occupied more like with my own woes. Then again, perhaps it is not so surprising; my parents have always kept their marital problems well hidden from me. Something not so hard for them to do considering the amount of time I spent at boarding school and now, living in Tuscany and only seeing them one or two times a year.

I can't actually remember the last time I saw them rowing, only the times when Pa was banned from the marital bed and exiled to a cot in his dressing room. My mother said that was because of his snoring but I know it was more to do with his drinking. He can go months without a drop but then suddenly he's away, often with his army pals, reliving their glory days in the officers' mess. My mother can't stand it and locks herself away but according to Pa she was once a drinker too: recounting the time in Germany, when she had split up with Bill, my biological father, and employed a girl to accompany her to bars at night just to ensure she got home safely afterwards.

My mother has always suspected Pa of having affairs; he is a handsome, outgoing charismatic man, quite the opposite in character to her; she is more like me: diffident, difficult, certainly not extrovert or outgoing by nature. Apparently, he has been having an affair with Sue, a work colleague in his Edinburgh office. Ma says she gave him an ultimatum that he refused: Pa says she wouldn't give him a second chance, although my belief is she painted him into a corner and he wouldn't back down. Whatever! The result is she has moved out of Belton, our family home and gone to London. Over the phone to me, Pa declares he is in love with Sue, saying she makes him feel alive again. She is four years younger than Carolyn, which feels a bit weird! I haven't met her yet, but I'm pretty sure I saw her in his office last time I was there; she has red hair, is tall, and stands out, and as I recall she was staring at me over her shoulder, as if I was a person of interest to her, which puzzled me at the time but then I thought nothing more about it.

I am surprised that at my age I feel so effected; the ground shaking beneath my feet once more, just like I would have done when I was a toddler; a sense of abandon echoing down all those years, because while my mother was trawling the bars to get drunk, I was left in the care of a foster family for a few months. Even today, if Carolyn has been away in Rome for a few days and is due back, Voss and I will be out on the veranda, like a couple of anxious puppies, looking down the valley eager to catch sight of her car headlights and know she will soon be home.

Notwithstanding these insecurities or maybe as a result of them, I find I am gently prizing myself away from Carolyn. It's almost as if my parents breaking up has been a catalyst for me to act.

Climbing out of Cesare's jeep, he points to the row of four terraced houses, buttressed against the sky in an impossible embrace; concertinaed together and plunked down in the middle of nowhere without a seeming rhyme or reason to exist except perhaps to be closer to God. Cesare is a young pig farmer who lives past Martin's place, out in the remoter mountainous region on the Tuscan-Umbria border. He looks more Austrian than Italian: short and burly with a ruddy complexion, rusty stubble and the curl of a red moustache. Sometimes we have a drink together in Bar Signorelli, if he is in Cortona on union business and recently, he has been showing me properties for sale around his area. Case *coloniche* are cheaper out there, yet close enough to Cortona to feel her umbilical pull.

"That one on the left at the far end belongs to the priest, but he only visits occasionally on weekends so you wouldn't be disturbed," Cesare enthuses.

"The house for sale is there on the right at the opposite end."

Taking in the view I can only describe the location as magnificently bleak: a barren, windswept hilltop with a distant ragged line of glassy mountains tinted pink and blue, melding almost into the far-away Adriatic. We clamber over rubble to gain entry to the building; the first floor has partially collapsed but the walls are standing and the roof appears to be intact. Next door, parts of the roof are buckling and the central tower is starting to implode, which could be a problem. The walls are a powder blue wash and feel Mediterranean, in stark contrast to the frigid atmosphere outside. I have been reasoning it is a good time to view houses because in winter you probably see them at their worst. There is a balcony upstairs with a pretty loggia, and immediately adjacent to the building is a tobacco-drying tower that comes with the property and would make a great studio. None of the other houses Cesare has shown me so far have been remotely suitable, but I can see some potential in this one and ask him to set up a meeting with the owner. I want to show the house to Bernardo as well and take a closer look at the structure so he can give me a better idea whether or not he thinks it is worth it and an estimate of the costs involved in making it habitable again. Cesare won't be there this time but has primed me beforehand that the owner Davide is a young school teacher from San Leone, who recently inherited the property and is desperate to sell.

Feeling a little sheepish, I give Carolyn some lame excuse and leave the house to meet Bernardo down on the main road as pre-arranged. She knows nothing of my comings and goings so far and keeping it a secret makes me feel like I am sneaking out to meet a lover.

Davide is eager to greet us as we drive up to the house; over-eager and nervous because he won't look me in the eye but keeps bobbing his head, pulling his cap off, and like a tic, running his fingers through his thinning dark hair before stroking the cap back into place. I introduce Bernardo and explain that he is going to take a closer look at the house, so we quickly move inside and leave Davide fretting outside. I enjoy visualising and speculating what could be; checking out the available light is always important, and dreaming about building my own studio and owning my very first home, while Bernardo, more pragmatically: measures, prods, thumps, writes in his pad and clambers onto the roof for a closer inspection.

When he is done, looking flushed after his exertions but satisfied, Bernardo, who has a smile that moves up in unison with his face, draws me aside as we leave Davide loitering out of earshot.

"What was the asking price again?" asks Bernardo, totting up numbers in his notepad.

"He is asking 59 million but I reckon there is room for manoeuvre. Cesare told me he is desperate to get rid of it."

"And how much land is there?"

"Davide told me two hectares, but most of the land is over there on the other side of the public road where the olive trees are, which is not ideal."

"The house being attached could be a problem in the future because you never know what will happen next door, but given the size, I would say 59 million lira is a good price: the overall structure is sound and somewhere around 40 million should cover the costs of doing it up."

My brain begins to swell. His estimate dovetails almost exactly with what I can afford and suddenly I feel giddy at the prospect of throwing large sums of money around, playing the big shot.

I have invested my inheritance in shares and against the advice of my stockbroker, a family friend, insisted he follow a high-risk strategy, which in a bull market has paid off handsomely. A chip off the old block, I like to think, referencing my father, pleased with my business acumen and good fortune, having managed so far to live modestly off the dividends without touching the capital.

Suddenly I am swept up in the fever and before I know what I'm doing, I swagger over to Davide and make him an offer on the spot of 54 million. It literally pops out of my mouth! Which, without pausing for breath, Davide eagerly accepts, momentarily taking the wind out of my sails and wiping the smug look off my face.

"With the proviso," Davide continues, grabbing his window of opportunity, "17 million is in cash."

I flash Bernardo a questioning look and can see he is momentarily nonplussed by the speed of events but, recovering quickly, confirms that paying a percentage in cash under the table is standard practice in Tuscany. So, we shake hands on it and relieved, I think now we can all go home, except Davide isn't finished; he insists on driving back to Cortona immediately to see the lawyer and sign the *compromesso*, the preliminary contract. Lamely I comply; right now, you could probably lead me over a cliff and so Bernardo and I race off after Davide in the car. Events are beginning to spin out of control and thank God the lawyer's office is closed by the time we reach Cortona on Saturday afternoon. Instead of feeling elated I have plunged back to earth with a resounding what the fuck am I doing? I haven't even considered the ramifications with Carolyn or how I am going to tell her. Davide of course is disappointed and put out that the office is closed but we arrange to meet again in Cortona the following Monday and Bernardo and I saying goodbye move off to Bar La Posta, where Angelo and his wife Mireille greet us cheerily from behind the counter.

"Prosecco," I say, putting on a brave face as we enter the small bar. Mireille smiles and asks me what we are celebrating. She still retains a hint of a French accent, otherwise you would take her for an Italian. Framed photographs of Angelo and Mireille posing outside the bar with French

President Mitterrand adorn the wall; he was the mayor of Château-Chinon, which is Cortona's twinned town, and has been a regular visitor here over the last decade.

"I've just bought a house out at San Leone," I explain, filling them in on some of the details. Angelo brings out the bottle of Prosecco from under the counter and fills the two flute glasses Mireille has polished and placed on the bar in front of us, rolling her eyes when she hears the story and pointing two fingers at her temples she cries out:

"Are you out of your mind?"

Angelo, the more placid of the two, comes round from behind the counter to shake my hand and says warmly,

"Congratulations: good for you."

Back home, panic sets in almost immediately: how am I going to tell Carolyn? A very sobering thought, and this is not the first secret I have had to keep from her.

The next day, I slip out for another look at "my house", feeling as bleak as my surroundings, and it becomes blindingly clear that I can't go through with it. An embarrassing situation, but it has to be faced and better to address it now than let it run on. Returning home, I call Cesare from Margherita's to let him know I am backing out and although he is irritated, he spares me the ignominy of informing Davide myself. One step forward, two steps back: typical Pisces.

Chapter 23.

Carolyn returns to Australia periodically in order to work as a doctor's locum or in the psychiatric unit of one of Sydney's main hospitals. I did accompany her to Australia the last time she went two years ago, bailing on a Tuscan winter, as we travelled to Australia via South America, but this time round I have decided not to go with her. A sign of our times.

We very nearly didn't make it to Australia at all last time because of Voss; he was badly mauled by a dog only a week before our scheduled departure and required urgent medical attention and care. Voss is a dandy dog who sometimes underestimates his charms especially when it comes to his rivals for a bitch on heat. It is not unusual for him to go walkabout around the valley and be gone for a few days, eventually making his way home safely but on this occasion, we found him on the doorstep early in the morning, whimpering and shivering uncontrollably. Great strips of rancid smelling flesh and fur had been stripped off his back and were dangling loose. Carolyn freaked out, bundling him up in a blanket and we rushed him off to the vet in Camucia. A pitiful sight: him being sewn up heavily sedated and splayed out like a floppy soft toy on the vet's table. Will he ever learn? Normally Amelio takes him in when Carolyn leaves the country, but Voss needed special care and after some serious soul-searching whether she could leave him or not, she decided to kennel him with Dr. Halliday, the vet in Arezzo. Poor fellow, caged up and deprived of his freedom for three months before he was well enough for Amelio to come and reclaim him.

It's a sad send-off at the airport for Carolyn. Nothing has been said as such, but the possibility we won't be seeing each other again weighs heavily on my mind. She turns and waves before passing through security control then turns again and blows a kiss before disappearing into the departure lounge. Even Voss isn't his usual perky self, as we troop back to the car.

Avoiding the big question, I throw myself into preparations for the two exhibitions I'm having this year: a solo show in Munich followed by a group show at the Crane Kalman gallery in London, both of which my Aunt Tante Eliette had a hand in arranging.

Rupert drops by the studio, cradling his newborn baby girl, Lucy, and for the first time I begin to feel a paternal stirring in me and a sense my biological clock ticking; or is it simply a need to compensate; to fill the void left by my parents splitting up by creating a family of my own? Carolyn has always been so adamant not wanting children and I have never really tried to change her mind. It's hard to believe but Jef is about to become a father too. He and Marina are moving to England so he can take up a post as a news producer in the ABC's London bureau: not a bad promotion for a photocopy boy.

I sketch Lucy fussing in Rupert's smitten arms and when she finally allows him to put her down, he poses for me; the central figure in a painting giving vent to the turmoil I feel inside; a man charging down a long alley of cypress trees,

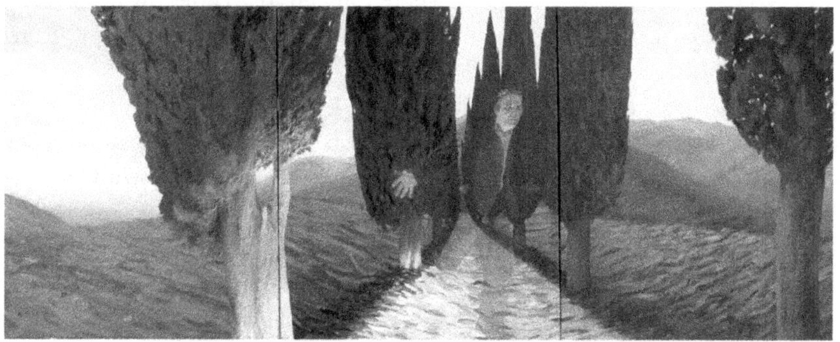

Flight of Faith.1984

caught in the headlights of a car like a startled rabbit: caught outside the rabbit hole? Has the spell finally been broken? That this is actually a place in time and I am now out of time?
Rupert's arms are outstretched as if he is about to take off, the lower half of his body dematerialising, vanishing altogether. Cortona, cushioned by the psychedelic colours of a winter sunset, is glimpsed in the upper left corner of the painting with Valecchie buried in shadow on the opposite side. The bold brush-strokes of the ploughed fields sweeping through the foreground from left to right are like a tide in motion, the whole reminding me of Moses parting the waves, leading us to the promised land! Or am I heading out of one?

Finding good titles for my paintings has always been important to me and the title of this one is suitably ambiguous: Flight of Faith. Is faith being routed or is it taking wing? Am I running away, fleeing, or am I flying towards something new? This much I know, because in truth I have already drawn a line and it is only a question of accepting what my heart feels but my mind finds difficult to accept: that the relationship is over.

On a trip to Rome, Jef is the first person I tell about my intention to leave Carolyn and ergo Tuscany: a cathartic moment making it public for the first time. Confronted by my failure, Jef's reaction is typical of someone in a steady relationship, not wishing to see the status quo disturbed. He thinks I'm being cowardly, especially the way I have ended the relationship over the phone.

"You should've waited for her to come home."

He is probably right but I just don't have the heart to face her here. I did offer to meet her half way in India, where I intend to go after my exhibitions in Munich and London but she made it pretty clear that she didn't want to see me. EVER!

So the wheels have been put in motion. I shall tipi-toe out of Cortona and leave Rip Van Winkle peacefully asleep and blissfully unaware, but before I do, I am painting that view of paradise again, the one that will be so hard to leave behind: the entire stretch of the Valdichiana seen from ringside Cortona, adding that meteorite I saw for good measure and two lovers in the foreground lying side by side in an eternal embrace. Peter says I can store my paintings in a closet in the apartment, which takes a huge weight off my mind about what to do with a growing number of paintings even though quite a few of the large ones will be going to Munich with me and Ernesto, from Bar Unica on the Corso, has agreed to hang the Valdichiana painting in his bar "while I am away".

It is two and a half meters long and Bob helps me to carry it from the studio up to the Corso. When we have it secured on the wall and stand back, the old ladies on their tea morning burst into spontaneous applause! My final curtain call; *stranieri:* we are like fugitives, one by one slipping across the edge of dawn's borders: lone figures that suddenly appear in the town in the morning and just as mysteriously slip back into the night at day's

Part 2: Lucignano 1985

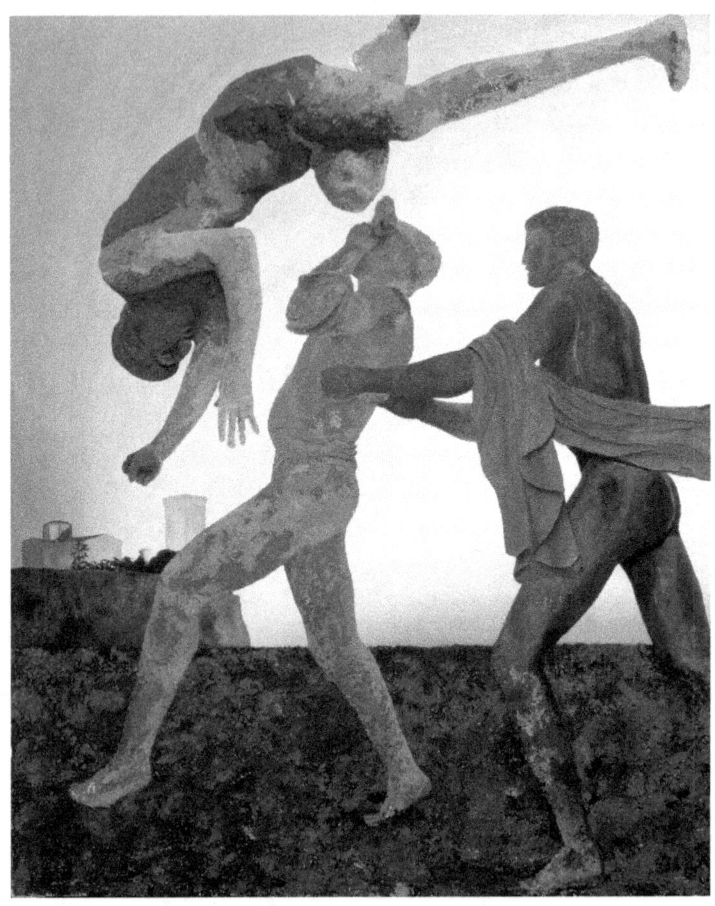

Balletto Pompeiano a Lucignano.1988

Chapter 24.

Sixteen months later and I am cooling off on the old tiled mosaic floor of Sabine's new garden apartment near the centre of Florence. I am having what I can only describe as my first out-of-body experience. I'm not even sleeping, just worried about my future on a lazy Sunday afternoon during a July heat-wave, when the floor suddenly opens like a trapdoor, plunging me into free fall through a bottomless ocean of blue. Powerful G-forces are pressing in on my face, cold air streaming along my flanks, and out of nowhere I am soaring high above Gullane, the village in Scotland I used to call home, above the golf links, like one of the goshawks I used to watch as a boy when out walking on the cliffs by the shore. And then I am back again on Sabine's floor.

She is sleeping peacefully on top of her bed, exhausted by the heat and in equal measure my self-pitying tone. My new girlfriend Judy is arriving from Australia in a few days and I am beginning to have serious doubts. I hardly even know her and to think she not only dumped her boyfriend for me but also quite her job to come and be here!

Sabine cuts me short when I start lamenting my situation and only admonishes:

"You wanted the bicycle, now pedal it!"

Sabine is probably the most generous person I know with her time and puts me to shame when I consider how jealously I guard mine, but she's seen it all before and is not about to get sucked in too deeply into the machinations of my commitment problems.

"*Bon Dieu*! Get over it and have another glass of wine." Losing patience.

In fact she can't wait to meet Judy and is busy planning a welcoming party for her in Frascati with Roby and asking my advice on what she should wear for the occasion. Sara too, Sabine's American friend living in Montevarchi with her husband Allen, is swept up by the occasion and full of enthusiasm:

"When is Judy arriving? You must be so excited that finally she's going to be here!" Genuinely happy for me, as I smile weakly, hiding my dread.

It was never my intention to return to Tuscany but then I hadn't considered the Tuscan factor, the force pulling me back from as far away as Australia, where I ended up after staying in India for six months.

When I shuttered and locked up Carolyn's house, I thought it was forever. I walked Voss down the hill to Amelio's, who—losing some of his usual aplomb—started to fluster and blush, flapping his arms about, not sure whether to surrender and give me hug as we bid each other farewell. I kissed Voss, he muzzled me back, dropped the key into Michaelina's, stopped off at Dante's, the carpenter, and could have sworn I saw a tear on Margherita's cheek when I went to see her at the shop on my out of the valley. I didn't say goodbye to Noemi and Emilia, only told them I was off to India, which troubled them enough.

Sabine moved off her mountain outside Prato and bought an apartment in Florence soon after she and Roby called it a day; they remain good friends and we can still all see each other, thank God; unlike Carolyn and I. I had not counted on just how difficult it would be seeing her again and how much that has impacted on my feelings towards Judy. I needed to collect the last of my stuff from her house so I called her to arrange a time. Down from Florence, I was staying with Bob and Jane for a couple of nights in their new place above San Martino, after the Hotel Belvedere was sold and they were obliged to move out.

I received a frosty reception from Carolyn when I arrived and Wilfred the German neighbour from the hill opposite was there, making himself useful in a handyman sort of way, charging around with a hammer and fixing a leak in the roof. Carolyn hardly said anything and kept her distance, hovering behind the kitchen bar as if that would shield her from my presence while I was sorting through my books in the cabinet. Not even gifting her my treasured volume of Jung's collected works elicited much of a response or leaving behind my Bang &Olufsen speaker, the one with the extra-long lead; only dear Voss was pleased to see me and I was grateful for that.

Wilfred, unexpectedly, called me the very next day; asking me to meet him for a pizza at the pizzeria in Vallone, where much to my chagrin, he proceeded to pour out his bleeding heart to me: about how much in love he was with Carolyn and how difficult she is to fathom and asking me for my advice. Bloody cheek—I could have strangled him on the spot! Her coldness towards me was upsetting enough, then to learn she was messing around with him was really too much!

I am depressed and questioning whether I've done the right thing in asking Judy to join me from Australia. No, let's be honest—I didn't just ask her, I charged in like a knight on my horse, overwhelming her in Melbourne, entreating her to drop everything for me to come too Italy: her boyfriend, her teaching job, her flat, everything at the drop of a hat; Judy, the other secret I had kept from Carolyn, because we had already met and had a brief affair in India, when I was on my way back to rejoin Carolyn, who had gone on ahead because she was still worried about the state of Voss after his savage mauling six months before.

I still have not found anywhere for Judy and I to live, which is an added pressure, except for here at Sabine's for the month of August when she'll be away in France on her annual holiday. Hand in hand with the property boom and the slow death of *Equo Canone*, the Italian rent laws that have regulated rents and protected tenants' rights, comes an increasing demand for holiday homes: making long-term cheaper rentals much harder to find. Carolyn's landlord in Rome has been trying to evict her from her flat in Trastevere for some time and is now offering her money instead; a *buon uscita* (cash sweetner) to vacate the flat and thereby avoid lengthy court proceedings. John, an old friend of hers, a writer from New Zealand, and one of the group of Australians who fled Greece with her at the time of the Generals and settled in Rome, has been more defiant and is fighting his eviction alongside the other tenants in his tenement block in Trastevere. A huge protest banner draped across the front of John's building proclaims: "*Palazzo occupato*!" But he doesn't hold out much hope for a victory because, Trastevere, the old populist quarter in the very heart of old Rome, has become a fashionable place to live these days and is much sought after.

Chapter 25.

Judy's arrival does little to dispel my dismal mood. You'd need Semtex to blast me out of this one—what is wrong with me? I was so determined to make her welcome but instead I am at war with myself and only making it worse. Judy has such a bright smile, already heading in my direction before I spot her in the international arrival hall, a sprig of yellow wattle pinned to her lapel. At least I have turned up to meet her!

Her introduction to Italy is via the Rome *raccordo* ring road: heading straight for Frascati from Fiumicino airport through early morning rush-hour traffic. Italian driving is therapy for me, it puts me in another zone, as I move effortlessly on and off hopelessly complicated ramps, and weave seamlessly in and out of the four lanes of traffic that girdle Rome like a dragsters' velodrome. Italian roads are not for the faint-hearted, Judy clutches her seat belt I don't even wear mine. On the autostrada, insinuating yourself into the conga line of lorries beating playfully down on you is a heroic task; or navigating opposing traffic in the narrowest of streets in small Tuscan hill towns is akin to a miraculous feat. The motorist rules! And then there is nothing more pleasing than driving down the Corso in Cortona, parting pedestrians left and right like a Moses parting the waves.

Sideways glances at Judy and I realise what frightens me is here we are setting off on a new life together and we hardly know each other. Apart from the week we spent in India together we had less than six weeks to get to know each other in Australia. I pray I am not on a rebound from Carolyn, that's all. Eyes on the road. Fellini-esque high-rise blocks march out of the old city to greet us across the intervening wastelands of industrial and domestic squalor. A continuous warp of flaking plastic lines the route, like detritus flapping off an ancient barbed wire flood-line. I absolutely love this: the chaos, the pollution, the completely un-aesthetic, the imminent danger of a meltdown. I could go on, but for the moment Judy doesn't appreciate the finer points of the pandemonium I am trying to extol, especially at this time in the morning after a long-haul flight.

We exit the *raccordo* and reach calmer waters. Frascati, sparkling in the sun, welded onto the side of the Alban hills, Sabine and Roby ready to greet us on the terrace of Bar Belvedere in piazza Roma. Sabine has her film-star sunglasses on under a straw hat decorated with papier-mâché flowers, and she is wearing a simple, flowing white cotton dress à la innocent maiden. Roby always greets me with "*fratellino*", kid brother, before we hug, which strictly speaking isn't true because I am a few months older but perhaps it's his patrician nose, the classic perpendicular Roman nose that gives him the right. He has thickened around the waist since I last saw him, a sure sign of over-indulgence and too much time spent in Frascati *osterie* in between jobs. These days, he travels the world as an underwater cameraman filming marine life for documentaries, as well as working

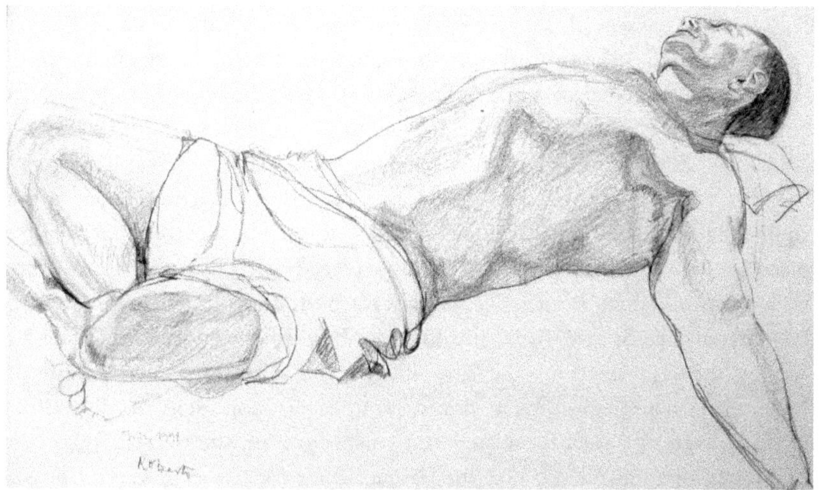

Roby.1985

on film sets as a clapper loader in nearby Cinecittà. Frascati is chock-a-block with small *osterie*; it's part of its charm: dimly-lit cellars filled with wooden vats and tables that in summer are shifted onto the pavements, where the locals bring their own snacks to eat and the innkeeper makes sure only the wine from his vineyard is being imbibed. Sabine makes a great fuss over Judy and thankfully takes charge, while Roby acts as our guide for the day and I can take a back seat and brood. Roby is greeted by nearly everyone we pass in the street and Sabine is no stranger either. Although Frascati is on the point of being swallowed up by Rome—you can see the dome of St. Peter's shimmering through the polluted haze, and the relentless suburban advance across the plain—it still feels like a small country hill town, a Cortona of the south.

Roby is taking us for lunch to a favourite trattoria at nearby Lago di Nemi, a lake formed in the bowl of an extinct volcano, rimmed by woods: Diana's fabled hunting grounds. En route he demonstrates the remarkable properties of a local hill; stopping the car on the lower gradient he suggests we all get out, tells us to watch carefully, then takes the hand-brake off and steps away from his Renault 4, which instead of rolling backwards as you might expect, begins to inch gingerly up the hill! We want to know if it is a miracle but Roby just shrugs and chuckles proffering no further explanations.

Roby has converted the attic of his parents' villa on the Colle Maria, just outside Frascati, into a roomy, one-bedroom apartment. There is an outside staircase that leads up to a huge concrete terrace leading across to his private entrance. The view, directly facing the tumbling sun, is a gently rolling landscape filled with vineyards regularly punctuated by similar-looking modern, two-storey concrete villas. Roby's dream is to live on a boat and sail round the world but he also likes the idea of earthly security and having a place on *terra firma* to cast his anchor—a place he can lock the door to and leave at a moment's notice but will always be there for him on his return. Fortunately, like Sabine, Roby speaks good English and Judy doesn't feel left out of the conversation; she says she has been taking Italian lessons in Melbourne in preparation but doesn't sound very confident of the results. By early evening she is exhausted and crashes out on the pile of Rajasthani cushions Roby has piled up on the parquet floor for her. A game of chess is beckoning us and I can take Judy back to the albergo later. Roby, determined to retain a competitive edge, has been boning up on opening gambits, still smarting from the trouncing he received at the hands of a grand master playing over a hundred games of simultaneous chess in the piazza. Judy is beautiful in repose, the strain of arriving drained out of her face, no signs remain of the bemusement of my very muted welcome, one cupped ear protruding through her soft, silky light brown hair.

"Like an Indian princess," Roby remarks looking down at her, and I have to agree, she is beautiful.

Before returning to Florence, Judy and I are detouring to Campagnatico, a hill town in southern Tuscany where David Malouf, an Australian writer, has invited us to stay for a couple of weeks. Judy is impressed when I tell her, and slightly in awe of the visit. "I taught one of his novels, Johnno, at school in Victoria." She explains. I had never heard of him before and was surprised when she told me he is a well-known author in Australia. Judy is insisting we visit the English bookshop in Rome before we go, where to my surprise she unearths two of his titles that she wants him to sign.

I first met David sharing a couchette compartment on an overnight train to Munich from Florence; I was on the final lap of leaving Italy for good and on my way to London via Munich where I was taking down my exhibition. We started talking as you do on train journeys and quickly discovered friends in common and found ourselves commiserating over how hard it is to make a decent living from our work. I bumped into David again a few days later, this time in Munich airport, but we didn't make too much of it except to say hello and briefly catch up. Then fast-forwarding nearly one year, I was walking down Oxford Street in Sydney and surprised to hear a voice calling out my name—there was David again, bounding through the crowd on the pavement towards me, a short, compact, balding man in gold-rimmed spectacles, holding onto the strap of his canvas shoulder bag and as amazed as I was to be bumping into each other again, this time on the other side of the world!

David is busy stripping down and repainting his windows and shutters when Judy and I arrive. His modest, two-storey village house is wedged into one of the narrow, potholed streets behind the central piazza. The ladies are lined up in the street outside their front doors sitting in camping chairs, gossiping to the clack of knitting needles. Campagnatico is a sleepy mediaeval village in the foothills of the Maremma, well off the beaten track as far as tourism is concerned yet close to the Tyrrhenian coast. Children chase pigeons around the empty piazza, flat feet clapping on the flagstones. The men are playing cards at tables in the back of the central bar and the old lady behind the counter doesn't even know where Scotland is after asking me where I was from, then becomes deeply suspicious of Judy pulling a fast one when she calls home collect on the phone in the bar without the counter ringing up a single digit on the meter.

Judy drinks in the atmosphere as we stroll around the village with David. People everywhere address him respectfully as Professore and he looks the part: at ease in his surroundings, thoughtful but good-naturedly returning the salutations.

"See that grocer's over there?" he asks Judy, pointing to the other side of the piazza. "It's owned by a fascist."

"You mean they are still around?" Judy asks incredulous.

"Actually, they never went away my dear, they're still a political force with their own party—the Italian Social Movement." David responds, amused.

"The fascists are the ones with the statues of Alsatian dogs on their front gates, that's my theory." I offer.

"Being a fascist—or a communist for that matter—is not something to be ashamed of in Italy." David continues in his pleasant high-pitched, boyish voice.

"Cultural differences," I chip in. "My mother is always warning me about them. Did you know, David, when we were in Grosseto yesterday, Judy thought all the people milling around the piazza were out on strike!"

"Well how was I supposed to know?" Judy smiles.

"The reverse can also be true," chimes in David. "An Italian friend once told me how he spent his first week on arrival in Sydney searching for the piazza where he presumed everyone would be gathering in the evenings before dinner!"

David is working on the première of the Australian Opera's production of Voss at the Adelaide festival, and Judy and I take side trips into the country while he puts the finishing touches to his libretto: an adaptation of Patrick White's novel Voss. I can't help thinking of "my" Voss, appropriately named by Carolyn after the main character in White's book: a real-life 19th century explorer/adventurer who journeyed into the Australian outback and became lost, never to be seen again. During our stay, David has introduced us briefly to a very frail-looking Italo Calvino, the Italian writer; and Jeffrey Smart, a well-known Australian painter who has a house near Arezzo, dropped in, offering me some encouragement with my work by confiding he was nearly 50 before anybody took any notice of his paintings and gave him his first big breakthrough in the art world.

Judy, I am discovering, is extremely well read and she has been holding her own in august company, despite her initial nerves; much better than me, as my moods swing unpredictably and God knows what kind of impression I am making or if I will be welcomed back.

When it is time to leave, Judy presents her books to David who obligingly signs her copies of *An Imaginary Life* and *Child's Play, the Bread of Time to Come.*

Chapter 26.

The vision I held of Judy when I first laid eyes on her in India was a vision of the tarot's Empress, seated on her sandy throne wrapped in a halo of gold and fringed by a forest of dark green coconut palms; the mother, if I am to be the father, of a new nation, although that was not a conscious thought then, rather one that distilled in my mind over time.

Perhaps it was my desire to meet Judy again that gave me the strength to leave Carolyn, even though I had no right to assume Judy would want to see me or even remember me; not after an absence of three years. I certainly had no clue about Christian, the man Judy subsequently fell in love with or that coincidently he was also there in the Woodstock café on Kovalam beach in India, seated directly behind me on the day that Judy and I first met. Nor was I aware on arriving in Australia, just how much fate had intervened on my behalf, if I can put it that way, because Christian was shot and killed in a bar in the Phillipines a year after they met. His death was over a trifle; asking a barman to turn down the volume of the radio was enough to see him killed.

Unfortunately, seeing us alone together now in Sabine's flat paints an altogether different picture. I am withdrawn, sullen, long faced, hardly capable of speech, huddled over the black marble top table, endlessly playing computer chess on a small pocket machine. The incessant automated bleep bleep bleep is driving Judy crazy and it's a miracle we have survived a full month together. The only time we make love is in the middle of the night when I am half asleep. I suspect the only reason we have hung on this long are one: my feelings of guilt and two: her not wanting to lose face by returning to Australia so soon after her big send off to Italy from Tulamarine airport in Melbourne, when no fewer than her ex-husband and two former boyfriends, including the one she dumped to be with me, plus her father, mother and sister Sue, were all there in the departure lounge, waving her off on her daring adventure with such great fanfare. It took me a while to summon up the courage to take Judy to Cortona, mainly because I couldn't bear the thought of bumping into Carolyn and when we finally went I deliberately chose to go in the afternoon, when I knew nobody would be about. I wanted to introduce her to Noemi and Emilia.

Bob told me while I was away Noemi had accosted him in the Corso one day, brandishing my last postcard from India and demanding if he had any more news of me. Noemi had heard about Indira Gandhi's assassination and the massacres that ensued while I was there. Both he and Emilia were relieved to see me back safely, and typically welcomed Judy — la Giuditta— with open arms, noting Voss's absence, but politely skirting around the subject of my ex *la Carolina.*

Judy's first impressions of Cortona are disappointing considering how much I've been talking it up, but if I'm honest they weren't that dissimilar from my initial response, except I found a rabbit hole to dive into almost immediately on arrival and Judy has yet to find hers.

Finally, Sabine is back in town, having recharged her batteries after a well-deserved break in Paris and on to her mother's in Dinard; sun tanning on the beach and eating sand carrots and crêpes with beaucoup du vin, whilst out admiring the young talent strolling the promenade. She is delighted with the way Judy has looked after her garden and I can see they are going to be firm friends, given the chance. Judy is conscientious, someone you can rely on. She is a gardener too and filling in the silences between us she has been watering, planting, pruning and generally keeping busy tending to Sabine's small backyard.

With good timing and good fortunate for us, we are headed back to Campagnatico where David, through a friend of his, has managed to find us temporary accomodation in a *casa colonica* converted into holiday appartments, that will be available through September and October. Unfortunately, he won't be there because he is going home for the premier of Voss and will not be back until next year.

Amazingly my spirits start to lift as soon as we pile into my car and head out of Florence towards our new home. (I have a theory that you either love Florence or you love Rome, but you never love both). Suddenly I am reminded that planet Tuscany still exists; such was the hole I have been digging for myself and much to Judy's surprise and relief she discovers that I can actually engage.

On the road! Heading for Etruscan country once more, Campagnatico still connected to Cortona to the north, with Tarquinia further south along the coast, and places inland like Pitigliano: an Etruscan town carved into the sheer tufa cliffs, surrounded by flat country slashed through with mysterious ravines. It must have been the Etruscans who imbued Tuscany with its timeless quality and I feel at peace once more, even excited at the prospect.

The *casa colonica* we are staying in is divided into two apartments, but we will be the only ones there. Olive trees stud the hillside behind the house with woods further up towards the ridge. Razor-sharp fields of stubbled wheat swoop round the front and tumble down to the fields of maize swishing like tall reeds along the dry stony riverbed of the once mighty river Ombrone; the river that served the Etruscans as a major shipping route from West to East. The arid ochre landscape, dolloped with green, bursts into orange flame in the intense flood of early evening sunlight.

Campagnatico, only a few kilometres away, is a typical walled hill village, 600 metres above sea level, founded around the tenth century. Its ageing, tightly-knit community is distinctly contadina and sedate but erupts into life soon after we arrive with the annual "*Palio dei Ciuchi*", the great donkey race. Everywhere there are flags and banners and bunting decorating the village, people in mediaeval costumes and milling crowds. Professional jockeys wear the colours of the four *contrade* (quarters) and ride the donkeys bareback. Bedlam reigns as well as high passion. Stewards are finding it difficult to marshal the donkeys together in one line behind the starting rope and there are numerous false starts, while the spectators, ever more agitated under the hot Tuscan sun, are hanging over balconies and perched precariously on the Etruscan walls, occupying every inch of available space. Finally, they're off, the rope drops to the ground and before we know it, the race is over, the course is so short it's hardly fifty yards? However, a great tumult ensues with applause, tears of joy, hurled insults and the usual scuffles, but nothing that the celebration feast in the piazza later that evening can't resolve.

To reach the coast from the house we by-pass nearby Grosseto, then negotiate the Aurelia, the old Roman road that now serves as a motorway, bordered on one side by an unbroken chain of camping grounds and discothèques, trattorias, bars and petrol stations. The beach is buffered from the holiday sprawl by a national park of majestic umbrella pines that fringe the coast. Judy frowns when I drive through the forest (only following the well-worn car tracks) in order to park closer to the beach. She is a seventies earth child, environmentally conscious; I can't even throw a tangerine peel out of the car window without eliciting a scowl.

She laughs at what we Europeans call a beach: this awkward, litter-strewn sliver of sand that tapers off into the tepid, surf-less Mediterranean with the factory stacks of Piombino belching grey smoke into the listless blue skies on the northern horizon. But as I point out, at least we can sip aperitivi whilst enjoying the sunset from the illegally constructed beach shack right on the sand.

Judy bowerbird, she heads for the local tip in Campagnatico, dragging me along behind her, loading up the Fiat station wagon with all kinds of junk: coloured medicine bottles, discarded Chianti flasks and leaking rusty watering cans or a mouldy wall hanging with a putto and fruit motif. At last I can settle down to some painting, albeit between two single beds in the spare room, where I have to be careful about not dripping paint on the carpet. Inspired by the Etruscan tomb frescoes we recently visited in Tarquinia, I'm troweling the cement like impasto I have been using to imitate fresco grounds, over the entire canvas now.

I am Pan the Shepherd playing a double flute, in a flowing white tunic edged in turquoise braid, herding a flock of sheep through the bronze and gold fields of harvested wheat.

Judy kneeling naked by a stream is Aquarius, the water bearer, pouring water from an earthenware jar or she becomes a warrior seated on a horse, a blood tipped sword pointing to earth as a battlefield of Roman and Etruscan soldiers is finally pacified and I am laid to rest.

"Ninotschki! Fantastic news!" Tante Eliette billows down the phone in her wonderfully deep, husky smokers' voice. She always exudes an aura of glamour, a Lauren Bacall in the way she dresses and the way her chestnut tresses tumble down over her shoulders.

"You'll be very pleased to hear the Southerns are happy for you to rent the villa for six months over winter, so you don't have to worry any more on that score!"

She has no trace of a German accent now, unlike my mother who retains an undertow. Along with my grandmother and their younger brother Adrian they arrived in London to join my grandfather towards the end of the last war: forced to abandon the family estates in Silesia and trek across Europe as refugees, fleeing the Gestapo first and then the advancing Russian army.

Tante Eliette has been holidaying at her friend's the Southerns and Judy and I drove up to meet her for lunch. The Southerns were in London at the time but have a house near Lucignano, a hill town on the west side of the Valdichiana, only thirty kilometres from Cortona and on returning home Tante Eliette promised to ask them if they would consider renting out the small guest annex, she had been staying in, over winter. Coming back from the bar in the village, I am gladdened by the news and much relieved. Our stay in Campagnatico has seen a dramatic lift in our spirits, rekindling something akin to love, yet even so I can not take anything for granted as far as Judy is concerned, not after my recent behaviour! And now that we have somewhere to move on to, it is still with some trepidation that I ask her if she wants to continue on our journey together?

Judy is at her desk and leans back in her chair, kicking away from the wall with her bare feet; then tilting her head and turning towards me, she flashes me one of her beatific smiles, girlishly anointing me with her almond eyes and says yes.

Chapter 27.

Lucignano is a fortified mediaeval village built in an elliptical shape with the Comune (communist run) and the Collegiata (the Catholic Church) facing off at the summit; only in classic Italian style neither congregation necessarily excludes the other. The village is unusual because there isn't a central piazza within the walls; instead, people congregate outside the top gate opposite the public gardens.

The Southerns' house is about two and a half kilometres outside Lucignano, down a treacherous, winding *strada bianca*: known as the white road because of the ghostly white colour of the gravel dust that powders the verges and banks with each passing car.

The Southerns aren't due back until Christmas and Dina their housekeeper, a short, middle-aged barrel of a woman, is at the house waiting to greet us on our arrival. Shaking hands, Dina clasps mine in hers for far too long, a play on her lips, milky brown eyes staring up at me as if she has gone into a trance and is about to tell me my fortune.

The villa is a recently constructed one-bedroom apartment built over the garage and adjacent to the swimming pool, annexed to an L-shaped loggia. A well painted racy fresco of a bacchanalian scene adorns the entire length of the wall alongside the pool: depicting an orgy of nymphs, sprites and satyrs cavorting in a glade by a stream. The windows in our villa facing the pool are set high up thus preventing any casual observer from looking down.

The main house, a tastefully restored *casa colonica*, is hidden from view behind a rise thirty meters or so from our villa. It sits at the head of a valley, a broad peluosed avenue flanked by wooded slopes with Brahman cows grazing on the far side of a stream. The sun dropping to the horizon creates a blistering, shining path along the axis of the valley floor, perfectly aligned with the Southerns' back door and kitchen terrace.

This has been a wet autumn; drifts of sodden leaves are piled high in roadside ditches and you can hear the raindrops plopping through the trees as they free fall from leaf to leaf before splattering onto the roof of the villa. When the weather clears, Judy, skirting the woods, walks down into the valley to pick mushrooms; there are numerous varieties and she usually comes home with a wicker basket fully laden, making sure to show them to Dina first as a precaution. Dina pokes through them keenly, screening out any she considers to be suspicious and she places each one she is not sure of into a pan with garlic as a test.

"If the garlic turns black do not eat the mushroom, throw it away immediately." She warns. "Cooking with the garlic you can find out which are the poisonous ones."

Unlike the hunters, mushroom pickers go out one by one, jealously guarding their treasures. Tuscans take mushrooming very seriously and around here signs nailed to the trees abound: "Mushroom picking strictly forbidden". According to Dina, winking, nobody takes any notice, especially where porcini (boletus) are concerned. These highly-prized mushrooms are difficult to find, even though they can be as big as a side plate, because they grow at the base of trees mainly covered in leaf mulch. When harvested correctly in the Autumn, they will grow again and again in the same spot, hence the need for secrecy. A kilo of porcini can fetch as much as 24 thousand lira; often sold from cardboard boxes by *contadini* standing at the road sides.

I have muscled out a studio space for myself in the garage underneath the villa, between John Southern's old army jeep and their washing machine, with the raised steel roller doors being the only source of light. Hardly ideal or appealing; it is damp and the concrete floor is cold and my feet are beginning to swell. Judy brings me mugs of coffee and her mother is promising to send us both a pair of Australian Ugg boots, which have wool linings and according to Judy will be perfect for the job.

Judy leaves the oven door wide open when she has baked the bread, just to eke out the extra heat. The window in our tiny kitchen is permanently dripping with condensation, but still remains the only room we can heat effectively with only an open fire place in the sitting room. Judy wasn't prepared for winter conditions and spends a lot of her time huddled up in bed with a hot-water bottle and her book. Now she is starting to look depressed! I hole up in the kitchen with my copy of LaPulce, which comes out fortnightly and carries small adds for houses to buy and rent in Tuscany. Sabine and I have muted the idea of putting our money together to buy a place, even taking a look at one, but for the moment this plan has been shelved. On shopping expeditions to Arezzo Judy rifles through the bins in the only charity shop we have found so far, snaffling up long coats, woolen jumpers, beanies and scarves, some items finding their way into my side of the wardrobe. In Italy it's not considered per bene to wear second hand clothes, unlike in Australia, where "op-shops" are part of the culture, and something Judy misses, especially on weekends in Melbourne when she would be running around the charity shops and markets and chasing down garage sales through small ads in the papers.

Judy is pragmatic when it comes to money and a tad wary of me: convinced I am a spendthrift! The kind of person who takes a taxi even if the bus is approaching the stop. Heeding her advice when I was in London, I bought an Italian car, the Fiat station wagon:

"For ease of servicing and to save money on the cost of spare parts." she said before I left Australia.

Something that would never have occurred to me.

I regularly go for walks in the valley, following the bogy, rubble-filled tractor track that skirts the edge of the woods from the house. There is never a soul about and the sweep of the valley floor, carpeted with alfalfa, feels like a private park or like I am in a scene from Blow Up, one of my favourite films. With the first frosts, the frozen rivulets of mud sparkle in the moonshine and my breath turns pale blue like a vaporous speech bubble. It is hard to imagine this small valley becoming a four-lane super highway, which according to Dina is exactly what has been planned. She has shown me the road map with the proposed route clearly marked by a red and white slash and says the only reason it hasn't been built so far is because the landholder is a wealthy and well-connected Architect from Milan and he and his wife, a Contessa, are well connected and vehemently opposed to it. At night we can sometimes hear the mechanical drone of the autostrada del sole, which is disconcerting enough.

Judy is struggling with her Italian and thinking about enrolling in classes again. Coming back to Italy after an absence of over a year, I was concerned too, about the state my Italian would be in and still can't fathom out how it has improved in the interim. You should hear Bob now, or Robert as he insists on being called these days (becoming quite feisty if you forget), rattling off in Italian like a rapid-fire Gatling gun; there is no stopping him. I get it too; he takes the scattergun approach, safe in the knowledge that at least a percentage of words will hit their target and be understood. I am less brazen, lacking in confidence at first, unless that is, I know the person I am talking to well.

Dina has already warned us off her cousin Angelo who is the Southerns' "*contadino*" and looks after their land, consisting of a small vineyard, an olive grove and the *orto* and garden. Dina says Angelo has a big mouth and I need to be careful what I say around him but so far, I find him personable enough, putzing in on his vespa twice a week. He looks more like a Moroccan marathon runner: wiry, with a a shiny boney face, and with short, frizzy, salt-and-pepper hair. He has been trying to sell me his red wine and Judy and I have already been for a tasting at his place in Croce, a small frazione of Lucignano about five kilometres away. He lives in a relatively new double storey rendered house; the kind the contadini have been flocking to in droves; his living room suite is still wrapped in the original protective plastic covering. The yard is spacious enough for his orto and a large shed where he keeps his pig and outside the door are his rabbits, squashed into milk crates, stacked in a tower one above the other. He owns a separate block of land where he tends his vines and olive trees, with an old rusty exsanguinate fiat cinquecento, abandoned by a small dam, useful as a shelter.

Angelo supervises the wine making at the Southerns, utilising space at the back of the garage where they have what looks like a large terracotta oven that is actually used for ageing the wine. Gunilla Southern, very thoughtfully, left us a few bottles of their wine in chianti flasks on our porch before our arrival but unfortunately the wine had soured by the time we opened them; although now that we have sampled Angelo's wine I suspect that is the way he likes it.

John Southern has designed a demountable wooden framed greenhouse that Angelo assembles under the loggia for the winter months. He trolleys in the lemon trees in their large terracotta pots from around the swimming pool and covers them inside the greenhouse with sheets of clear plastic for added insulation. Occasionally I join him there when he is on a lunch break. He tears chunks off a white unsalted loaf and serrates slices of salami with his penknife, sometimes bringing leftover pasta with him and drinking his undrinkable red wine from a plastic mineral water bottle.

Last year Tuscany went through the big freeze, with temperatures falling to minus 15 degrees Celsius, which I missed thankfully, being in Australia pursuing of Judy.

"*Dio lupo*!" Angelo laments. "Even the hunting season was cancelled!

"And it wiped out most of my olive trees and burnt the vines black."

Shrugging philosophically in between mouthfuls:

"Big frosts happen from time to time; the trees even need the frost because it keeps them from growing and gives the oil that particular tangy flavour, you know spicey. We produce the best olive oil in the world as a result! But even so, *Dio buono,* last year was too much! It has decimated the landscape. Did you know there are some places where one side of the field was affected and the other side was not?"

Tuscan olive oil: the finest in the world! How many times have heard that said! Certainly, it is true that just about everyone owns a few trees and makes their own oil. Every November a posse of Carolyn's friends descend to help her with the olive harvesting. Amelio always emphasised to me the need to prune the trees in such a way that you create a bowl shape out of the branches, making the olives more accessible to pick. Now days the contadini put nets down under the trees to catch the olives but before that they strapped on special wicker baskets at the waist, allowing for hands free to rake the olives off the branches. Amelio took the olives to the mill, the *frantoio* where they are cold pressed under great granite stone wheels and turned into 'green gold'. Carolyn always complained about how she had to smuggle the oil back into Australia because of the strict custom controls surrounding foodstuffs.

"The problem now" Angelo continues "is that olive groves are being ripped out but the trees will never be replaced, even though the government is offering generous subsidies to replant them." And waving his penknife in the air, Angelo frowns, "I know some are claiming the subsidies without bothering to put in the trees after."

Chapter 28.

It's freezing standing outside painting the view from the Southerns' driveway; wearing mittens, blowing hard on my fingertips, stamping my feet; it still beats painting in the garage and presents me with a new challenge. The woods form a backdrop with the gentle curve of the drive lined by young pine trees and a generous chunk of cerulean sky streaked white above them;

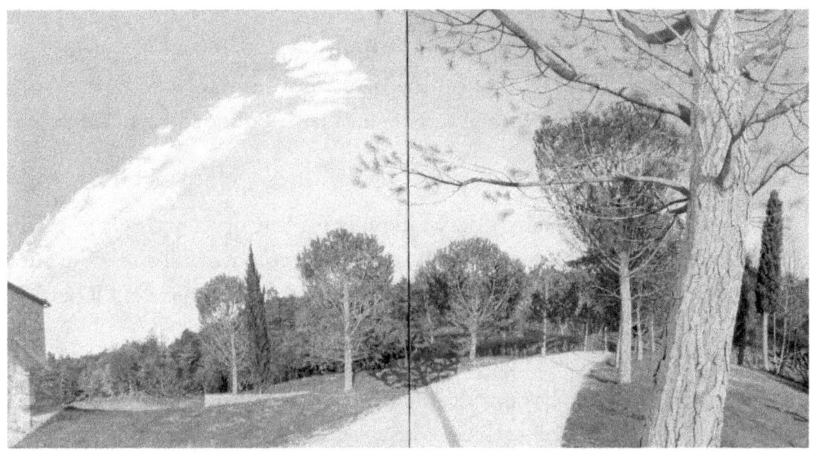

SouthernComfort.1985

the Southerns' house only a bookend to the painting, which I am calling Southern Comfort. So focused am I on details that I haven't noticed the passage of time as traced by the woods; transiting from the autumn colours on the left of the canvas, to the defoliated winter trees on the right. I don't usually paint like that from one side to the other but I like the unintended effect. So much of painting is purely accidental and takes you by surprise, opens your eyes only afterwards, as if another hand is at work without you consciously realising it.

Sitting rugged up in a camp chair behind my easel is nothing compared to

Bob stooping over his easel in a snowstorm; an immovable bulk, icicles like barnacles clinging to his beard, snow piling up on the wide brim of the Kookaburra hat that I brought back for him from Australia.

Bob (I can't get my head around Robert) is currently painting *en plein air* around Santa Caterina: the country midway across the Valdichiana, between Cortona and Lucignano. He has decided to record the landscape here throughout the seasons and towards that end has managed to persuade a local farmer to let him store his canvases and materials in one of his disused cantinas. This means Bob can commute easily every day on his *motorino* without having to depend on Jane to ferry him and his equipment to and fro in her new Renault 4 car. Bob doesn't drive and has no intention of learning.

Just down from the Southerns along the *strada bianca* is a *casa colonica* with a ceramic sign on the bank at the entrance: Artist Studio Open, and out walking one morning, Judy, ever curious to explore, pulls me reluctantly in behind her. An old, green Morris Minor estate with UK plates sits abandoned under a cypress tree on the bank above the road and I can see a small, well-tended garden with a pergola and lawn bounded by fields behind the house.

"*Permesso? È permesso?*" We call out.

Presently, a small upstairs side window is yanked open and out pops the face of a middle-aged woman with a brightly coloured silk scarf wound around her head, who calls down in English, "Hang on a minute, I'll be right there."

An overwhelming cat smell blasts us from the house as soon as she opens the ground floor door, shooing a cat back in gently with her toe.

"Sorry 'bout that," she says nervously, slipping out and closing the door behind her. She has delicate moisturised skin and unwinding her scarf reveals her thinning wispy ginger coloured hair.

"We have to keep the cats locked up during winter or the hunters will get them. There are eleven of them, you know; people keep abandoning them on my doorstep; it's such a pity but I don't have the heart to turn them away."

"That's probably the reason they leave them." I observe.

"The other day we saw someone chasing a pheasant down the road in a cinquecento; they were trying to run it over, can you believe!" Says Judy indignant. "And they drove right into the field after it too!"

"Poor creature, so typical! Don't you just hate the hunters? Whenever they come around here, I play loud classical music out of the window just to annoy them and hopefully scare the birds away!" Vicky says in a quavering voice, introducing herself and turning to Judy:

"Do I detect an Australian accent? I'm from South Africa myself."

"Yes! I'm from Australia."

"And I'm Scottish," I say, shooting Judy a dangerous look. Judy has been having great difficulty distinguishing the Scots from the Poms, much to my annoyance and one time even went so far as to call me a German and contradict me in front of a Scot who was querying my English accent!

"Are you the artist?" Judy asks, taking my hint. "We saw the sign at the entrance."

"Good Lord no! That would be Sheldon, or Shelley as everyone knows him. He is American."

Vicky seems personable enough and doesn't hesitate to invite us in, leading the way round by the garden to a locked gate at the bottom the outside staircase. The open face of the loggia is secured by chicken wire to keep the cats in and at the top of the stairs is an ancient yellow and green parrot squawking on a perch in his cage. Showing us into the kitchen, we are met by Shelley and introduced. The walls are chocolate brown and the kitchen is dark and unappealing. Given a quick tour of the upstairs, Shelley then beckons us back down the stairs and into his studio in the converted stables below. He has to restrain a huge, growling, blue-tongued arctic chow as he opens the connecting oval glass doors into his studio and Vicky, taking over, drags the dog out by its collar.

"Stop it Billy, behave!" And calling after us "would anyone like tea?" Then disappearing into another room with the dog.

Shelley is about my age but Vicky is significantly older. He looks every bit the artist: tentative, portly, with a full dark beard hollowed out on the chin and long wavy chestnut hair neatly hooked behind his ears.

"Shelley, that sign at the top of the road by the cemetery; is that yours?"

I venture, curious about an official-looking sign post that I pass on my way to the village:

"Rocchetto Art-Studio 2.7 km→ ".

It's similar to one of those official signs you normally see pointing you towards a museum or church or somewhere of historical significance.

"Perugine, the Mayor, is a friend of ours and gave us permission to put it up." Shelley replies stroking his beard.

“And do you find it brings more people to your studio?" Asks Judy politely.

Shelley has a way of looking through you without pausing to look at you. He shrugs, appearing mildly bored.

“Oh, maybe a few curious visitors like you, but nowadays it’s mostly by appointment only.”

Shelley’s paintings are prominently hung on the pale-yellow walls of the converted stables and together with a smart green moquette carpet the place has the air of a gallery.

“Do you like the carpet?” Asks Vicky, re-entering with the tea tray.“It's new. We were given it by Muriel Spark, the writer, as a thank you for looking after her cats. She lives in the area and is a cat lover too.”

My attention moves from the carpet to the walls, glancing around at Shelley's work. The paintings are mainly impressionistic landscapes: olive trees in fields with poppies or irises, views of Lucignano with sheep or cattle grazing in the foreground. Dominating one wall however is a large painting of an interior with an Afro-American family seated around a table finishing their evening meal. Unlike his other work it is very colourful and more expressionistic.

“I painted that in America.” Shelley explains. “It’s a family I knew in my home town of St Louis.”

“Shelley's family is big in the transport industry there, but he didn’t want to be part of the family business and ran away to Europe so he could do what he really wanted, which was to paint.”

Perhaps the redeeming factor in his landscapes is the fleck he creates with the brush stroke and his use of thick paint creating a pleasant swirl across his canvases. But I can see he has difficulty drafting figures; a portrait of Vicky makes her look arthritic and a self-portrait has him holding a brush in a very withered hand.

“Nino's an artist.” Says Judy merrily.

"Oh! Do you paint too?" Asks Vicky.

“Yes, and I'm in desperate need of a studio. We are staying at the Southerns' and I’ve been working in the garage but it's so damp I’ve had to decamp outside to paint.”

“Oh, Shelley paints *en pleine air* all the time.” Replies Vicky breezily, and is at pains to point out how difficult it is to paint *controluce* successfully:

“Shelley’s forte you know. He’s only interested in showing us what is beautiful," she says approvingly, almost dotingly.

"None of that psycho-babble you get in modern art these days. Besides he doesn't have any of those mental problems needing to be expressed!"

I nearly splutter into my tea. Judy shoots me a furtive look. Vicky is clearly an eccentric and a little highly strung, and obviously worships Shelley. He takes it all in placidly as if it is his wont, and we sit back and reflect on her words, nibbling on our dry biscuits to regroup. One of the older cats hobbles in across the carpet.

"Hello, Hey You!" And Vicky scoops the three-legged creature onto her lap before taking up her train of thought again.

"Shelley is quite well known you know, but it wasn't always so. When we first arrived here three years ago, we were almost broke and had to barter paintings for food and even wood for the fire on one occasion."

"How did you find this place?" Asks Judy.

"We lived in Edinburgh then moved to Florence and were on our way to Umbria driving down the autostrada in our old faithful Morris Minor, rest in peace, when Shelley noticed Lucignano in the distance and on a whim decided we should come here and take a look. Not long after, Shelley was in the bar at the top gate making friends with the locals and asking about places to rent and one of them brought us down here. It was being used as a storage dump by the farm but the farm manager agreed we could rent it and sent down a few of the farm workers to clean it up for us. This is part of a big farm estate and I must say they have been really good to us. Mozzoni our landlord is an eccentric architect from Milan and his wife the Contessa, her family used to own the Corriere Della Sera; they own most of the land around here." Vicky continues.

"He must be the one holding up the highway?" I venture.

"The *superstrada* you mean? Yes, that's him, he's been fighting it for ages through the courts, hasn't he Shelley?"

Shelley nods confirming, adding:

"Luckily for us his wife is an environmentalist and President of the Fondo Ambiente Italiano.

"That's the equivalent of the National Trust" adds Vicky.

"Unfortunately, if the road ever gets built, it'll come straight over our hill." Shelley indicates the vineyard across the road from the house, not twenty metres away.

"She's a friend of the environment minister so they mix in the right circles. You know how Italy is" Vicky interjects. "The funny thing about Mozzoni is, he only rented Rocchetto to us, because we are foreigners and because Shelley is an artist."

"Really?" I say, pricking up my ears.

"That's probably because being foreigners he can kick us out more easily. But being an artist might have helped. I know he paints watercolours." Vicky says.

"Does he have any other houses for rent? We would fit that bill!" I say probing.

Judy sideways me as if I'm out of order asking, but explains: "we have to be out of the Southerns' by this April."

Vicky doesn't miss a beat.

"Oh, funnily enough they might have somewhere. They used to rent the house up the road but it's been left empty for the last couple of years. Would you say Shelley? Remember that Swiss couple were living there before? What was his name?"

"The Contessa wanted the farm to go biodynamic and she brought in a Swiss expert to oversee the project." Shelley explains.

"And the farm workers still laugh about the attempt." Says Vicky chuckling. "Because it didn't last that long! Don't you remember Shelley? They weren't allowed to us chemicals and had to hand til all the land. Why not ask about the place next time you go up to the farm to pay the rent?"

"That would be nice." I encourage.

"Have a look on your way home: Poggio Spinoso, it's the place on the right, set back from the road just before you get to the Southerns." Vicky enthuses when we say our good byes.

Chapter 29.

The Southerns are in residence for the Christmas holidays so I have pulled the easel off the drive and retreated into the dreaded garage; John Southern has considerately offered to park his old army jeep outside, freeing up a bit more space yet unfortunately does little to alleviate the sense of desolation. John is very pucker English and so is his wife Gunilla, although she comes from Sweden: a tall, striking looking blond in the fresh Nordic tradition but starting to put on a few pounds with the onset of middle age. John is typical English ex-public school: stiff, very self-assured and scrupulously polite, a military type. He is a big man with puffy cheeks, that make his eyes look sunken and smaller than they really are, giving him a faintly menacing look. Besides working at Lloyds of London he has an interest in a company that provides security to foreign dignitaries.

My father is spending Christmas with us but isn't bringing Sue along "because I don't want to cause a fuss with your mother." He says.

It has been nearly two years since they broke up and my mother is still finding it hard to accept. She can't let him go and the fact that he doesn't want a divorce remains a source of comfort and hope to her. I think he needs to be a little more forthright, after all he and Sue are now living together in Switzerland and the situation couldn't be clearer. My mother thought I should be doing more to bring them back together and now scolds me for not taking her side completely so I am left walking a delicate line between them.

Notwithstanding her marital woes, or perhaps because of them, Ma has taken on a completely new and unexpected direction during my time away. My mum! She used to be so straight but now calls herself a New Age healer! My mum, who freaked out when I painted a portrait of her with a tarot card stuck in her hand. Now when I tell her about my out of body experience at Sabine's, she just laughs:

"Ach Du, you needn't be alarmed; I astral travel all the time!"

Nowadays my mother's skills channeling the ascended masters Katumi and The Lady are impressive. She sits quietly in her chair, looking at you, hands folded sweetly in her lap. She does not go into a trance as she articulates her inner voices and when fielding my questions, it almost feels like I am just having a normal conversation with her, except the words are not hers but those of the master she is channeling. She looks the part too: like a pilgrim, with her snow-white hair cut straight at the shoulder, her violet smock tops and floral cotton pants or simple loose dresses with leather sandals and cream socks on.

Belton our family home in Scotland has been sold and my father is now talking about moving from Geneva to San Francisco to head up a new venture capital business backed by Seiko. He is convinced a groundbreaking wrist watch pager that works through FM frequencies is going to

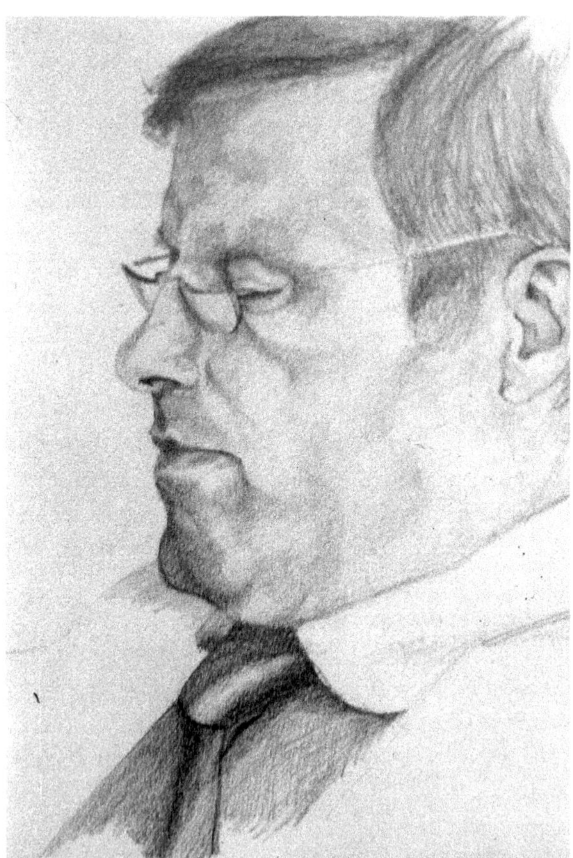

Pa.1978

revolutionise the world. I remember one time in Belton when I was still at school, how excited he became talking about a new technology he was about to introduce into the retail division at John Menzies: a black plastic keypad that fitted snugly over the mouthpiece of the phone. He gave me a demonstration dialling then punching in numbers on the keypad, explaining gleefully:

"This way we can automatically order stock for the shops directly from the warehouse."

He was mildly disappointed that his enthusiasm wasn't met with any amazement on my part.

The days are crisp with brilliant cerulean skies overhead, as we make the customary rounds of hill towns in my father's beloved silver Mercedes-Benz Roadster, me in the back feeling conspicuous with the top down, Judy enjoying the slip stream through her lengthening hair. The festive season is here with the Southerns inviting us over for drinks on Christmas Eve and we have invited a few people for Christmas lunch. Vicky and Shelley have already thrown a pre-Christmas bash. Pa drank too much and gave the party his version of a goose-stepping German segueing neatly into a diatribe on the IRA, (he was a major in the army and served in Korea and Aden) and declaring how, if he was in charge, he would put the lot of them up against a wall and machine gun them. Our German neighbours Gisella
and Heiner were shocked and I took him home early to avoid further embarrassment. "Women!" he declares the next morning still feeling belligerent: "they expect men to make all the decisions then don't give us a second chance if we get just one wrong!"

It's Judy's turn at the Southerns', drinking too much schnapps with Pa and I having to guide her home, one on each arm. Consequently, the next morning, I suddenly find myself in charge of the Christmas lunch with ten people coming and Judy, too hung over to leave her bed but calling out instructions for the fish from the bedroom. Judy is a brilliant cook; she ran a restaurant once; the Edinburgh Tea Rooms in Beechworth, an old gold-mining town in Victoria and thankfully she has already prepared the desert in advance, appropriately named tiramisu ("pick me up"). Pa is impressed by my efforts. His forte is cooking porridge (cream and brown sugar), and he makes good scrambled eggs, butter no milk slow heat, and brews a good tea without stewing it. (During school holidays he would bring me a mug of tea in bed every morning before he left for work.) Judy says her father Phil can't even boil an egg, so I can claim brownie points here.

Judy rallies by the time our lunch guests arrive. My father has apologised for his outburst the other night and although solicitous, Vicky greets him a tad warily. I can see by his smile however that he is going to be a charmer today. He has that ability to bounce back with verve, like the radiant Leo he is. Judy is an Aquarius and feels more chastened.

Sabine arrives with her American friends from Montevarchi, Allen and Sara, and their neighbour Tim, a Welshman with impeccable English manners and the prerequisite understated humour. Sabine is concerned for Judy's health and tells me what a good boy I am stepping in. Tim buys and sells vintage Jaguars but is currently in Tuscany staying at a friend's, hoping to kick-start a new career for himself writing film scripts, churning them out by the dozen on his new computer. His father Stephen is an art director and has recently won an Oscar for his work on *Out of Africa* with Robert Redford and Meryl Streep.

Allen, as promised, has brought a case of his excellent red wine, including his spectacular'82 vintage; the first instalment in a barter agreement we made in exchange for one of my paintings. Both Allen and Sara are academics: he specialises in the history of food in the Middle Ages and looks the part with a distinguished Afghani beard—or is it a Solzhenitsyn? And Sarah teaches History at the Syracuse University in Florence, focusing on women' issues. They live in rolling wine country north of here, in a well-appointed classic Tuscan villa that sits on the knoll of a hill, skirted by his small vineyard.

Tim has been trying to get his hands on a few cases of Allen's wine for ages but it's a limited production and Allen has been resisting his enticements even though they are good friends. In exasperation Tim has offered to buy half my consignment at a wonderfully inflated price and as Judy has been asking me lately if I ever sell my paintings, I am happy to oblige him and gain more brownie points at the same time. Sabine too has finally succumbed and bought a painting of mine; she balked ever so slightly at the asking price, I could see it in her eyes, but she resisted the temptation to bargain me down.

Dan and Marion arrive late, an eccentric middle-aged couple from San Fransisco staying in Trequanda; they don't know for how long. Dan, tall and gaunt with a ghostly grey complexion, is recovering from a spleen operation and looks permanently glum. He is an old radical tragic from the beat generation and Haight-Ashbury days, who is writing a book, he claims, on the industrial-military complex. Dan is big on conspiracy theory. His sparky wife Marion, with long, salt-and-pepper gypsy hair, is a textile artist who creates wearable art; "knicker less!" According to Judy, who was probably the only one to notice, blurting it out later in a pique of jealousy: "Surely you realised she was chasing you around the room all afternoon? It was like a game of musical chairs!"

After the lunch, Shelley draws me aside to let me know he's spoken to Cassagni the *fattore* (farm manager) for the Mozzonis, about the empty house Vicky was talking about over the road. Apparently, the farm manager is willing to show it to us in the New Year even though according to Shelley, Cassagni told him "It's not really for rent." Weird but probably more a Tuscan attribute; never commit unless you absolutely have to.

Chapter 30.

I have introduced Bob to Shelley, thinking maybe the three of us could put on an exhibition together in Cortona. Vicky is keen on the idea and has invited us all around for tea to discuss it. Palazzo Vagnotti is the obvious venue she suggests as she knows the priests who run the palazzo and promises to have a word, maybe do a deal. Palazzo Vagnotti was originally a church seminary but with the drop in priest recruitment over recent years it is now being used purely as an exhibition space: the annual Cortona antique fair is held there, as is the Georgia University students' end of year show and of course, Bob had his sell out show there when he first came to Cortona, a feat he has yet to repeat.

Vicky works tirelessly on Shelley's behalf, promoting his art and organising his affairs and at the moment is busy writing the text for a monograph on his work that they intend to publish as a hardback with extensive colour illustrations of his paintings. Sometimes I wish Judy would look at my work in the same adoring way Vicky looks at his.

Shelley has organised a time for Signor Cassagni to show us Poggio Spinoso as it is known, which Vicky informs us means prickly knoll. Only a hundred yards down the road from the Southerns', I have already been over to check the place out and found it to be a tantalising prospect. Vistas in all directions, the solid, large L-shaped stone house is built on the saddle of the ridge surrounded by fields following a succession of undulating wooded spurs that tumble into the Valdichiana.

Cassagni arrives late for our appointment, bowling up the short drive to the piazza in a cream-coloured Renault 4, apologising by way of a bearish grin to Judy and me as he hoists his lumbering frame out of the car, only to realise after rummaging through his jacket pockets and tipping the contents of a plastic briefcase folder over the car bonnet that he's left the keys behind at the farm.

"No matter, follow me, you can climb in through the kitchen window."

Cassagni signals in a pleasant rumbling baritone and leads us up the outside staircase to the entrance. The double window only needs a gentle push and swing open freely, together with the inside shutters clattering against the wall. Cassagni declines to follow us in.

"Not at my age, I'll wait for you outside."

Scrambling over the sill into the kitchen, the huge fireplace immediately strikes me; it could easily seat four people and still leave plenty of room in there. Two planks serving as benches flank the raised stone hearth, above them are rows of brass-handled aluminium pots dangling from nails driven into the joists supporting the chimney hood. Directly underneath the hearth

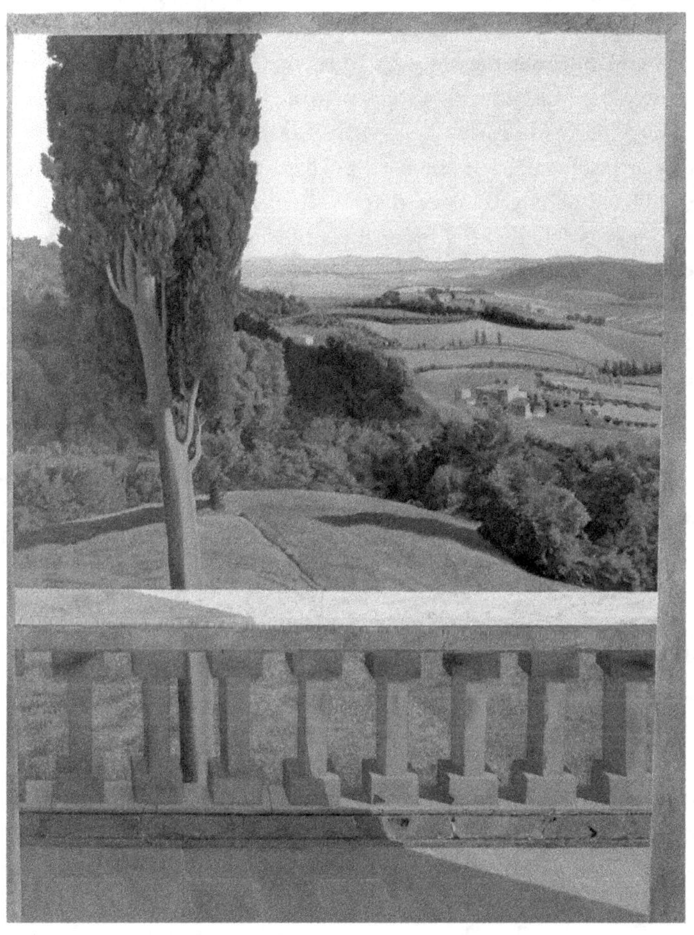

Poggio Spinoso. The kitchen view.1986

there is a long wooden drawer that pulls out and has etched two grooves into the terracotta paving beneath. Judy surmises it might have been for drying clothes or linen.

"Did the contadini use sheets then?" We puzzle, although that seems unlikely. The kitchen is basic; no fridge, an uncomfortably low porcelain sink and a small *cucina economica*, the classic wood-cooking stove. A very long rustic oak table in front of the fireplace occupies most of the kitchen space with an antique dresser over by a door that leads through to the back of the house. We explore each of the seven rooms in turn; most have two sets of windows and opening the shutters wide, the light floods in. The walls and ceilings are whitewashed with a thick marone stripe skirting the floor.

"It's big," moots Judy.

"It's got potential." I moot back enchanted. "I could have a studio and you could have a study, think of that."

The house is filled with a cornucopia of furniture from antique divans, a love seat and upholstered chairs, to a four-poster bed in one room and a green art deco bedroom suite in another, with marble dresser tops and painted floral motifs intertwined in gold ribbons. Everything is slightly worn around the edges but it has charm even if paint is peeling off the ceilings and beams and the wiring is tacked onto the wall, some of it sagging where the studs have come loose from the plaster. Cassagni is waiting downstairs to show us the long stable, crammed with ancient rusty farm machinery, and a a couple of cantinas underneath that are empty except for a few glass demijohns coated in cobwebs and some loose roof tiles. I am won over and hardly daring to know, ask him if the house is for rent?

"It might be," he replies cagily "for a limited period."

"And how much would the rent be in that case?" I venture.

"Let's suppose five million lire for one year."

Five million seems a bit stiff and taking a punt I suggest four million might be fairer. Judy looks at me astonished.

"After all," I say to Cassagni, "there must be a value in having tenants looking after the property rather than leaving it empty?"

"Haha." Laughs Cassagni looking amused but unpersuaded by this old argument:

"Sooner rather than later we are going convert Poggio Spinoso into holiday apartments, so it really doesn't matter either way."

Signor Cassagni clunks the door shut and slides back the driver's window to say goodbye, sinking further down into the canvas car seat.

"Look, I'll mention your offer to L'Architetto Mozzoni and see what he thinks. You're an artist, right? Well, you have that in your favour at any rate."

Taking off down the drive, his head barely above the window, he looks like a biker riding a chopper.

Judy isn't so convinced either.

"It's expensive and way too big for us." She says, cautious.

"Are you kidding me, where else are we going to find a house like this?" I say, stomping off.

Chapter 31.

Two weeks later Cassagni passes by with the wonderful news that Mozzoni, has accepted my offer and agreed to rent us the house for a year. I am ecstatic. Cassagni has invited me to come up to the farm (Campo Forte) to sign the lease; to cap it off, he has offered to hand over the keys beforehand and let me set up my studio before we officially move in, in April.

I am not sad to be leaving the Southerns'; the villa is comfortable, perfect for the summer months but cold and damp over winter and although offering us a life line, it's been a miserable time for both of us. Judy isn't as keen as I am on the move; she still thinks it's too expensive and too big for our needs but she is coming around with the prospect of starting a garden and faced with the fact that nothing other has presented itself.

She has been collecting rose cuttings from Gunilla's garden and sticking them into billycans that line the porch. Gunilla has an English garden and won't let Angelo anywhere near the roses anymore, not after he hacked into them this winter when she was away. He was really offended, protesting he was only pruning them and didn't turn up for work for the next few weeks. Gunilla practically had to beg him to return because her orto desperately needed work in preparation for this spring.

Campo Forte is a pleasant fifteen-minute stroll from the Southerns'; down into the valley, veering off to the right, stepping stones over the ford, ducking under the padlocked metal bar across the road that was put there after an outbreak of foot and mouth disease; up the hill flanked by woods, following the rutted tractor track to the plateau, past open fields and on to the farm.

Campo Forte, a large solid *casa colonica*, presides over the farmyard like a brooding hen: workshops, tractor sheds and chicken coops, behind them the cattle pens and the new, enormous steel hay barn and the silos. Odd bits of farm machinery are scattered around the fringes of the yard, some under covers, some abandoned in long grass on the banks or in the shadow of the main house. Cassagni is late again so I hang around the yard and when he finally appears, he struggles to unlock the door of his office; a small converted cantina below the outside stairs of the *casa colonica*, across the way from the stables where Mozzoni keeps his horses.

Mozzoni himself, lives on another part of the farm. It's as if Cassagni hasn't ventured into his office for years, reluctantly opening the shutters, stirring up great motes of dust, glimpsed in the buttery rays of morning sunlight filtering through the grimy window panes. He keeps his cap and coat on as if he has no intention of lingering and we sit on either side of his metal desk and get down to business.

"There are a number of conditions attached to the lease," sliding the paper across the top, "which runs for one year."

He opens a fresh manila folder and writes the name of the house: Poggio Spinoso in bold letters on the index tab, and urges me to read the lease first before signing.

"In addition to the rent you will have to pay the water rates, approximately 600,000 a year and the electricity bill comes to the farm so you can pay it when you pay the rent, quarterly."

I skim down the list: farm has right to use the piazza by the side of the house and access to the surrounding fields via the property at all times; they want to keep the stable under the house and one of the *cantine* for farm use and the workers can use the outside tap, and so on. No big deal, I am eager to sign along the dotted line.

"I'm proposing to do some maintenance work on the property before you move in." He says agreeably.

"We need to level the piazza because it gets waterlogged and put more gravel down on the driveway. Also, I want to replace the old weatherworn kitchen doors and put new French doors in."

What's more he is offering to install a wood-burning stove in the house but it would be too much to ask for an Attwood. I heard Gunilla has recently ordered one because her mother is coming to stay next winter and I only wish she had thought of it before. John finally installed the stove we ordered at Carolyn's and notwithstanding the price I wouldn't hesitate to recommend it to anyone.

Judy starts cleaning the villa a week before we are due to move out; she is being over-conscientious as far as I am concerned but expects me to help her wipe down all the doors and window frames to get rid of any invisible residue mould. Gunilla and I are embroiled in a niggling argument over the electricity bill, which she claims has been unusually high during our stay and is now expecting us to pay it all, even though the electricity was included in the rent as part of our agreement. I refuse of course, although I have offered to settle in part, which she has turned down and we are currently at an impasse. We had had already had a misunderstanding when we first moved in after I thought the rent she originally quoted for was in Lira but instead she insisted was in pounds, almost doubling the rent.

Dina winks knowingly when I tell her about the electricity.

"I told you so!"

Apparently, it was Angelo who told John that we left the outside light on every night and frequently loaded up the washing machine.

Dina surprises me when she comes to say goodbye, offering me one of her rabbits and putting a finger to her lips as if to say I need you to keep stum! About what I have absolutely no idea! But I suspect it has something to do with her irregular hours while the Southerns' were away. Politely I turn her offer down and then assure her that everything is okay.

Poggio Spinoso was originally a small, 18th-century woodcutter's cottage that has been progressively added on to; the uneven roof levels and the mixture of tiles: the slate, the classic old rounded terracotta *coppe* tiles and the modern square roof tiles all tell the story as does the mish-mash of masonry: the *pietra serena* and flint stone, terracotta shards, the Sienese brick cornices, lumps of white travertine, and the ugly modern anti-seismic breeze blocks around the kitchen door that somebody started to render then never finished the job.

Today, the woods have receded and the house sits on a balding pate of couch grass surrounded by a sea of ploughed earth, buffered from the incoming fields by banks of scruffy quince hedgerows and outlying clumps of blackberries. The view from the kitchen balcony is dramatic, extending all the way to the cupola of San Biagio below Montepulciano, glinting in sunshine thirty kilometres away. Luckily, the king size, four-poster bed, which almost fills one room, is demountable, because set in motion is a great dance of furniture circling the house, as Judy and I try out different variations: where to have our bedroom, where to have my studio, where to put her study. The four-poster has been ingeniously designed out of heavy, honey-coloured Venetian door panels that hinge together at the four upright posts making it easy to dissemble and reassemble. Cassagni has promised to send over Fernando, one of the farm workers, with the tractor and trailer to take away a surfeit of iron bedsteads and anything else we don't need.

The inventory of the house comes to five typed foolscap pages on top of which I am expecting a consignment of furniture from Scotland. My mother is going through an anti-material phase and hardly wants to keep anything so I offered to take a heavy upright piano, a seventeenth century refectory table, a Knole sofa and an Empire sofa that both belonged to my grandparents, plus other more useful items like bed linen and blankets and matching Yves Saint Laurent bath-towels!

I put in a request to Cassagni for the farm to fix the damp in the bathroom and tile the shower recess, which is just a bare wall, tentatively asking if they could put in a new bath while they are at it? As a result of my request, we have had our first visit from our new landlord wanting to assess the situation for himself. Mozzoni arrives with Cassagni in tow, who waits in the piazza while Mozzoni marches straight into the house with his Baden Powell hat on and his muddy boots, saying nothing more than a brisk *buongiorno.* He is a wiry, white-haired man in his seventies with a thin moustache and has a boyish precocity about him; only pokes his head round the bathroom door for a cursory look then turns on his heels and marches straight out again, making a passing comment, which I didn't catch, about the painting (Flight of Faith) hanging in the middle room. I am slightly put out; not a hint of a welcome, not even a handshake, every inch a feudal lord, haughty with his contadino tenant.

Cassagni returns a few days later, calling up first from the bottom of the stairs "MacDonald" then after a beat climbing up and discreetly tapping on the kitchen window without showing himself, as etiquette demands, then waiting for me to appear on the balcony before stepping forward.

"L'Architetto has agreed to fix the shower but doesn't think a bath tub is necessary. But not to worry" he continues conspiratorially: "We'll put one in for you anyway and no one will be any the wiser!" Cassagni has also agreed to connect the phone if we pay half the costs and with the proviso, we let the workers use it in case of any emergencies. SIP, the telephone company, will have to erect five new poles just to connect the line to the nearest junction box only a hundred yards up the lane. From the house I can already count nearly one hundred and eighty telegraph and electricity poles marching higgledy-piggledy across the landscape: through fields, by the sides of roads and cutting swathes up and down distant wooded slopes.

Come the evening, the Valdichiana is a birthday cake of blazing lights threatening to banish the night altogether. Balls of light hang like clouds above every village and far-flung discotheques fill the skies with laser beams. New streetlights are frog marching down the white road towards us from the village and on a distant cleared hillside behind the house, a military exclusion zone rumoured to be a missile dump is lit by row upon row of fairy lights. Even our Persian neighbour has installed huge white globes around his swimming pool and behind him the Napolitano has trained amber spotlights, the kind used to illuminate historical sites, onto the façade of his modestly restored holiday cottage, that he runs on a timer so they go on even when he is not there.

For Tuscans there is nothing so conspicuous a status symbol as electric light: more than that, it serves to affirm their very existence because to remain in darkness, to be invisible, can only mean to not exist and therefore unimaginable.

Chapter 32.

These days in my new studio! Cassettes playing, coffee in hand, cigarette lighted, newly stretched and primed canvas enticing, turps and linseed oil fragrances, paints freshly squeezed out onto a glass palette, brushes handy in an earthenware jar and I am back on deck at mission control. I don't even need to leave my chair to watch the sunset.

I can see Vicky's house in the middle-distance and Shelley struggling across the *strada bianca*, disappearing into the vineyard opposite, struggling with a large canvas bobbing up and down above the rows of vines like a great white sail. He is putting the finishing touches to his work in preparation for the exhibition we have organised in Cortona at Palazzo Vagnotti.

Posters announcing the show have been put up in shops and bars all the way to Arezzo. Every poster needs to be franked by the Comune for a small fee, before it can be displayed in public, or else you are liable to be fined ;not that anybody really takes much notice. Shelley had a batch of left over prints from one of his exhibitions, with a picture of a landscape and all we had to do was take it back to the printer with the added text: *Quattro Pittori in Toscana*: Four Painters in Tuscany.

Unfortunately, we are now only "Three Painters in Tuscany" and it is too late to change the poster. The fourth artist, a Columbian girl, dropped out at the last minute, much to the annoyance of Shelley, who is blaming Bob for stuffing things up. Shelley and I had yet to meet Esther as she was only included in the exhibition on Bob's recommendation and apparently, she has been unexpectedly called back to Columbia.

Palazzo Vagnotti is a cavernous exhibition space with rooms off a central corridor stretching the entire length of the building, including a small theatre down at the end with a small stage and a balcony. There is plenty of space for each of us to occupy two rooms and also combine our works in the corridor if we want.

Off to a bad start, I should have realised this isn't going to work; not with two large egos involved. It's only been a few days and tensions have been steadily rising. About what? I'm not sure, nobody will say, except there has been an incident and Bob and Shelley are no longer on speaking terms and neither are Vicky and Jane, which is very strange; Vicky will defend her man to the last, however unjustified, but Jane is normally so mild mannered, she is genuinely kind and much more the conciliatory type. When I ask, Bob remains unusually tight-lipped and Shelley simply shrugs and wanders off.

The one thing they can agree on is that they don't trust each other enough to leave the other alone in the gallery with their work, which in the current circumstance is only exacerbating the situation. Shelley and Bob are patrolling the corridor like two battleship commanders just itching for the slightest pretext to start a full-scale war. At least I can slip away, although I had hoped we would organise a roster and give everyone a break from the tedium of being in attendance all day long.

I invited Carolyn to the opening but she never showed, which is probably not surprising; but then I've been half expecting, half hoping to be surprised by the sight of dear Voss careening round the corner of Piazza Signorelli in his familiar busy sideways gait, nose to the ground, but alas no sign of him either. All the same, I keep a close check on the visitors' book just in case Carolyn came and signed her name when I wasn't there.

Notwithstanding Carolyn, it feels so good to be back in Cortona on a daily basis: Carolyn has been inside my head for far too long, keeping me at arms' length. I admit I have felt intimidated, or guilty maybe about the break up, or even just scared about raking up old emotions, especially with Judy now being here. What joy on hot afternoons cooled by the shaded stone; listening to the familiar squeal of the swifts as they wheel crazily around the piazzas, or watching the fat pigeons only pretending to hop out of your way, or witness once more the unmistakable rapture on the faces of tourists, sitting in the piazzas drinking cappuccino or sipping their *aperitivi*, dreamily writing" wish you were here" postcards and actually meaning it; wanting to share the moment with the whole world. It makes me wonder who amongst them might be the next to slip cross the border and remain. Rip Van Winkle town casting a spell doesn't change.

One of the first people I bump into along the Corso is a grinning Noemi, wearing his usual black and white Juventus strip with his old tracksuit bottoms and scuffed Nike trainers and waving his hands as soon as he sees me. Noemi is hobbling more than before, but we decide to go further down for a coffee in Piazza Garibaldi, where he duly brings out my dog-eared postcard from India, folded in three so it fits snugly into his wallet. I'm chuffed even amazed that he has hung on to it for this long.

Noemi can't stop flirting with Francesca behind the counter, a shapely, well rounded, good-looking woman with long black hair, who rebuffs his advances good-naturedly; all the same, Noemi can't help himself by the door as we are leaving: cupping his hands suggestively on his chest he bursts out:

"It's a pity your heart isn't as big as your breasts!"

Emilia sneaked into the exhibition one morning on her shopping rounds and I wasn't there unfortunately to give her the tour. Bob told me; a quick loop, signing the visitors book and she was gone, hands full with her heavy plastic shopping bags. Knowing her, she was probably relieved that I wasn't there. At least the next time I am over for lunch she will be able to compliment me and say what a good exhibition it was.

I make a lousy salesman. In the UK, just out of school, I only lasted one day attempting to sell double-glazing on a Luton housing estate; we were bused out there from central London, our doorstep pitch was aimed primarily at the wives, yet more often than not it was the husband who appeared at the door, leaving me flummoxed and floundering for something cohesive to say.

Bob has no such problems when it comes to selling his art, happy to buttonhole anyone right from the start, while Shelley stands back and allows Vicky do all the talking for him. It is ironic then, that nearing the close of the show, I'm still the only one who has actually sold a painting. Yet even there, in keeping with the general tone of the exhibition, my sale has caused a minor ruckus with Vicky practically accusing me of stealing her client: Joachim, a German tourist who she met in Lucignano and who she invited to the exhibition expressly to see Shelley's work.

Luckily for me, the van he drove down in is large enough for him to take the painting home with him.

I decided to celebrate the sale of my painting at the Pizza in the park; run by young Massimo with the financial help of his father, Il Professore, who along with his wife helps in the kitchen and on Saturdays put on a special lunch for their regulars, mostly the expats, sitting outside together at a long table under the sweetly perfumed *Tigli* trees. Quite often they put on exhibitions, inviting local artists to display their work on easels they set up in front of the restaurant along the *parterre.*

On my way I bump into Marc, a young American composer, who Bob introduced me to at the opening of the exhibition. There is an edge to Marc and an understated sense of humour that I like so I invited him along: a fellow traveller perhaps. He is in Cortona for a month on a working holiday, putting the finishing touches to a work he has composed for piano and digitally programmed to be performed on a computer.

After our pizza, Marc and I move on to Imola's wine bar. I have the foresight to call up Judy and let her know I probably won't be making it home tonight and by the end of the evening I am in such a drunken state that Marc has to carry me back to his place to crash. By a coincidence, he has been renting the same apartment off via Guelfa that Ron used to live in and Rupert took over after him, living there up until his marriage.

Collapsing on the bed Marc leaves me to watch the room spinning round and around my head. Please stop the world I want to get off! I stagger for the bathroom but not in time; instead, find myself vomiting into the kitchen sink; it is filling up so fast with *penne al pomodoro* that I begin shovelling them out of the third-floor window with my hands, and struggle back to bedroom where I puke out of the bedroom window.

Very early in the morning I am woken by a persistent sound of distant scrubbing and bleary eyed, pushing the curtain back, I can see an old lady in the garden below washing down a stone bench directly under my window. Seeing me she angrily fists her scrubbing brush in the air, shouting:

"Was this you? You animal! What a disgrace: I should report you to the police!"

And pointing to the bench I had spewed over last night:

"This is my husband's favourite seat, don't you know!"

I mumble an apology and quickly duck back inside, feeling mortified.
Hurriedly getting dressed, I tiptoe out of the apartment, scribbling a short note to Marc, too embarrassed to face him in person and as I am exiting the building, I notice bits of pasta lodged onto the roof of a car parked at the front entrance.

Marc calls me at home in the afternoon sounding very irritated:

"Hey Buddy, what the hell was going on last night? What's the story with the old lady downstairs? This morning, the paramedics were carrying her husband, who just had a heart attack, out of the apartment and she almost accosted me on the stairs with her umbrella."

She must have thought Marc was me, I realise. But surely what happened to her husband had nothing to do with the events of last night?

What if they did? Was he there? Sitting on his favourite bench when it started raining with vomit?

The final word on the exhibition belongs to the art critic, Romano Santucci from *La Nazione*, whose review is published only a couple of days before the exhibition closes.

Vicky organised the article and as far as I know she didn't need to pay him for it, which according to Roberto is standard practice in Italy; often done in the form of donating a painting to the critic's private collection.

"Like being a card-carrying member of a political party, if you want to get ahead as an artist you will have to play the game." Declares Roberto.

Roberto remains staunchly apolitical and a stoic, almost belying his own advice.

Romano Santucci. *La Nazione*

'A splendid group show. It is a love of the Tuscan landscape that unites these three artists.
Robert has crisscrossed Cortona painting views of the mountains and the Valdichiana, offering us a complete snapshot of the area at different times of the year. He paints from life; experiencing nature at first hand in all its purity … Robert repeatedly finds new subtleties and juxtapositions between light and shade. Shelley paints in nature as well, rotating his canvas according to the transiting sun. His painting is lively and fresh, full of inspiration. The composition of his work, while falling within the impressionist style, is nevertheless imbued with a vibrant sense of joy and sensitivity–the texture is malleable, the greens, greys and blues sit side by side without contrasting violently. Nino is also inspired by the landscape but in a symbolic way: in his compositions, the synthesis of his work distils a notable and pleasing mystery. His language is flowing, tinged with melancholy and offers us through nature a certain intimate suffering, which the painter proposes in his vision of harmony and colour...'

Chapter 33.

There was no actual garden to speak of at Poggio Spinoso except for a couple of farmhouse roses climbing the wall of the *forno*, abutting the old sunken *orto*. There are crocus and clumps of iris that crop up along the banks down to the surrounding fields where earlier in the year I noticed bunches of wild daffodils growing. An almond tree behind the *forno* produces bitter almonds, the kind used in Armagnac and I can almost pick the cherries from the branches of the tree outside one of my studio windows.

Three scrawny looking cypress trees scattered around the perimeter, are probably in the early stages of bark canker; an airborne fungal parasite spread by insects that attacks the crown of these trees and moves slowly down killing it. It is classified as a pandemic and with no antidote in sight it is playing havoc with the iconic (if not native) Tuscan landscape. The cypress tree originates in Persia and was introduced into the Tuscan landscape three thousand years ago by the Etruscans. (Who else!)

Judy was part of the self-sufficiency movement in the early seventies, living on a rural property in Victoria Australia, with her first husband Tony and she looks the part again: a real country girl, dressed in a turtle-neck under an oversized man's sports coat rolled up at the cuffs, a blue beanie pulled down over her ears, hair overflowing! An Amazon girl wielding a *zappa* (the Tuscan hoe) ready to hack out a thick-rooted, half-dead bridle creeper climbing up the walls of the house, then steadily moving around the house's perimeter, creating new garden beds, planting zinnias, lambs' ears and phlox; annuals, but only because she doesn't know how long we'll be here for. A jasmine in a terracotta pot is doing its best to attach to the wall and cover up the breeze blocks surrounding the kitchen door, with an existing wisteria wending its way around the red brick balusters on the balcony wall, and smaller terracotta pots filled with petunia, chrysanthemums and anemones lining the top.

Cassagni (like most Italians who visit) is horrified at the idea of flowerbeds slap up against the building and dismayed by the ivy I am training along wires on the upper wall under the bedroom window, to hide the mismatch of white *travertina* stone, warning us about highways and a multitude of pests finding their way into the house. If I thought I was going to be let off lightly and only admire Judy's efforts, I am soon disabused of the notion and handed a shovel to dig over the *orto*, about thirty square metres. She expects me to cut the grass as well:

"After all," Judy points out, "what's the use of having flower beds if you can't see them?"

Her idea of a good birthday present for me is the Flymo: an electric mower. Shelley leant me an old petrol push mower of his that promptly broke down, leaving me with a costly repair bill and the suspicion that he knew it was about to crash all along.

There is a concrete silo that abuts the bank on the other side of the orto; made up of three small compartments, with separate heavy concrete doors. It is more like a bunker or nuclear shelter, but the thick slabbed concrete top makes it ideal as a terrace/entertaining area. Along the South side there is an eight-foot drop, so I have embarked on constructing a classic Tuscan fence (squares with interior diagonals); using the long wooden poles that I have pilfered from the vineyard as stilts and anchoring them into the silo wall. Cassagni has recently ploughed under the vineyard on the other side of the piazza in front of the house, which included a row of *uva fragole*: sweet Isabella dessert grapes that are delicious and taste of strawberry.

A few asparagus crowns and Jerusalem artichokes are growing in the orto, otherwise it is mostly compacted clay, the kind that isn't friable and won't be shrugged off a spade so easily. Martin highly recommends a no-digging method of cultivation that sounds appealing to me right now because the orto must have been a lazy builder's graveyard once, judging by the amount of terrazzo, broken roof tiles and lumps of concrete I am striking buried underground.

I am regularly dispatched in the car to the farm, to fill up large plastic bin liners with manure from the dung mountain in the cattle yard. Cassagni rations me to one big bag per trip but I usually sneak another one or two in after he leaves me to get on with the shovelling. Judy can't get enough of it, constantly feeding the soil to nurture it back to health. Before you know it she has brassicas in the ground and *cavola nera, insalata,* trestles for sweet peas and stakes for the tomatoes, rows of pepperoni, melanzane and plans for sweet corn and strawberries, not forgetting the rosemary hedgerow and bay tree she planted as well as a herb garden and the potato patch I have dug as an experiment, next to the compost behind the *forno.*

It is hard to get Judy to slow down once she is in motion except for Chernobyl and rumours of a nuclear cloud drifting our way across Europe has everybody scurrying indoors. Health inspectors wielding Geiger counters are starting to check shop produce for traces of radiation. The situation is confused and people are besides themselves at the real prospect of mushrooms becoming inedible for years to come if those isotopes ever hit the ground.

The media is even suggesting that breast-feeding could pose a danger. Jill and Paul, friends of Judy's from Australia, on a year's sabbatical and renting a house near Siena, are expecting their first baby and shrug it off as if nothing in the Australian manner; determined to brazen it out and have the baby as planned in the alternative birthing centre in Poggibonsi. Paul has Italian heritage and is keen to call the baby Nino, if it is a boy. Far from feeling flattered, this makes me anxious, being over-possessive about my name and fervently hoping it's going to be a girl.

I consider Nino to be *my* name. It's how I sign my paintings. In fact I am the only Nino I know. The only reason I was christened Hermann in the first place was because Nino was not a prescribed name in Germany at the time of my birth. My parents however persisted with Nino and the name caught on; nobody has ever called me Hermann and when my step father adopted me at the age of five, Nino also became my official name.

Tim, our friend who writes film scripts, has written an article about me for Next, a small circulation art magazine published in Rome in English and Italian:

"… Now if I was writing a bestseller and needed a name for a successful international painter, Nino MacDonald would be about right …"

I do wonder what the fate of Hermann Leonard Pöhling, the German would have been as opposed to that of Nino Douglas Alexander MacDonald the Scot. Would we have turned out the same?

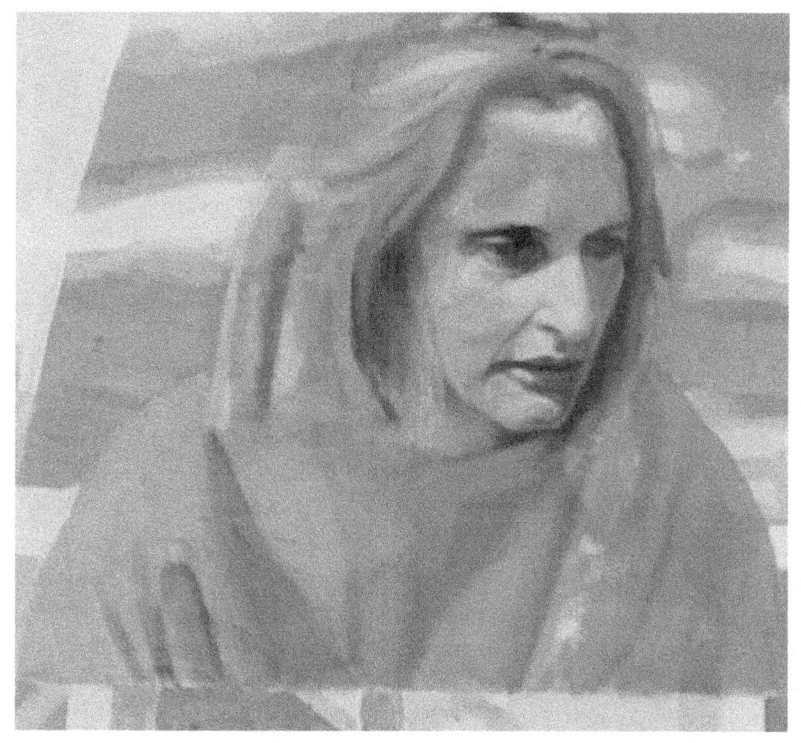

Judy.1986

Chapter 34.

Perhaps it's the fallout from Chernobyl that has turned my head so drastically; Vicky is already blaming the hydra-headed tomatoes in her *orto* on the radiation; then the life-size bust she was modelling of me in clay exploded in her f*orno,* just about summing up the state my actual head is in. Certainly, the big black cloud hanging over Poggio Spinoso had Marina concerned: "You can see it from miles away!"

But by now Marina had already had the misfortune of watching me reading a newspaper at the breakfast table that I was holding upside down and must have realised that our few days together were already numbered.

Judy, Marina and I had driven up to Sabine's for lunch; Judy was leaving the country for her *permesso di soggiorno* (permission to reside) and I was bringing my painting *Breakthrough* to hang in an exhibition in Florence that Roberto had invited me to participate in: *In Memoria Di Chernobyl.* Judy had to sit on Marina's lap all the way to Florence just so I had the space to transport the painting in the back.

My affair with Marina started innocently enough: fellow artists collaborating on a painting together with a canvas set up in the garden at Poggio Spinoso, Judy present but not participating.

The psychology of collective painting has fascinated me ever since a trip I made to Tangiers in Morocco, where I fell in with some local boys at a cafe on the outskirts of town and we spent our days drinking mint tea, smoking kif and drawing together on sheets of paper that we passed around between us. Only then it was different; as an exercise in sublimating artistic ego, it was more about exercising caution, gingerly skirting around each other's' markings so as not to give offence. With Marina it is quite different, we go for it; like driving bulldozers through each other's work, no restraint and no recriminations either because we come from a place of no ego, or try to, like a breath of fresh air.

Marina has other ways of stroking my ego, especially if she is enthusing about my work. Judy thinks I should be doing more landscapes so that I can sell them like Bob, and it offends me that she doesn't understand the calling.

The mission is everything; not that I consider myself chosen, more like a finely tuned instrument that is in harmony with fate; that I am a human receptor, channelling a message but not the creator himself; a belief bolstered by the perception that the privileged circumstances of my life all seem to conspire towards facilitating that end. I can dedicate myself to painting and not have to worry about making a living. Judy is not convinced, she thinks the privilege is counterproductive, that in fact I lack the motivation to succeed and I should push myself more to get out the door (the studio that is).

In my other ear I have my new age mum telling me that worldly success is not the important part; that even if nobody ever sees my work, it is the very act of painting that imbues it with the energy that can reach right the way round the world.

Marina and I behaved badly that lunch at Sabine's, flirting openly in front of everyone. Afterwards, ostensibly to hang my painting, we skipped off before the rest, leaving Judy behind and I could see how distraught she was and how Tim went to comfort her as I was closeing the front door.

With Judy out of the country, Bernardo was shocked to see Marina and I holding hands in Bar Signorelli; I think he had designs on Marina himself and so were Dan and Marion: that night we were cuddling in the back of their car on the way to the pizzeria to meet Marina's friend Hans. Judy barely tolerates Marion, not after the Christmas episode and then again, a few weeks later, when we had dinner with them in the Ristorante Napoli in Sinalunga and Marion spent the whole evening dominating my attention on one side of the table while Dan button holed Judy on the other. After they left we had a stand-up row and I ended up walking all the way home from Sinalunga: a good twelve kilometres.

It was Marina's friend Hans, a German sculptor, who suggested we go to the hot springs that night after our pizza. I didn't fancy the idea as it was cold and dark outside with blasts of ice fog on the roads and Marina had to cajole me into it. Hans, strands of dishevelled thinning blond hair, hunched over the steering wheel peering through the windscreen, his bulky chisel-battered fists swiping at the condensation, finally turns down a mud frozen track and parks his van in a clearing in the woods; the stench of rotten eggs is strong as steam caught in the headlights is rising from the denuded gully up ahead. The ground is a ghostly white carpet but also sparkly with crystal particles glittering in the high beam. Even the horse shoe ring of oak trees crowding the clearing, are dusted in white.

Stripping off naked outside in the dead of night when it is freezing cold, doesn't sound very enticing but the occasion and eeriness and isolation of the location pulls me right back into my comfort zone as soon as I slide down into the steaming tub of bubbling hot water. Fully immersed, the five of us are humming and hawing.

"Hans is the one who first had the brilliant idea of heaping up stones under the water outlet there."

Marina points to a large white PVC pipe resting on a ledge above us, gushing a constant stream of water into our tub, which in turn is overflowing and filling up two more pools set out below us, then gently cascading down the hill into a stream about thirty metres below.

"Go on tell them what happened Hans."

"I live close by here and out walking one day I stumbled across this area. Evidently the spa at San Giovanni reroutes the spring water here to the top of the gully when the Spa closes down for the winter. I realised if you pile up the stones underneath you can create a vessel to hold the water in. You see how the sulphur creates this white coat like plaster over the stones, fusing them together in an impermeable barrier."

"As you can see." Marina makes a sweeping gesture. "Through word of mouth the idea caught on; with more people coming and starting to do the same thing Han's did."

Two shallower terraced pools fanning out below have been added; not as deep but cooler in water temperature and room to float around in.

I had never met Hans before that night although coincidently, Judy and I have been to his house once. We were on our way to see Dan and Marion in Trequanda, attempting a new short cut across the Crete Senesi that I had discovered, clearly marked on the map but that in reality didn't exist. The road winds through the semi deserted hamlet where Hans lives, before petering out on a muddy plateau, which is where our car slid and bogged in a ditch. The evening was stormy and for no particular reason Judy and I chose that night to dress up, which we rarely do; she was wearing her favourite Thai silk dress with expensive Italian shoes on, I wore my smart bespoke tartan trews and we ended up covered head to toe in mud, trying to push the car out of the ditch; wheels spinning mud spurting, flashes of lightening shifting all around us in fading light. The first place we came across looking for help was Hans's; a light was on in his house but nobody came to the door and ultimately, we were rescued by a Sardinian shepherd just down the road. We must have looked a sight on his porch, but not withstanding the notoriety of Sardinian shepherds at the time (after a series of high-profile kidnappings), he invited us in to dry off in front of his fire with a glass of wine, gave me the phone to call Dan to come out and get us, then offered to tow the car out with his tractor in the morning, even refusing to be paid for his efforts when I offered him cash.

I feel so seedy now, standing on the platform in my old threadbare, gabardine school mac and scuffed tan leather boots; waiting for Judy's train to come into Monte San Savino station. A five-day stubble is roughing up my face and I have my sunglasses on, even though it is overcast.

Judy is obliged to leave the country every six months in order to renew her *permessso di soggiorno* and she has been away, in France, for little more than a week. Now, stepping down onto the platform, all she needs is one look at me to confirm her worst suspicions. Although I know my halfhearted fling with Marina is definitely over, my stomach is churning with the turmoil inside, as I don't understand myself how I will react seeing Judy again for the first time since my behaviour at Sabine's; but the moment comes as a revelation, suddenly looking at gold again: the Empress, undaunted, walking side by side with me through the destruction of that riot-torn fishing village in Kerala, where we first met: past the smouldering charcoaled huts and the policemen stationed there to keep the peace between the Moslems and the Christian factions, telling us 'no problems', 'everything under control' with a sideways shake of the head, their loaded Enfield rifles casually resting on their laps or slung over the backs of their chairs, lined up down down the middle of the village. Judy had shorter, blonder, beachcomber hair then, that made her ears poke out, a sarong modestly tied at the neck still enough to turn anyone's head.

I saw Marina too out of the corner of my eye at the opening, sailing down the aisle at Palazzo Vagnotti, looking like Cleopatra with her coal-black hair and sharp Elizabeth Taylor eyebrows; her white teeth set ablaze by a bright vermillion smile. Vicky introduced us at the exhibition; Marina, the artist from Rome with a house on the other side of Lucignano, who Judy and I had heard so much about previously because Vicky couldn't stop telling us how sorry she was for Marina's ex who she had banished to a shed in the garden.

As soon as we get home from the station, Judy informs me she is only here to pack a few clothes and that Tim is coming down to get her. Gentleman Tim! Such impeccable manners, he probably has plans for her too, swooping down to rescue a damsel in distress.

Judy has left me here on my own, it is winter. and Marina making a rare appearance after all the drama, finds me on my knees weeding banks as a penance.

"Coming here," she remarks, "there is a huge black cloud hanging over Poggio Spinoso; you can see it from miles away!"

Chapter 35.

Thankfully the airline didn't charge us the excess luggage on our return from India. My suitcase alone weighed a ton, filled with Judy's Aladdin's cave of stuff she had collected: rugs, khaddar, bed covers, brass kettle, a Tiffin carrier, heavy wooden statue of Shiva, lumps of carved stone discarded from temples etc... On the last leg, the bus from Arezzo, the driver obligingly made an unscheduled stop, dropping us off at the top of the hill on the corner of our road and we were able to hitch a ride the rest of the way down to Poggio Spinoso on the back of an Ape.

Welcome home my love, to a new start and a balmy spring morning with the quince hedgerows in full glorious bloom.The front door is unlocked, just as I'd left it three months earlier when I couldn't get it to close properly and had to abandon the attempt or possibly miss my flight to India; resorting instead to one of my mother's New Age incantations: conjuring up in my mind a long silvery tail of fiery light which I swoosh round and around like a sparkler, cocooning the house in its strong protective light.

Dan and Marion, who were giving me a lift to Terontola station, came early for a celebratory breakfast. Judy and I were getting back together after a hiatus of three months, but just to be safe we had decided to meet half way, back to where our story had begun in India.

My heart sank when Judy said she was leaving me that terrible day last winter, but somehow, I managed to forestall her temporarily and she phoned Tim to tell him not to come. Instead, we went for a long walk down into the valley below the Southerns and I let Tuscany do my talking. Judy decided to return to Australia to give her the time and distance, she felt she needed to work out how she felt.

"I guess it's time to hold our breath." I said, touching her arm at the departure gate, not convinced that I would ever see her again, spending the winter on my knees weeding banks as a penance.

Dan and Marion provided the champagne and juiced the oranges whilst I prepared the scrambled eggs. Unfortunately, by the time we arrived at Terontola my train was literally pulling out of the station and desperately seeking an alternative found there was none, not even a taxi, that would get me to the airport in time. What a disaster, except graciously, Dan agreed to drive me to the airport with Marion in tow a tad reluctant.

God! 1987 is turning out to be a stellar year, a roller coaster ride of emotions: Judy is back, then in August, as luck would have it, I sold all my shares at the very top of the bull market, only two months before the disastrous 'Black Monday': the massive global stock market crash. I have Dan to thank that; he's been banging on forever about the inevitability of a global crash, eventually panicking me enough to take action and dump all my investments, buying foreign currency instead (the Australian dollar).

Then in September, Judy is feeling out of sorts, curled up under a rug on top of our four-poster bed when I give her the news we have been anxiously waiting for.

"Congratulations, Mamma, you are pregnant!"

The lab in Sinalunga has just called to confirm the test was positive. Judy can hardly believe it; her first time pregnant at thirty-seven years of age. I am ecstatic and race out into the garden and leap up and down fist pumping the air, exulting in some primordial confirmation of my potency.

"Oh! you clever dick!" Is how my mother puts it when I give her the news over the phone and I'm sure no pun was intended.

Friends are asking us if we are going to the UK or Australia to have the baby: everyone has their favourite Italian hospital horror story, especially the *stranieri*, except Sara our American friend in Montevarchi is having nothing of it, declaring she has a friend who is an obstetrician in Montevarchi who owes her a favour and we should go to him. She will ask.

The only hiccup for Judy in her situation is not having universal health coverage and we can't afford to go private; I might have done well with my investments recently but we still have to live modestly in order to survive: going to India for example ends up being cheaper than staying in Tuscany even including the air fares. Up until now my GP in the village, Dr. Ricciarini, has accepted Judy on his patients' roll as a favour; he doesn't even charge her, which is so typical of Italian generosity and their willingness to bend rules. Anarchy and unilateral decision-making are at the core of this nation!

As a resident Judy would be covered, but she is reluctant to take that step because she thinks it would make her a bludger (an Australian term for scrounger); it would be too blatant an attempt to manipulate the system she says. Of course, I disagree, pointing out that far from it, Italians would feel flattered that she only wants to become a resident because so she can have her baby here.

Contrary to my nature, I became a resident soon after we moved into Poggio Spinoso. The motive was purely economic, after Judy discovered that the electricity tariffs are twice as high for non-residents. Most Tuscans will tell you it's better by far to stay well out of the system and voluntarily making yourself accountable to officialdom is plain stupid and I totally agree!

Normally, getting your residency is a complicated process, although, as I suspected correctly, with a word from Cassagni (ergo Mozzoni) in the ear of Vasco, the town clerk, my request wouldn't prove that difficult to process. Cassagni accompanied me to the Comune and it only cost 500 lira, the price of the official stamp that Vasco slapped onto the document with such gusto. He did insist, however, that I also apply for my *permesso di soggiorno*: something I had resolutely managed to avoid up until then. In the eight years I have lived in Tuscany, I am yet to be asked to produce one for whatever reason. Judy being Australian feels more vulnerable and she still departs the country every six months in order to renew hers, although if she became a resident the time would extend to every five years. On one occasion Judy practically had to beg the customs official on the train to stamp her passport for proof of re-entry and when he finally obliged, he stamped in the wrong year! Even that made absolutely no difference when it came to renewing her's at the Questura.

When I duly applied for my *permesso* at the police station in Lucignano, I was delighted to discover that proffering my blank English chequebook was sufficient proof of independent financial means! Two weeks later when it was ready, the Maresciallo himself phoned me; a very unusual step because this would normally be handled by a sergeant at the front desk. He made a big point over the phone of asking my permission to use the familiar person tu and to call me Nino. (Normally, unless you know the person well, the formal pronoun voi(you) is employed. Similarly saying goodbye, you wouldn't say ciao, but rather the formal address arriverdverci or in Tuscany even more formal still: arriverdella). The Maresciallo went on to invite me to collect my permesso from him personally at the station and duly I was ushered into his office and bid to sit down in front of his desk, feeling nervous about what would ensue. Instead, he pointed out a collection of art works he had on display on the walls of his office, and the penny dropped soon after having spotted one of Shelley's works hanging there! Following the script, it wasn't long before I was offering to donate one of my own paintings to 'the station' and could go home relieved.

This is Lucignano's courageous Maresciallo, who made headlines in the local press after he boldly stepped out into the road by the public gardens, at great personal risk, to apprehend some drunk hooligan dragster doing burn ups in his car and terrorising the locals in front of the main gate.

Sara has promised to ask Dr. Migliorini, the obstetrician who delivered her daughter Kira in Montevarchi, if he will consider wavering his fee and take Judy on as a personal favour and I have finally convinced Judy that she needs that residency if we are to go through with it here. A quick trip up to the Comune to see Vasco and an explanation as to why she needs one, and as I had predicted, once he understood he was only too delighted to oblige.

Finally, 1987 brings me the dreaded C word. Ma called to let me know that Pa has a brain tumour and I am going to London to be with him for the operation. After such an exhilarating year, I've been taking long walks down to the woods, feeling sick to the stomach; alternating between haranguing and pleading with God. Sue raised the first alarm from San Fransisco, where they have been living this past year, after he began complaining about ringing sounds in his head and then started misplacing stuff, even the car, notremembering where he had parked it. She brought him back to the UK for tests where he was diagnosed. The Doctors have been stressing to us the delicate nature of my father's surgery; warning us of the potential for further brain damage and loss of quality of life,
really only absolving themselves ahead of time; it can't get much worse: there is no retreating from this ailment, no room for doubt or hope, although Ma has been channelling The Lady, an ascended Master who says he will pull through.

Seeing Pa helpless and in a state of shock is an ordeal in itself; driving to the hospital in London from Kent with his sister Jean and Sue, I hold his hand for most of the journey.

Ma is insisting to the Doctors she is still his legal next of kin, sowing confusion, then looking to me to back her up all the way. I just want to focus on him; not organise meetings for her with him in pubs round the corner (of the hospital) just because Ma doesn't want to see Sue or her sister-in-law.

Oh God! Watching him trolleyed into the lift on his way to the operating theatre, the clunk of the lift doors sliding shut, and not knowing what will

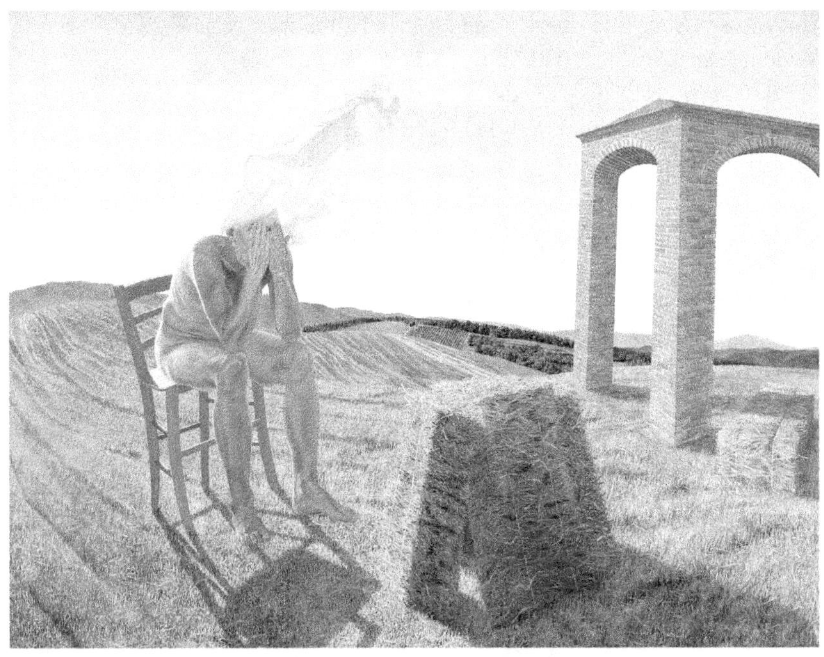

A year of dying quietly.1989

be. Then the next day, after the operation, his head swaddled in bandages, sitting up in his bed waving his arms around, miraculously, or so it seems, a recovered man, laughing and joking, nearing his old self' everyone so relieved.

I can return to Tuscany with some measure of peace: prepare for the upcoming addition to our household. Then, only two months later, my father announces that Sue is pregnant too! Completely out of left field, this is news indeed! And must have come as quite a shock to my mother, who always presumed he was infertile, they having tried unsuccessfully in the past to have a child.

Sue is on the cusp, age wise, and declares: "It's the most unlikely pregnancy ever!"

So now I get to joke on the phone with my father, about being the first cab off the rank and how I will be offering him advice on baby rearing. And yet, underscored by our attempts at levity, there lies the continued threat of a tumour that has not gone away but is, after the initial positive response on the move again. The news from Sue in Edinburgh, where Pa is currently undergoing a course of radiotherapy, is not so good:

"He went missing one day out on a walk and the police found him wandering around Edinburgh High Street without his shoes or socks on and brought him home."

Chapter 36.

Judy and I watch from the kitchen window with mounting horror as large earthmovers begin work trundling around the field in front of the shepherdess's house on the far side of the wood; not five hundred yards away as the crow flies. At first, we thought this might be the start of a new housing project and it has not exactly come as a relief to discover it's going to be a motocross track; apparently the land belongs to a farmer and his son is an enthusiast. A circuit with a series of high, ramped earth mounds is being bulldozed around the field and up through the woods below the cemetery.

Coincidently, one of the new proposals for an alternative route for the *superstrada* slated to go through Mozzoni's land, is via a tunnel under the cemetery exiting in the same field as the motocross track. Judy and I have already decided we can't stay here if the road is built and with the motocross nearing completion, the prospects either way don't look too great. A *superstrada* in front or behind us and a motocross track! So far, fingers crossed, Mozzoni has been successful in blocking the *superstrada* but I wonder for how much longer? The popular argument is that it will bring new economic prosperity to Lucignano and people are concerned about the detrimental effect the vibrations are having on historic Lucignano's foundations with an endless parade of lorries rumbling up and down the hill on their way to Siena or Perugia.

I attended a very heated meeting on the subject in the Comune, with people, most of whom are in favour, nearly coming to blows with officials over the issue, angry about the lack of progress and blaming Mozzoni, who isn't exactly flavour of the day, for the endless delays. This is a class war; locals resent his clout and the way he has been able to frustrate the project for all these years, especially now that it is fast becoming the last remaining link in an ambitious national road building plan known as Il Due Mari: a four-lane super highway joining the East and west coasts of Italy. Imagine that? All the way from the Adriatic and it has to go right through my backyard! As it stands, the *superstrada* bypasses Arezzo and comes to an abrupt halt in a field below Monte San Savino, only five kilometres away, sitting there like a loaded gun pointing straight at us.

Thankfully only a few motorbikes race round the new track on any given day, even so it can be irritating, like a dog yapping in the distance or the buzz of a mosquito close to the ear that refuses to be shooed away. Occasionally, I see the shepherdess leading her sheep up through the sliver of wood into the field that divides us. A stout woman, wearing a tattered red or blue bandana, with leather creased skin burnt black in summer. She tarries a while, leaning on her staff reading a paperback while the sheep are grazing before moving them forwards on their daily circuit. She is accompanied by two unruly Alsatian dogs who snap and snarl at the tremulous sheep, occasionally hobbling an unwitting creature's hind legs, and it's not uncommon to see her striding home with a sheep wrapped in her powerful arms. When I mention the motocross to her, she isn't unduly concerned by the noise; here, noise similar to electric lights only serve as a supplementary affirmation of life. Her closest neighbours though, an elderly German couple, who live right next to the track, are complaining about the clouds of dust billowing through their house because he fears his extensive collection of rare books will be ruined as a result.

As Sara predicted, Dr. Migliorini has agreed to take Judy on privately and promised to deliver the baby in Montevarchi's public hospital, about a forty-minute drive from Poggio Spinoso. My mother, born in 1929, reveals that my grandfather helped to deliver her on the way to the hospital in the back of a horse drawn carriage during a snow blizzard in Silesia; a feat I'm not hoping to emulate, and even though Judy and I haven't been attending prenatal classes, she has a stack of baby books for reference's sake. The one she looks at the most is "Baby and Child" by Penelope Leach. Judy is confident, I am mildly paranoid thinking of what possibly could go wrong

We go once a month for her check up at the good doctor's consulting rooms in the centro storico of Montevarchi and except for one incident, everything has been proceeding smoothly. The car battery was flat one morning and Judy overstrained herself helping me to push it out of the garage and jump-start it down the drive. Suffering abdominal pains, Judy thought she was having an ectopic pregnancy but Dr. Migliorini only ordered her to bed for a couple of weeks as a precaution and I duly learnt my lesson ministering to my lady love. According to the ultra sounds the baby is healthy, a weight off my mind, and we have elected not to know its gender, preferring to be surprised, although we have both had dreams it's going to be a girl with green eyes.

It is well past midnight when I wake up; from our bedroom I can see Judy sitting at the kitchen table intently poring over her pregnancy books. How can I adequately describe her beauty, the aura that shines through her glowing skin, similar to the translucence of an alabaster window in a Romanesque church. I swing off the four poster and busy myself making her a herbal tea, then sit quietly in another corner while she works out if her contractions have started in earnest or not. It takes a couple of hours, counting the contractions, then suddenly she is sure, it's action stations, it's happening and I am on the phone to Dr. Migliorini, embarrassed to be waking him at four in the morning but letting him know we are on our way to the hospital.

Judy is calm, I am full of butterflies but determined to drive with harmony, without haste, to savour this momentous event. More—as we drive over the mountain—to meld us with this blue hour, with the sky and the earth, the mountains and woods all perfectly poised within the deepest shades of cobalt blue; when time itself is perfectly balanced between night and day: I will take us through.

Screams literally greet us at the unattended entrance to the old Montevarchi hospital, erupting down an empty hospital corridor as we hurry in. Dr. Migliorini is already there, all business and efficiency but in good humour, he's seen it all a thousand times before. The good Doctor leans towards the traditional school and swears by the stirrups. If ever we tentatively broached the subject of alternative birthing in his consulting room, he would swat the very idea away, laughing, even joking, leaning over, elbow on the desk, reminiscing how he once dimmed the lights in the delivery room as a concession to one of his patients making similar requests.

Jill and Paul, Judy's Australian friends went to Poggibonsi, the only alternative birthing unit in Tuscany, but that is too far for us to travel. Jill delivered "littleNino" in a warm tub and to avoid any confusion I am now known to them as Big Nino.

Judy is parked in an antechamber, waiting for her waters to break, while a newly minted mother on the runway next door is taxiing to a halt, the same lady whose screams we heard earlier. Her husband has already accosted me in the hall outside the delivery rooms, anxious for news of his wife. I had none to give him except encouragement but puzzled, asked him "why aren't you in there with her?"

Looking crestfallen, he explained his wife had elected for her mother to be present at the birth and they only allow one person to be there with her. I feel for him, missing out on what should be one of the biggest moments of his life!

Frocked up in a green surgeon's scrubs, my long hair tucked into a clear plastic cap and wearing plastic over-slippers, I hold Judy's hand as she is trolleyed into the delivery room, discreetly propping my cassette tape recorder and microphone over in a corner on the floor. Everything is speeding up now. Judy is resolute, she pushes down, she pushes down, down, then … then …what is that? What am I looking at? I don't get it: it's like a spongy brain emerging! Momentarily stuck, some hectic activity, one last push and it's out ... and it's a boy!

A boy? Perplexed. What about our dreams? So convinced we've been, we haven't even bothered with a boys' name; I liked Olivia, Judy preferred Lilly. No matter, Dr. Migliorini hands me the scissors:

"Would you like to do the honours?"

Offering up the umbilical cord and patting me on the back afterwards, looking impressed.

"Congratulations, some men faint, they can't handle it."

Then turning to Judy admiringly:

"You Australians! So strong, so robust! Not a murmur even! None of that drama Italian women go for!"

He looks genuinely pleased and so do the midwives.

The onset of the dawn chorus of starlings is starting up outside. Darling boy, a Tuscan boy! A tiny slip of humanity snuggling into the crook of my arms before he is rushed away in a mountain of white towelling to be dried under a blower machine or is he being weighed? I am dazed, his tiny, tiny hand clamps around my pinkie finger as we introduce ourselves.

Absolutely exhausted but high as a kite, I drive back to Sara and Allen's place, where I will be staying for the next few days. I pop the cassette into the car tape deck and settle back to enjoy the instant replay, but nothing; I wind the tape forward, flip it over, push play again, still nothing at all, only the hiss of white noise of an empty tape and I realise with dismay that I must have forgotten to switch the recorder on!

The Doctor is keeping Judy in over the next five days, which is a relief for her; she's human after all; not quite sure what hit her and she needs time to recover her strength. They won't release her anyway until we have a name for our baby boy, and we are having trouble coming up with one.

Staff smoke on the ward, dropping their ash everywhere and on the first morning round after giving birth, the midwife hands Judy the wrong baby to breast feed! Judy only belatedly realising because his tiny cotton booties aren't the yellow ones Sabine knitted him. Sabine is the *madrina*, the godmother and rushes down from Florence to be with us.

Twice a day, crowds gather outside the crèche windows impatiently waiting for the clattering venetian blinds to be raised, revealing the single row of cots in front and a row of incubators parked behind them.

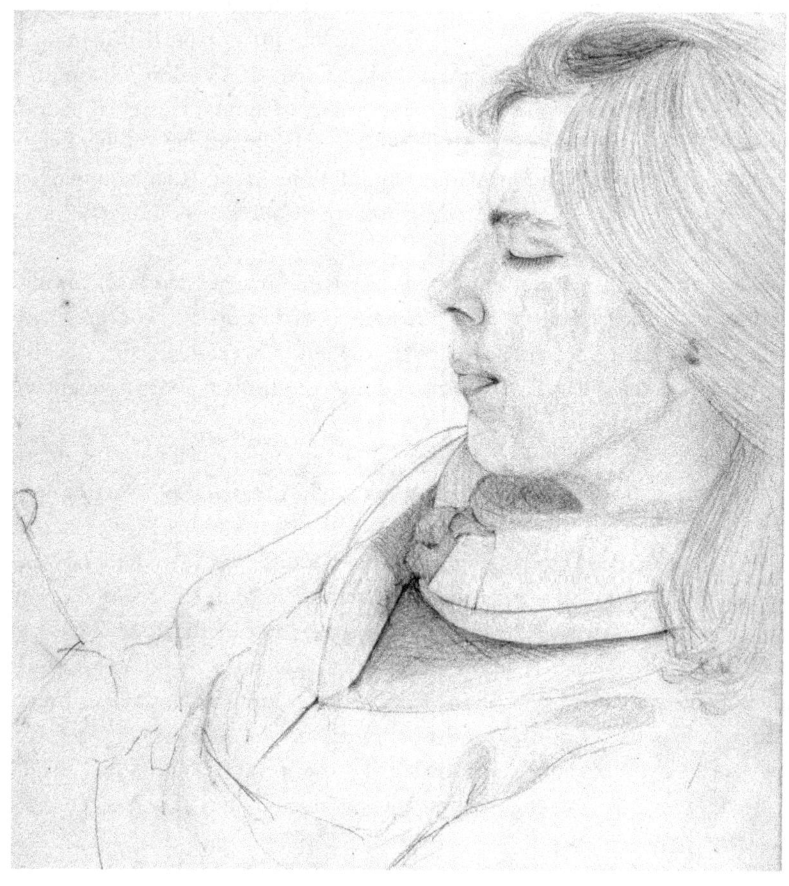

Antonia.1978

Little mites, what a welcome to our world! Hoisted shoulder high by burly nurses to be displayed to the delirious crowd on the other side of the divide, like a trophy on cup final day. Boys are dressed in blue, girls are in pink, the

traditional colours, like the large sash bows tied to the front door knockers of every household after each birth, announcing to the world if it's a boy or a girl. We are only at the beginning of June and already Dr. Migliorini is hailing 1988 as a year for the boys.

At the eleventh hour my cousin Antonia in London has come up with the perfect name: Cosmo. She is an art historian and informs us that the name is of Scottish-Italian descent; adapted by the Duke of Gordon in honour of his good friend Cosimo de Medici. And being a Gemini, Cosmo is also one of the Roman twins of that constellation, so it really ties in not only country wise but the bit of a hippy name, until I pointed out that another Scot, Cosmo Lang, was also an Archbishop of Canterbury in the nineteen twenties.

Six months later, Judy and I are taking Cosmo to Scotland for three months where we have rented a house in East Linton, to be nearer to my deteriorating father. Sue has given birth to Kelly, a healthy girl, so I now have a baby step sister who will be Cosmo's aunt even though she is younger than him by two months. Pa is now
undergoing chemotherapy treatment: the last resort according to the doctors who on top of everything else are pumping him full of rat poison to thin the blood and aid his poor circulation.

It is a tremendous shock seeing him now; a different man; he looks like a sad Humpty Dumpty waiting for the fall and no amount of love in the world will put him back together again. At least he gets out for a stroll now and again, leaning on his silver knobbed walking cane and sometimes we shuffle down to the pub at the end of the road, where, sitting up at the bar drinking shandy he laughs about the taxi driver taking him to the hospital when Kelly was born, congratulating him on being the proud grandfather! And is amused by the people he knows who pass him in the street failing to recognise him.

Antonia.1979

Cosmo and baby Kelly receive very little of his attention. Yet I remember him well when I was a child, encouraging me to use the side of the bath as a water slide, or fooling around on the bed tickling me until I am in fits of laughter. The lightness of his touch then; in our rough and tumble games; now no more than a half-hearted pawing with his daughter and grandson propped up on his lap, only there for the duration of a family snap.

Pa has been a practicing Christian all his life, dragging me to church with him while he had the power, yet I see the fear in his eyes now, visiting him in his hospital bed during a minor crisis, clutching onto his St. James' Bible as if he's been shipwrecked and it's his only hope of survival.

A parade of his old friends and business associates passes through the flat, sitting with hushed tones over tea; almost a wake, with sombre and solicitous looks. My father's false bravura still making plans for the future.

Chapter 37.

The Valdichiana at one time was a malaria-infested marsh: Chiana is an Etruscan word meaning "marsh"; flooded by the river Arno to the North, extending all the way to Chiusi in the South. Since the twelfth century, numerous attempts have been made to drain the marshes; Leonardo drew maps of the Valdichiana in the early 1500s as part of one such project that never got off the ground and it wasn't until the 18th century that the *bonifica* (the reclamation of the land) was finally achieved during the reign of the Grand Duke of Tuscany, Leopoldo II; hence the name of the farmhouses, commissioned by the Duke in recognition of the engineering feat, consisting of a vast network of heaped earth canals that still criss cross the plain.

From Lucignano to Cortona there are three possible routes and whichever way you go it's an easy thirty-minute drive. The agricultural heartland of the Chiana is a vast rumpled landscape of ploughed red earth, the tractors keeling like trawlers at sea with flocks of seagulls wheeling in attendance. In summer, the combine harvesters line up five abreast spewing out grain into attendant tipper trucks, or you might be greeted by mile upon mile of sunflowers, their heads rotating with the sun until bowed and blackened at the end. The landscape across the Chiana is dotted by the distinctive Leopoldine farmhouses, with their characteristic blunt central dovecote towers. According to Martin, swallows were encouraged to nest in the eaves, providing the *contadini* with an extra source of protein.

The Valdichiana is well known as a food bowl, but a thirsty cash crop with a quick turnover like tobacco has been taking over, soaking up water resources at an alarming rate as well as depleting the nitrogen in the soil through a lack of rotation thus leaving the fields sterile after only a few seasons. Overhead sprinklers and linear irrigation systems are a common sight, spurting out massive amounts of water and causing a steady drop in the water table as a result. The artesian well at the end of our drive has been dry since we moved in and the Southerns recently hired a water diviner, as people frequently do in these parts, to pin point where to sink a bore on their land, but in the end, they couldn't afford to drill down deep enough to reach the water table. Nobody harvests rain water from their roof and water just pours out of our down pipes spilling onto the ground.

Fortunately, our water supply comes from the privately owned Consorzio di bonifica via the *aquedotto* and is the same mineral water that people in Lucignano line up for at the drinking taps by the public gardens, often bringing with them crates of empty bottles to fill up.

Tuscany is now officially in drought and water restrictions are in force in Lucignano, which does not include us because we are not on mains water. At the height of summer Judy can spend up to three hours a day watering, split into two shifts: early morning and evenings, a labour of time due mainly to our feeble water pressure, which is gravity fed from three asbestos holding tanks sitting on a platform under the roof of the house in one of the back rooms.

Judy's garden has grown exponentially since we moved in and her obvious passion and good eye have even won over her initial detractors: Cassagni, the farm manager for one, but Italians in general, ever sceptical on seeing the flower beds along the house's perimeter. I think it was the tulips in full bloom that first brought Cassagni round to her way of thinking; he couldn't believe a Tulip could be black, and showed a child's delight in the discovery. His change of heart has brought another benefit with it; instead of the tractors accessing the fields via the garden between the *orto* and the house, thereby trampling on her borders and ripping up my lawn, he is proposing to create another route into the fields around the back of the garage next to the *forno* thus avoiding the garden all together.

Shelley was round last week and he blew his top with Judy because she was watering the orto, claiming Vicky was unable to water her garden as a result. Normally he is docile and disengaged but becoming so irate I had to ask him to leave and Judy swears she will never speak to him again.

Shelley and his neighbour across the road, the Milanese Todisco, share the same water line with us and recently we have been having issues with the reliability of the water supply. The water comes to us first from a junction at the top of the road then branches down to them. The amount is regulated by a valve that is housed in a manhole at the foot of our stairs. Our supply is supposed to be calibrated, drip fed into our tanks at the rate of one litre every eighty-four seconds, which equates to around a thousand litres a day. Unfortunately, the supply has proven to be erratic, sometimes nothing comes in sometimes only a dribble.

Judy is acutely aware of running our tanks dry and is forever dashing up and down the stairs from the garden to the piano room at the back of the house, standing under the platform where the tanks are housed and listening intently for the soothing tell-tale soosh-soosh of the water when it's flowing in normally or the intensely annoying plonk-plonk drip if it is only intermittent. I am then called on: out of my studio to scale the heights up to the platform, equipped with my torch, litre bottle and stop watch in order to check on the levels and if necessary, measure the flow. The metal ladder Vicky gifted us when we first came, just reaches the lip of the mezzanine platform if I place it almost perpendicular to the floor: it's about nine feet from the ground and quite a skill to squirm up without tipping it back, considering nobody is holding it for me. Judy will be waiting impatiently for me downstairs outside the window waiting for the news. "Yeees! Jude, can you hear me?" I shout from under the roof. "Water is only dribbling in and the tanks are down to about a quarter full." I can confirm.

Getting back down the ladder is even more dangerous than going up, sliding backwards on my stomach off the ledge first then jack-knifing onto the ladder, with my feet hoping to land on a rung.

Judy, fed up with the whole situation, has been nagging me to get the water problem sorted once and for all, but not knowing what to do and equally sick of the problem disturbing my studio time, especially now with the advent of Cosmo nibbling away even more of my precious time, I've decided to take matters into my own hands. Notwithstanding Cassagni's dire warnings NEVER to fiddle with the valve in the manhole at the foot of the staircase, I eagerly pull aside the heavy metal plate cover and on my stomach with a spanner in hand find the old rusty valve easily turns. Then for the first time ever, I can hear the water gushing into our tanks, not squirting but with an almighty wooshing: balm to my ears, and in my mind without really thinking it through, it seems like the problem is finally sorted.

The next morning however, Cassagni and an irate Todisco suddenly appear at the kitchen door while I have Cosmo on his back on the kitchen table, changing his nappy.

"*Bel prodotto*! (Nice work)," remarks Todisco as he comes in, leaving his Husky dog at the door, then launching into his tirade, accusing me of being a water thief. His water has run dry and he was in the middle of filling his swimming pool! In hindsight I realise there would obviously be consequences for my actions: if we are getting more water, then it stands to reason the others would be getting less. Cassagni isn't too pleased either, giving me dagger looks across the kitchen table, but Judy, she consistently surprises me, far from being cowed, is quick to get on the front foot and throw the accusations back into Todisco's face! In Italian too! "So where's all the water been going to before when we weren't getting any?" She says furious. "Barring an underground leak, it must have been going to you, because Vicky wasn't getting it either."

Cassagni, exasperated by the whole business, declares he's had enough and is sending in the Farnetani brothers to fix the problem: three brothers who have the contract to do all the plumbing and electrical work on the farm. They roar up the drive in their beat-up white Ducato van three days later. This isn't the first time we have encountered the Farnetani brothers. They were over once to fix the outside light above the stair well. It is too high up under the eaves of the house for me to reach there and a quick solution for them: park the van underneath, prop the ladder up from the roof, climb up and break the glass housing with a broomstick (because it wouldn't unscrew) and change the bulb (but leave the smashed housing in place). Unfortunately, the light blew again not long afterwards, and now I warn friends leaving the house in the dark that there are exactly fourteen steps to reach the bottom. I counted them, and to be absolutely sure, tested it myself by running down them with my eyes shut.

The Farnetanis arrive like a typhoon, conducting their usual whirlwind inspection of the scene and after the briefest of confabs set to work, grabbing their tools and rolls of pipe out of the tangled heap of equipment and materials in the back of the Ducato. According to them, all the old iron pipes will need replacing, which fortunately are easily accessible, being bracketed onto the outside of the walls, similar to the electrical wiring.

The brothers hustle about the house in a curious choreography of activity, shouting instructions through walls, hammering, ripping out, drilling, replacing, and are happy to show me the old pipes which they have rightly surmised, are rusted inside and choked with calcium deposits, obviously obstructing the flow of the water. When everything seems to be in order again and the valve recalibrated, the brothers depart in a flurry, chucking their tools back into the Ducato and slamming the doors, pleased with a job well done; leaving behind them, piles of rubble loosely swept into room corners and the butts of their cigarettes ground out on our floor tiles!

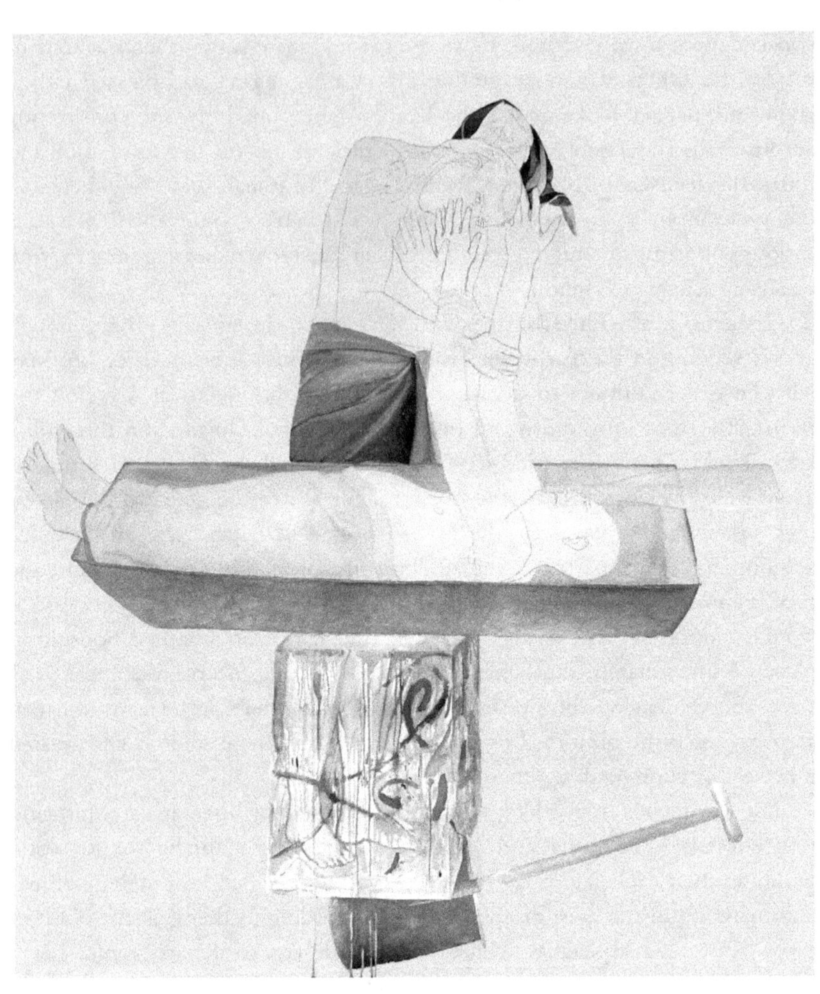

My father my son.1990

Chapter 38.

I knew as soon as I woke up that you must be close to death, a dream indelibly etched onto the back of my eyelids: the domed inky sky full of stars, the multi coloured laser lights on the polished marble slabs of a space-age cemetery. I am led into a room off to one side of the complex and you are there, sitting on a rug on the floor beside me, smiling, looking your old svelte self, healthy, buoyant, confident, and I feel so happy to know that you are well again.My father had already been moved from home to the hospice in Granton, ostensibly to give Sue a respite, but by the time I arrived in Edinburgh with my mother he had slipped into a coma. We were by his bedside when he briefly regained consciousness a few days later, opening his eyes, yellow eyes drowning in morphine, a supreme moment though, stretching his arms skywards calling out Schnirpi, his endearment for her, Ma bending over him mopping his brow as she took his hands, then turning his head sideways on the pillow and raising himself slightly, he looked right at me, arching both eyebrows imperceptibly, as if he was mildly surprised but glad to see me there, before sinking back into the pillow and the land of the dead.

He died two days later on July the fourth, Independence Day! Ma had already returned to London; the Doctors saying there was no telling how long he would last, and so I was with Sue in the immediate aftermath. I broke down completely seeing him laid out in the sanctuary, so still, one arm resting above the turned down satin bed cover. The same room I'd seen people staggering out of in huddles, not fully comprehending what they had just seen. I groped his bare arm, kissing it uncontrollably, the sight of his inert face overwhelming me, but strangely comforting too, as if seeing his body so completely drained of him, his life force: Douglas George MacDonald, could only mean he had gone some other place.

After, Sue and I sat at the top of Arthur's Seat overlooking Edinburgh, watching the flash of silver suns racing across the firth of Forth as we polished off a bottle of his best single malt whiskey, drinking to his memory while doing our utmost to drown our own thoughts. I don't think I have ever been so drunk driving a car, wending my way back to the flat through the streets of Edinburgh with Sue freaking out because there was a cop car tagging along behind us! Except there was no way I was going to end this night of all nights in a cell, not on the day of my father's passing.

I wanted to deliver the oratory at the funeral but the deacon advised against it; he said close family members don't usually make it through to the end and so he took on the responsibility himself, even though he didn't know my father. Listening to him at the pulpit, I should have insisted I chide myself, although I know in the end, I was relieved at being given an out. The church was packed, which was gratifying and after the service I moved to stand at the door to greet the mourners as they exited the church but Ma hustled me away, she didn't want to see anyone, which led to quite a few of my father's friends scrambling down the path after us to offer their condolences.

One man stopped on the pavement and doffed his cap as the cortege passed on its way to my father's final resting place in Broughty ferry, also his birthplace.

Judy didn't attend the funeral because she is pregnant again at five months and expecting in December, so we both agreed it would be better for her to stay at home with Cosmo. Taking into consideration our age: Judy is thirty-nine and I am thirty-six, we thought having two children close together would help us energy wise, since growing up together they will need less looking after and start entertaining themselves; being older only compensates so much in comparison to having children at a younger age. Apart from Sabine, there is no one we can depend on to help either, except perhaps Marina, who we can now count on as one of our closer friends! Judy gracefully buried the hatchet and gave peace a chance, helped no doubt by the appearance soon after of Enzo, Marina's new boyfriend and the fact that they are now an established couple and living together.

Sabine adores Cosmo and takes her role as *madrina* very seriously, knitting him jumpers in all the latest yarns and coming down to see us as often as her time allows. Judy's parents flew over from Australia almost as soon as Cosmo was born, providing relief for a short spell, and later, Ma arrived bearing bach remedies and blessings but she will never be like Judy's mum Vivienne, who took command of the household, cooking, sewing, washing cloth nappies, things my mother would never do. Judy is disappointed with my Mum but I say let her meditate or practice her alternative therapy on us instead. She has been in Ireland studying Alignment therapy under a New Age Master: a new therapy designed to trace and release energy blockages in the body by realigning our energy fields. I lie down flat on the kitchen table, fully clothed while she moves her palms above my body, hovering but not touching. I can feel an intense heat emanating from her hands even through my clothes.

This time round we know our baby will be a boy and are already prepared with a name. I want to call him Toto although Judy insists, we at least register him officially as Taddeo, which she feels has more gravitas. I reluctantly agree but can't help thinking about the history of my own name and also how patterns keep repeating themselves: Kelly for instance, my step sister, will grow up never knowing her real father just as I never knew my own.

Dr. Migliorini is the hero of our hour, obligingly taking Judy under his wing for a second time. Judy feels reassured in his hands, even if he is old-fashioned and has a clipped, slightly cocky manner that brooks no contradicting. I know we intrigue him with our "bohemian" lifestyle: his wife kicking off her shoes at our place when they came for lunch after Cosmo was born, wiggling her toes in the grass with pure delight, genuinely thrilled to go barefoot as if it was some kind of forbidden fruit.

Dr. Migliorini still talks up Judy's reputation at the hospital: those heroic Australian women, winking at me; and has asked Judy as a special favour to allow his wife to be present at Toto's birth, so keen is he for her to witness the phenomena. He warned us it could be quicker this time round, so Judy has erred on the side of caution and we arrive at Montevarchi hospital early in the morning only to be sent home again two hours later with the good doctor declaring a false alarm. Judy in the winter sunshine, looking lovely, carrying herself in a long flowing blue skirt and loose cardigan, casually picking wild flowers by the road side on the way home, only to be rushing back to the hospital later that same afternoon, just in time for her encore to the assembled company as we now have a second gorgeous son born on Christmas Eve: Toto, aka Taddeo MacDonald.

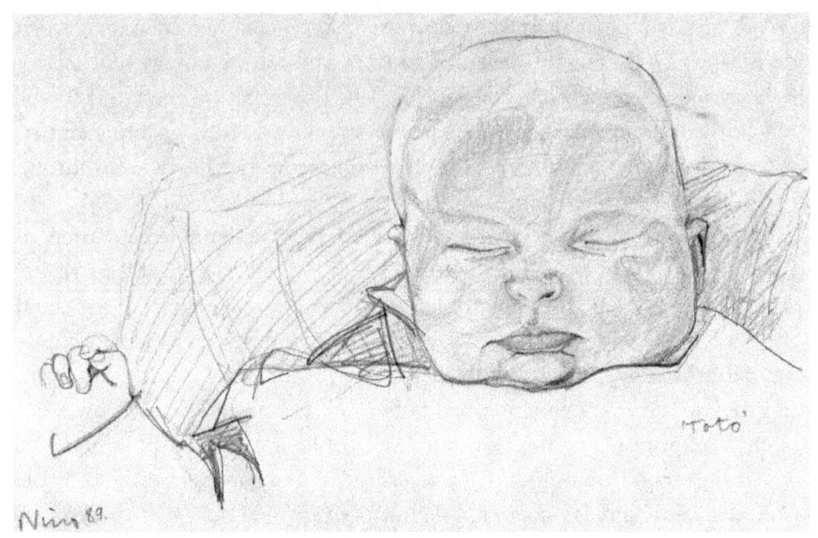

Toto.1989

Chapter 39.

Unfortunately, the Farnetani brothers' solution to our water problems proved to be short lived, and we are crossing swords with Todisco again. He frequently drops by complaining, demanding I go and measure the water, or brings Perugine with him, the ex-mayor of Lucignano, a plumber by trade, to do the measuring for him! Todisco is a good friend of my landlord Mozzoni so I have to be extra careful about how I deal with him, always mindful of maintaining the status quo with the farm, especially as the rent has remained unchanged for the past five years and the lease, according to Cassagni, is being automatically rolled over at the end of each year. Cassagni seems happy with our arrangement and presumably Mozzoni too, but you never can tell with him, he remains an enigma who I very rarely see and never have occasion to speak to.

Finally, with no solution in sight, Todisco decides to take matters into his own hands by excavating for a new pipeline to his place along the side of the strada bianca, bypassing Poggio Spinoso altogether but joining up with Rocchetto. Vicky isn't too pleased with the arrangement, she doesn't trust Todisco, but Shelley and Todisco are good mates.

At last we can all breathe easy; everyone is getting their rightful share of water and peace has been restored to the neighbourhood. In fact neighbourly relations with Todisco have greatly improved as a result and we are even invited over to swim in the pool or for the occasional lunch, much to the relief of mutual friends like Marina and Linda her neighbour, an American artist, who have had to straddle both camps for the duration of our struggles.

It turns out that Todisco is an engaging and entertaining character once you find yourself on the right side of him. A retired, award-winning environmental journalist, who in his later years has turned his hand to writing pot boilers, or romantic novels as he likes to call them, sporting suggestive titles such as *L'Alba delle Passioni* (Dawn of the Passions) or *La Bambinaia* (The Nanny) that are actually rehashes dressed up as fiction of his various torrid affairs with a succession of younger women.

With his trademark cheeky grin, he is still a regular guest on the Maurizio Costanza's talk show on national TV and appears across the networks. People recognise him in the street as I found out:

"Look! Isn't that Todisco?" I overheard one woman whisper to her friend pointing, as we were strolling down via Nazionale in Cortona together; although she didn't quite pluck up the courage to ask him for his autograph.

For two years running Shelley and I have been elevated alongside Todisco to the status of a VIP if you can believe what the local press are saying about us:

"*VIPS ON HOLIDAY CHOOSE LUCIGNANO*" ran the headline in *La Nazione* last year:

"*...The English sculptor (sic) Nino Mac Donald, who has found success and admiration in Italy...*"

"SO MANY VIPS ON HOLIDAY!" Screamed the headline this year: "For years now the well known German (sic) painter Nino MacDonald has made his home in Lucignano ..."

One day a sculptor, the next year a painter and I love the inference that I am on holiday; that old chestnut that being an artist is not a real job. Judy once had the cheek to label me "a Sunday painter" because I wasn't selling any work and when things go wrong between us I dig into my studio and conduct trench warfare, as we lob insults at each other across the way. Occasionally I can claim an outright victory as for example the day Gisela, a German neighbour (who my father had offended that Christmas at Vicky's) and her son Patrick, call in to the studio and decide to buy two large paintings! She bought Passage of Rtes and Patrick chose "Life line": one of a series of works I painted during my father's illness that, like Passage of Rights, was inspired by the Indian journey Judy and I undertook when reconciling the year before. Lifeline shows a turbaned man standing on the prow of a catamaran fishing boat throwing out a lifebuoy even though the boat is about to run aground on the beach.

Gisela kept quizzing her son. "Darling are you sure you can afford this?"

I'm trying to feign disinterest, fingers crossed behind my back, hoping she'll be quiet and let Patrick, hardly out of school, get on with it.

I have made the rounds of the galleries in London and Edinburgh, Milan and Rome, hawking my portfolio. Ideally, I would prefer galleries to come to my studio to see my work but in my experience that it is almost an impossibility and one of the few hasndycaps of living in rural Tuscany. A portfolio of photos is indispensable and whenever I have three or four new paintings, my friend Gianni, an architect from Arezzo and a keen photographer, will come down to photograph them with his professional Pentax format camera, yielding excellent quality 5x4inch colour transparencies. I first met Gianni at a lunch time gathering he was holding for his Aretini friends; a close-knit group of men who like Gianni, I have since discovered are fiercely partisan when it comes to their place of birth: identifying more with the Casentino, the rugged hilly bandit country north of Arezzo, as opposed to the rather gentler Valdichiana to the South.

You can picture the scene in Gianni's den, his drafting table pushed to one side; the guys standing around with a glass of red wine and passing the joint around, bantering to and fro with that familiar ease of old-old friends' talk. I was feeling distinctly the odd man out, hardly knowing anyone at the time, while Claire, Gianni's English wife and the other wives/girlfriends, rolling joints of their own (not Judy though) are down the hall in the kitchen preparing lunch and seeing to the children! Gianni is the consummate Italian professional: handsome with his long dark hair neatly parted down the middle and swept back in an arch: the self-assured looks, the *simpatico* easy-going smile, ironed white shirts and pressed jeans with calf skin loafers on.

My paintings are universally large so we whack them up outside on the garage door and photograph them in the available light. I have always felt photographs never do the paintings justice which, paradoxically can also work the other way, as I found out with the exhibition in Munich. Tante Eliette loves to show photos of my work to anyone who wants to look and amazingly, her cold calling Galerie Neuhausen on a trip to Munich, resulted in getting me a show; only once he saw them, the gallery owner took a dislike to my paintings and it became an unmitigated disaster. He would have cancelled the show if it was not for Lorenz, the fashion photographer I used to work for in London and who I was staying with, paying the guy to ensure it went ahead. Invitations had already been sent and my father and my grandmother, my aunt and others were already coming to the opening. Knowing my father would be there I deliberately had not invited my mother, which created huge problems in itself, but only because this was the first opportunity I had of seeing him on his own since their separation.

Nothing sold, which was hardly surprising considering the lengths the gallery owner went to distance himself from the exhibition, refusing to invite press, then sulking behind the bar he had set up in a corner of the gallery and going so far as to charge everyone for their drinks on the opening night. It was humiliating and I only saved face after my father stepped in insisting on paying for all our drinks!

Chapter 40.

Cortona promotes itself to the world as *La Citta d'arte* and as part of its cultural patrimony can boast Gino Severini's impressive mosaic: the twelve stations of the cross on Via Crucis as well as Fra Angelico's beautiful Annunciation of Cortona on display in the Diocesan museum. More broadly, since the Renaissance, the visual arts in Tuscany have remained an integral part of mainstream popular culture and in Cortona, local artists are well supported by the Cortonesi. Most households will have one or two original works of art on their walls, and bars and restaurants are always hanging works by local artists.

A case in point was Roberto, who I encountered in my early days living in Cortona, better known as Roberto Di Milano: an alcoholic, quasi destitute painter (since passed away from alcohol poisoning), who regularly haunted the bars along the ruga piana at night, selling his work while progressively getting blind drunk; a sad, gaunt figure with wild darting eyes, muttering incomprehensibly: dressed in a threadbare gabardine coat with a black artists' beret on; hawking a stack of small oil paintings secured under one arm, the paint hardly dry; paintings that in my mind were either the childish drunken scrawls of an alcoholic or the works of an unheralded genius. He would never tarry too long; he had purpose and must be moving on; standing at the bar, just time to down a glass or two of wine and sell a couple of paintings, which he did with surprising ease, often for as little as twelve thousand lire or the cost of a drink.

Club Gino Severini, where I held my first solo exhibition has long since closed its doors; Roberto decided it was too much work and Enzo went on to open a small private gallery opposite Bar Signorelli, which he rents out when he is not exhibiting his own work, and is very popular judging by the number of artists lining up to have exhibitions there, including Bob.

This year, Comune intransigence over offering local artists a place to exhibit has finally been broken, shamed by the success last year of an exhibition put on by a motley crew of eleven local artists including Marina and myself at Palazzo Vagnotti; under the banner of a new cultural association called La Sfinge (the sphinx). It was set up by Roberto and his friend Giandomenico, a popular high school teacher universally known as *Professore*. You will often catch them walking lock step through Cortona deep in talk-talk: Giandomenico taller than Roberto, postures instinctively, the full moustache, the pipe, the racy pastel sports hats worn at a jaunty angle, smiling, one hand loosely balled behind his back, or gracing his chin deep in thought, listening to what Roberto has to say before responding.

Roberto, sceptical by nature but also diplomatic, nevertheless feels vindicated by his success and gloats:

"After all these years, Alfredo our culture tzar, has suddenly realised he can wash his hands completely of the thorny issue of exhibiting local artists by letting us do the job for him! He is offering us Palazzo Casali and has even agreed to pay the printing costs of the invitations and perhaps a poster."

There is no Sfingism involved in the Sfinge: no manifesto, just an ad hoc group of local artists keen to show their work. The name itself derives from the statue unearthed at the Etruscan tomb in Sodo, where Roberto: painter, poet and also archeologist was one of the supervisors on the dig. You can visit the tomb with the sphinx in situ if you manage to rouse the old caretaker who lives nearby and has the keys; you need to ask her politely to take you down to the site and unlock the gate for you, she, no doubt dropping hints along the way that no-one is paying her for the service!

I will be sorry to see Lilly excluded from the exhibition this year, our newspaper cub reporter and probably the only living Goth in Cortona; she stands out with her lacy tops and torn jeans, jet black hair, black lipstick and black nail polish. As an artists' collective we have been pleasingly anarchic so far, without recourse to a selection criteria for our exhibitions but decided rather on a first come first served basis. Perhaps this year, now that we are under the auspices of the Comune for the first time, we are experiencing something akin to a dose of gravitas and Lilly unfortunately has been caught in the net; the victim of a whispering campaign conducted behind her back, as the novelty of her naive paintings of mermaids and sunsets suddenly seem undercooked.

1992 is shaping up as a busy year for me; besides exhibiting with the Sfinge in Cortona, I am having a show in London, in the windows of the Harvey Nichols department store, a stone throw from Harrods. My cousin Antonia, who now works as a curator of sculpture at the Victorian and

Albert Museum approached the store on my behalf, with a proposal to exhibit, to which they readily agreed, much to my surprise and delight. Doors opening! The reasoning behind the idea was simple: if the Mountain won't go to Mohammed, then Mohammed must come to the Mountain; if I can't get galleries to come to me to see my work, I will have to take my work to them. Harvey Nichols has a strong reputation for innovative window displays, so where better a place to showcase my paintings? Right in the middle of London, on public view for two weeks, twenty-four hours a day!

I will have to organise the transportation of the twelve large paintings going there, which is no easy logistical matter and I rue the fact that no gallery is going to turn up at my door with a truck and do it all for me! I have been down to the lumberyard and am in the process of constructing three large boxes each measuring 2000 mm x 1700 mm x 20 mm deep, that will weigh a ton when they are completed and packed. In Italy legally exporting works of art requires a licence, which in my case means crating the works and transporting them to the Belle Arti (The Ministry of Culture) in Siena, where each painting is unpacked and inspected before the crates are sealed again with the official lead seals of approval. The rationale is an attempt by the Italian government to stem the flow of stolen artefacts leaving the country. As if an art thief is going to apply for an export licence. In order to save me a lot of bother, I certainly didn't for my exhibition in Munich! I thought I was being so clever reserving a first-class sleeper and taking the paintings with me on the train, even bribing the attendant not to stow the paintings in the luggage compartment. All went to plan except I was spotted by German customs offloading the works onto the platform in Munich and subsequently detained by customs officers threatening to impound the paintings unless I paid the import duty.

I drove up to Munich with Judy to bring the paintings back in my car and going through customs, covered the paintings with a tarp, placing two camping chairs on top; surmising correctly that the custom's officer would see us as just another couple of tourists going on a camping holiday.

MISSING!

HAVE YOU SEEN THIS PAINTING?

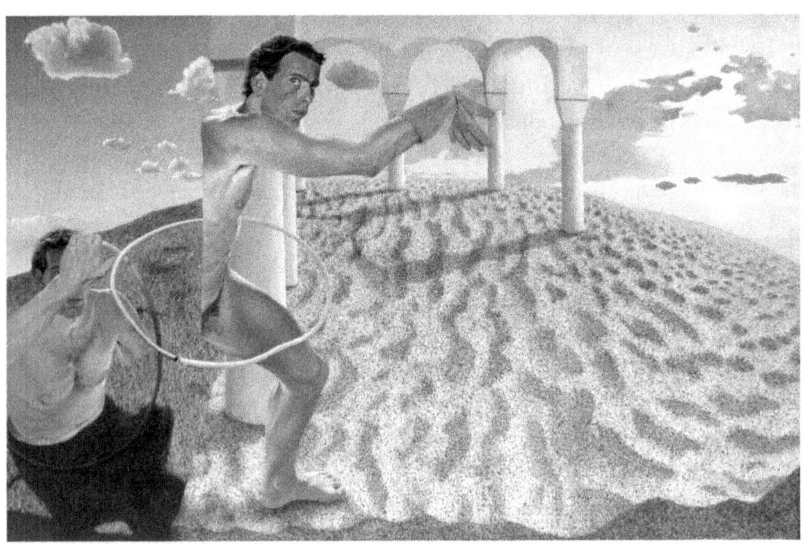

Heaven's Rush.1979

REWARD OFFERED. LAST SEEN IN MUNICH CIRCA 1985

Chapter 41.

Judy and I are woken by the unusual sound of gunshots ringing out in the dead of night. Our first thought is what on earth would anybody be shooting at in the dark? Then, has somebody been murdered? Judy is an avid reader of the crime reports in the newspapers. The next morning, armed Forestieri rangers knock on the door and explain that poachers have been seen operating on Mozzoni's land and seeking our permission to set up a stakeout for the night in our garage. I didn't think to ask what could be poached at night but I do marvel at Mozzoni's clout, turning a government militia into his own private force. After an uneventful night the Forestieri, tired and disappointed, leave empty handed the next morning; the poachers long gone whoever they are.

People are always showing up at the house unannounced: that's part of country life! They come asking for directions, or can we use your phone our car has broken down. Gunilla (her name meaning 'Battle Maiden') regularly charges up the drive on foot chasing after Bugsy, her new black pug dog, without so much as a hello or a goodbye. For reasons unknown, whenever Bugsy, trailing his lead behind him, escapes from home he makes a bee-line straight for Judy's garden and pees all over Judy's plants.

A complete stranger startled me in the bath once when nobody else was at home; having a bath in the middle of the day is one of my secret pleasures. I was amazed to see a hand first, then an arm then a female head appears round the half open bathroom door and so was she; startled to see a face staring back at her. She recovered remarkably quickly, enquiring innocently if this was the *agriturismo* (farm stay) she had been given directions to from the village? I said no and by the time I managed to climb out and wrap a towel around my waist and follow her, she was already half way down the drive in the company of another lady, I noticed, watching them from the kids' bedroom window. A quick round of the house and I realised too late a much cherished silver christening cup had disappeared: a gift from my grandmother with Nino engraved on it in her very distinctive hand writing style.

On one occasion a pensioner couple drove up in their camper-van and casual as you like proceeded to set up their picnic table and bring out their lunch under the massive evergreen holm-oak tree; claiming they thought the house was abandoned when I stormed out across the piazza to confront them! (Like an indignant Englishman defending his castle). The notion of trespass is still an alien concept to the Italian mind.

One morning on another occasion, a car raced up the drive and five men bailed out and disappeared behind the *forno* (pizza oven) without so much as a shout of "*permesso*". I was painting on the kitchen balcony at the time and saw them arrive; really annoyed, I rushed down to confront them brandishing a paintbrush, wearing only my shorts and turning the corner round the *forno* found them standing in a huddle together on the bank above the field, deep in conversation; I was made to look a fool as they largely ignored my protestations and ever since then, with one of the men, whenever we pass each other in the car we will glower at each other.

I found out later from Cassagni that they were the committee of the local hunting club and were there deciding on the boundary for a new no hunting zone around Poggio Spinoso: something actually in our favour. Periodically areas are placed out of bounds to the hunters for up to two or three years, in order to give the wild life a chance to recover (sic) from the annual onslaught. Vicky says Mozzoni only acquired the fields around Poggio Spinoso and Rocchetto as a quid pro quo to the hunters, allowing them to hunt there and hoping to keep them at arm's length from Campo Forte, which he regards as his own private hunting reserve, although the reality is that hunters will go wherever they please. In previous years I have had to watch as the hunters set up their camouflaged hides on the edge of the fields facing the woods below the house, blasting away at anything that flew out.

Silvini, the retired farm *muratore* turns up at Poggio Spinoso whenever he damn well feels like it, usually on a Sunday, which really irritates the hell out of me; there to pick up building materials he has stashed away in one of the *cantinas* under the house and more often than not we will end up in an argument. Vicky had the same problems with him storing stuff in her cantina but eventually managed to get him out. I swagger, threatening to throw him off the property and he tells me to fuck off I don't have the right. Jef happened to be staying the last time there was a confrontation, and he called Silvini "*un maleducato*" (impolite) which was hilarious considering the heat of the argument and how Silvini swears like a trooper. Ma took pity on him though when he was tiling our bathroom and putting in the new bath: she was sleeping in the guest room next door and had to put up with his constant cussing as she attempted to meditate. Judy wasn't so forgiving, insisting he redo some of the shoddy tiling work around the shower recess after I had refused to call him out on it.

Jef is back from London with Marina and their son Martin, and they are living in Milan now. He decided to turn down a big promotion to New York with the ABC and came back to Italy for Marina's sake because she was feeling homesick and missing her family.

"Hell! At my stage of life, I'll take being a big fish in a small pond." He moots, papering over his initial disappointment, but in recompense he has landed a great new job at Canale 5, one of Italy's top commercial TV stations, producing his own current affairs program: Monitor.

Martin, Cosmo and Toto go out into the fields together to play. Martin is leading being the older by a couple of years, and encourages them to tip a big cylindrical hay bale down the hill! Jef and I are sitting on the kitchen balcony watching with mounting horror and left furiously gesticulating and shouting as we realise what is about to transpire, yet helpless to intervene because we are too far away. The bale picks up speed and actually flies over the *strada bianca* into the field on the other side!

Right on cue, here comes Fernardo, one of the farm workers, driving his cinquecento and only missing the bale by a few seconds. Boy am I in the doghouse with Fernando after that one and so are my kids, although Martin the innocent remains Jef's baby boy and can do no wrong. I suspect Jef is a soft touch and Martin needs his mother Marina to keep him in order.

Campo Forte is regimented like an army with Mozzoni as the commander in chief, Cassagni the faithful lieutenant and Fernando the trusted sergeant in the field; vestiges of *mezzadria*, the system of sharecropping that has existed in Tuscany since the Middle Ages and was only finally dismantled by law in 1982. However, culturally ingrained, Mozzoni is still a *padrone* and some of the *contadini* still doff their caps to him.

Under *mezzadria*, landowners exercised an absolute power over the contadini who were landless and treated as serfs. Crops were tithed and it was strictly forbidden for them to sell any surpluses. Housing was at the discretion of the padrone and as unsecured tenants, the contadini lived under the constant threat of eviction. Just to survive, homeless contadini often became brigands and as a measure of how exploited the contadini were, they themselves formed militias to protect their padrone's lands from the brigands!

There is a popular *contadino* saying: "better dead as a child than an ox" meaning they could always have more children, but an ox was more valuable to them. It wasn't until after World War II that the *contadini* were finally given title to the land and offered generous loans to stay there by successive governments attempting to stem the drift off the land and into the cities as the Italian economic miracle of the 50s and 60s gathered pace. Mozzoni employs at least eight men on the farm and it's not unusual to see a gang working the land around Poggio Spinoso. Some days there can be as many as five tractors all lined up on the piazza, each with their attendant ploughs, bailers, trailers, tanks. We are the eye of the storm with everything whirling around us, short frenetic bursts of seasonal activity, when Poggio Spinoso becomes a strategic staging post for machinery and farm workers as they marshal in the piazza before fanning out into the fields.

The noise of the farm machinery doesn't bother me either, not like the autostrada does, not even the caterpillar tractor clanking up and down the ridge all day long, with Fernando driving and Giulio standing up behind him, cranking the levers and sowing the fave beans. Not even the roar of the combine harvester as it swoops in at the back of the studio, drowning out my music and whipping up howling gales of dry debris and dust, forcing me to close all the windows. Rather, I feel nostalgic for summer holidays spent in Ayrshire in Scotland, on Uncle John's farm: standing up on the combine harvester beside him, a red polka dot handkerchief tied around his sweaty neck, or Philip, Uncle John's right hand man, tying me up in a sack and sending me back to the main house like a parcel because I had been annoying the men in the yard.

The farm workers no longer shelter in the open space under the house, even lighting fires in there and instead take their breaks sitting under the Holm-oak, or in winter, they stand around a fire built on the piazza, burning off the olive tree pruning's, unless that is I can pilfer them first; the dried leaves and twigs make excellent kindling, crackling and exploding into life on the hearth.

The men are such a noisy rabble: listening to them during their lunch breaks, it never ceases to amaze me how much they still have to say to each other after a life time continuously spent in each other's company; much of it is banter and bluster, shouting over the other to be heard: Madonna this,

Dio lupo that, yet always delivered with passion as if the fate of the world could hinge on every single word.

Cassagni is an odd mixture of old and new. You could easily mistake him for a contadino, (apart from his height and girth) but as the *fattore* (farm manager) he also has a surprisingly corporate bent, always preoccupied with efficiency and the bottom line. He loves to tease me about his plans to turn Poggio Spinoso into holiday appartments and I can never be sure if he isn't half serious!

His attitude to land clearing is: "if you have to go round it, better pull it down!" And if anything, Mozzoni has to rein in his *fattore* in because already having ploughed under the vineyard next to us, he is now threatening to do the same to San Leone, the vineyard opposite Vicky and Shelley.

Occasionally Fernando takes Cosmo, pleased as punch, up into the cab of his tractor when he is cutting the hay, or he hoists Toto into the bucket seat of the parked caterpillar tractor, to play. As a toddler, Cosmo's favourite pastime was pedalling his toy tractor through the hay bale tunnel I had built for him on the piazza, with baby Toto propped up behind him in the little green trailer, both of them watched over attentively by our stray mutt Lila who appeared there one day and simply refused to go away, sitting patiently on bank above the piazza for days on end, until we finally relented and invited her inside.

Chapter 42.

The irony of being a foreigner living in Tuscany is that you automatically stick out at the same time as becoming more invisible. It is a good situation to be in because it allows for a great deal of freedom of movement; there is no great weight of expectation placed on you to conform to local standards, other than to the norms of civil society, because as an outsider you represent no real threat to the status quo.

However, with both Cosmo and Toto attending *asilo* (pre-school) this situation is beginning to change and Judy and I are slowly being reeled in and put under closer scrutiny by the Lucignanese. When we threw Cosmo's first birthday party at home and invited all his school friends, instead of just dropping the kids off and coming back later to pick them up, which would seem to be the norm, parents arrived in droves and stayed all day long, curious to take a good look inside our house and also discover a little bit about how we live!

Initially we spoke English at home but now that the boys are in nursery they are insisting on Italian. It brings a lump to my throat when I think we are bringing up two little Italians! Charming as well because both of them are picking up the local chiana accent. Currently, Judy and I are speaking in English together; the boys speak in Italian; Judy speaks to the boys in English but I am speaking Italian with them, fearing of an ever-widening communications gap between us. Judy is determined to keep the English going even if they only reply to her in Italian.

It is a bizarre coincidence that I have German as my mother tongue but only speak English and talk in Italian to the boys. I can empathise with their situation because it happened to me at their age in exactly the same way when coming to London from Düsseldorf and starting at nursery school. I would only speak in English to my mother who was trying desperately to encourage me to carry on speaking in German with her.

The *asilo* in Pieve Vecchia is on the road to Foiano, half a mile on the other side of Lucignano. It is a nondescript, one-storey 1970s building with wheelchair access, divided into two classrooms with two teachers looking after around twenty kids aged between three and six. In Italy, formal education begins at asilo where the children are taught to read and write in longhand/shorthand and learn rudimentary arithmetic. They are also assigned homework. The weight of the school books they have to carry in their backpacks, back and forth to school everyday, is quite alarming. The school has an impressive, professionally equipped kitchen run by Rita the cook, a crusty old *contadina* with a crone's warty face and a huge heart. She lives just round the corner from the school with her son who is a doctor, in a well-appointed modern villa; a good example of the intergenerational shift in Italian society over the last few decades.

Rita rides on the yellow school bus to the village every morning to buy the meat and fresh fruit and vegetables for the school lunch. Toto's favourite dish is meatballs with salad, and he likes to remind Mamma Judy that nobody cooks *polpetti* quite like Rita does. We have discovered that Giuliano the school bus driver once lived at Poggio Spinoso and his son was born there he tells us. He drives the bus right up to our house because we are the last stop on his school run and the piazza offers him a convenient circle to turn around. Once we offered to give him a quick tour of the house and garden and he declared that apart from the garden nothing much else has changed. He collects the boys at eight-thirty every morning Monday to Saturday; they are there ready and waiting outside, hair combed, smartly dressed in their pressed blue with white collar *grembiule* (school smocks), heavy school packs slung over the shoulders, and he drops them off around three after the siesta at school, sleeping off Rita's lunch. "*Oh Dio*! Cosmo has sniffed a boiled sweet up his nose and it's stuck!" His teacher Ornella, from the *asilo,* cries plaintively down the phone at me, as if it's potentially a life-threatening situation.

I race off to school and we drive to the nearest *Pronto Soccorso* (A&E) in Foiano, five miles away; a small cottage hospital, where a doctor with noticeable alcohol breath and visibly trembling hands tries to dislodge the pea-sized object with a pair of tweezers, but quickly relents, he is shaking too much, declaring we need to see a specialist! Racing across country to the hospital in Arezzo, forty minutes later, the ear, nose and throat specialist with his miners' lamp clamped to his forehead takes one look up Cosmo's nose and announces:

"There's nothing there!" Gently reminding us that sugar melts.Cosmo remains unperturbed throughout the incident, perhaps slightly amused at all the fuss, but he isn't letting on, he keeps things close to his chest. We do have our share of real dramas with both boys suffering from asthma. More serious attacks have landed them in hospital on several occasions. One time saw baby Toto placed in an oxygen tent, looking like a plump Bedouin camped in the middle of the hospital ward and loving the attention. Women (Marina dotes on him) all say Toto has bedroom eyes, oriental like his mother's but with lazy, drooping eyelids.

The boys usually call me Nini although they occasionally let slip Mamma: being so used to having me around the house.

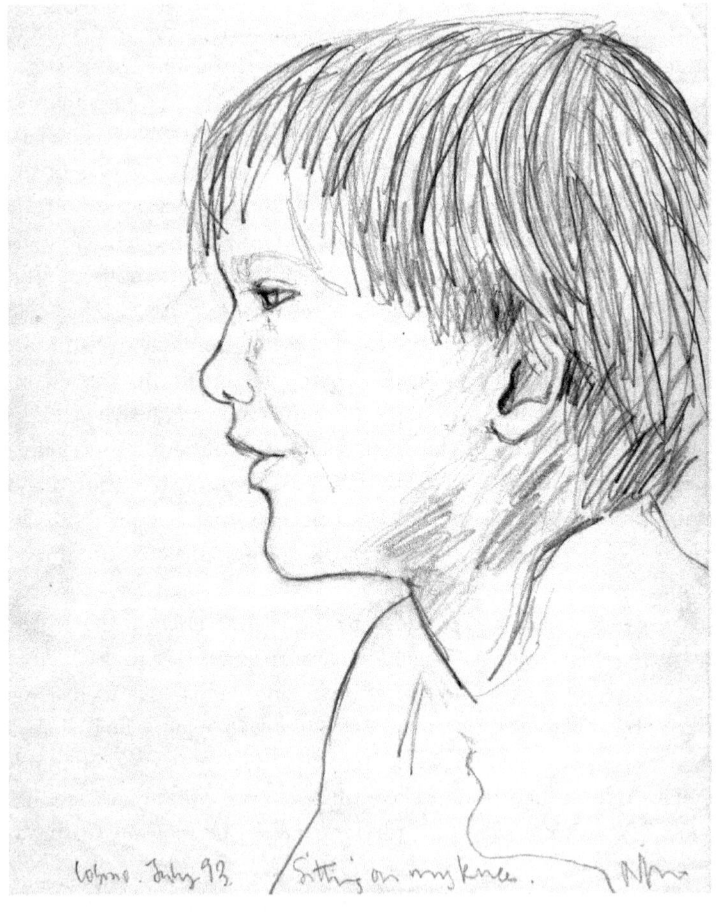

Cosmo.1993

Painting at home means my studio is a revolving door of domestic concerns, so I often work at night when the household has quietened down and I am left alone. I am grumpy in the mornings, at least until I have had my first cup of coffee and smoked a cigarette, waiting for everyone to have left the house before I get up. Judy and I used to take it in turns to dress the boys, tie their shoe laces, prepare breakfast and see them off to school but now Cosmo has discovered he can do it for himself, with Toto following his lead soon after. I think it gives them a sense of adventure and being grown up. Long may it last! All we have to do is prepare their *merenda* (snack) the night before and leave it out for them, only giving a quick shout goodbye have fun and a wave from the bed in the morning as they go out the door and wait in the piazza for Giuliano to arrive. With everyone gone (Judy has found a job, working three days a week, so she loads the washing machine downstairs under the house on her way to work) I still have a few household chores to complete before I can get back into my studio: tidying the kitchen, making all the beds and sweeping the floors and I hang the washing out later, usually when I put a second pot of coffee on. The clothesline is behind the forno strung up between the two almond trees. If the farm workers are around, working in the fields, I will purposefully delay this chore until they have gone; they would laugh at me doing 'womens' work' and although I am fine with doing housework, I feel self-conscious in front of them. Gabriele our postman surprising me in the garden one morning as he zoomed up to the house on his vespa while I was hanging the washing on the clotheshorse, was embarrassing enough. Judy is teaching English literature and the history of Cinema at the Amity school in Arezzo; a highly unusual private boarding school set up in the mid-eighties as "a behaviour modification facility"for problem kids" from wealthy American families.

The school is housed in a beautiful renaissance villa set within its own grounds, just outside the city walls; gilded but all the same a rich man's version of a borstal school, not that these kids are young offenders in the criminal sense. Nevertheless, at the beginning of term the students' passports are taken away, money is confiscated and runaways— some managing to get as far as Rome—are inevitably hauled back in the school's white Transit van. I know how that feels like having run away from Fettes, an all-boys boarding school in Edinburgh, when I was sixteen.

Judy thinks her students at the Amity school are angels compared to

Shepperton Tech in Victoria, Australia, where she once taught and in the case of Amity, she believes it's the parents dumping their kids far from home, who are the real delinquents. She is enjoying the work, especially getting out of the house more regularly and as a bonus has been given a free hand to devise her own course material; the school curriculum puts a huge emphasis on its program of cultish West Coast, emotional growth therapies: techniques originally developed in the sixties by the CEDU schools in California.

Chapter 43.

Impromptu landscape-painting competitions, known as *Estemporaneo* are popular events during the summer months in villages up and down the Valdichiana. Anyone can enter, and all you need to do is turn up in the early morning of competition day with a blank canvas, which the organisers will time stamp on the back and you are ready to go; returning in the early afternoon with the completed work, which will then be exhibited and judged with cash prizes awarded after.

The *Estemporaneo* in Lucignano is organised by the Pro-loco, a not-for-profit volunteer organisation set up to promote the interests of the village. This year they are offering prize money to the tune of a million lire, which is pretty decent by any standards for just a few hours of work! The finished paintings will be hung outside under the loggia below the Collegiata and taken down at the end of the day, whereas in Cortona they are exhibited in the Council chambers for at least a couple of days.The standard in these competitions is always pretty low and so I fancy my chances; already mentally composing my off the cuff (sic) valedictory speech! However, Luca, an acquaintance of mine and is on the panel of judges this year, sounds a word of warning, pointing out the existence of a small cabal of 'professional' artists who apparently follow the *Estemporaneo* circuit around each year and according to him, regularly scoop up the prize money.

"They make a living out of it." He claims. "You always know the ones by the slick, glossy, heavily stylised paintings they produce."

"You must be kidding me!" I exclaim, genuinely amazed.

"No. They have a formula too: every painting is essentially the same with only a few details rearranged here and there to fit in with the different locations! Another dead giveaway is the kitschy gold frame." "Guaranteed to dazzle the judges I suppose."

"Let's just hope that you're not one of them."

"No no, not me I promise! I can't stand them; I'll be looking for a little more originality!" He protests.

I hadn't thought about a frame! Shelley is big on frames. He has often lectured me on their importance:

"If you are at all serious about selling your work then you have to spend the money on good frames. Believe me the investment will be worth it."

Bob makes his own frames and has also given me lessons; long tedious sessions with his mitre saw then nailing frame lengths together outside his house. It is actually quite an art if you have the patience for it. We used to go together on the occasional foray in my car chasing down wholesale deals on lengths of framing wood, but I never could get the hang of it.

Dutifully, having had my canvas stamped on the back, I am driving down the hill past Lucignano towards Monte San Savino, then turning left onto the long winding driveway that leads to Campo Forte. The old pole barrier that used to block the entrance has been permanently shoved aside but serves as a reminder of the extraordinary security measures the Mozzonis undertook when *Le Brigate Rosse* (The Red Brigades) were an active threat in the seventies. It was rumoured that Mozzoni's wife La Contessa never traveled outside without an armed bodyguard and her Alsatian dogs.

Like Mozzoni, she remains an enigmatic figure, someone I have yet to see even after all these years. I can count the number of times I have actually met Mozzoni on the fingers of one hand and remember our conversations word for word, they were that short: passing Mozzoni on the driveway with a group of his hunting friends, I pulled the car over and waited for him to catch up because I thought he had signalled me to stop.

"Good morning Architetto. Did you want to speak with me?"

"No! I was signalling you to slow down. Don't drive so fast!"
He snapped and walked on.

On another occasion, this time driving to Campo Forte to pay the rent, I saw him walking towards the farm and stopping the car and leaning across the passenger seat to wind down the window, I offered him a lift, even though he literally was only yards from his destination! That time he just looked at me askance.

I have already scouted the view I want to paint in advance: a spot at the edge of the woods up past the farm behind the mustering yards, and no sooner have I unloaded my easel and table from the back of the car, when I hear the sound of another vehicle approaching from the road above. This doesn't surprise me. I knew I would be red flagged for driving straight through the yard at Campo Forte without stopping and sure enough Virgilio appears up behind me not thirty meters away. He is immediately recognisable because he always wears the distinctive long feather plume in the peaked cap of his Alpini regiment.

"What are you doing here, what do you want?" He shouts down.

Perhaps he hasn't realised who I am, although surely he would have recognised my car? Not many UK plated cars drive through the yard! I've never exchanged words with Vigilio before although we do recognise each other in the street and nod. His wife Maria is Mozzoni's housekeeper and they live at La Badia, Mozzoni's official residence on the farm, only two hundred meters from Campo Forte along the same drive. Virgilio is a rather gloomy straight laced ex-military man of pensionable age, employed on the farm as its custodian. The Mozzonis are based in Milan for most of the year and jealously guard their privacy when they are in residence here, which would account for Virgilio's zeal. They are probably here.

"Good morning Virgilio, it's only me: Nino the tenant from Poggio Spinoso. Sorry, I didn't mean to disturb you but it's the Estemporanio today and I would like to paint this view. I hope you don't mind." Rather begrudgingly, he concedes the point and leaves me to get on with it. You can't go anywhere in Tuscany without being noticed. Antonella, the shepherdess's daughter, will be the one to have alerted Virgilio on the phone as soon as I drove through the yard. She lives with her husband in the apartment above Cassagni's office at Campo Forte and occasionally drives the tractors for them when the farm is shorthanded. Her two boys Marco and Nicola go to the same *asilio* as Cosmo and Toto and are good friends.

Finally settling down to the business at hand I unfold the breakfast table to lay out my materials, squeeze paint onto a glass pane, unscrew the lid on the jam jar with the turps, pour the coffee from the thermos, light up a cigarette and start blocking out the white canvas: the woods framing the broad meadow, the stream running through, a wooden fence cutting across the middle to break it up a bit. Why did I choose this view? I find it less inspiring today, perhaps the light has changed? Actually, it is a challenge to paint an intelligible landscape in just a few hours yet still I feel resistant; why am I doing this again? Oh yes, it's the money! Better polish up my speech.

The awkward tripod feet of my easel inevitably sag because I can never get the butterfly wing nut tight enough on the shank to support the weight. (The same unwieldy easel I purloined from my mother and she claimed was the reason she stopped painting)

The cloudless sky makes the painting easier, just a good wash of cerulean to ultramarine blue; best not to lay the paint on too thick, mindful of drying times, of flies sticking to the canvas and wet-on-wet oil paint turning into a muddy quagmire of colour. A fast-food painting: yes junk.

Back in Lucignano, I watch as Luca and the other judges trundle across the piazza to where our paintings are hanging, biro and paper in hand, inspecting each one and making notes, then trundling back to the jury room to consult. Luca says it is a numbers game, whoever gets the most votes.

"They didn't get my vote." Luca assures me and sharing the
indignation I feel at the final results .

"I didn't even get a commendation!" I pout.

Luca was proved right though as one of the so-called cabal painters took first prize with his frothy chocolate box floral themed painting with added vague architectural references.

To my surprise Luca bought my landscape, probably a canny deal because it was dirt cheap, but I was flattered all the same and promised to provide him with a frame.

"Next year" he says confidentially "I will make sure you are a judge so we can really make a difference."

Chapter 44

The local angling club has fenced off the small lake (more like a large dam) at the bottom of the field across the road from my studio. It lies hidden behind a screen of trees, so I only catch glimpses of the shimmering water in winter time. After an accidental drowning there, Mozzoni, mindful of insurance issues, offered the anglers the sole use of the lake on the condition that they erected a chain link fence all the way around the perimeter. Once, when I thought I was giving up smoking, I found myself scaling that fence, knowing full well I could scavenge cigarette butts on the ground around the barbecue area. Fishing competitions are held twice a year, when the lake shore is neatly pegged off into numbered compartments for the competitors and the week before competition day a flatbed truck carrying a huge metal tank filled with trout arrives to re-stock the lake. On the day, the Vigili close our *strada bianca* to two-way traffic and cars park bumper to bumper along the verges of the field opposite Poggio Spinoso, some driving up onto the field itself if parking spaces are no longer available close enough to the lake. Last year the damage the cars caused forced Mozzoni to create a makeshift parking area, dumping a ton of rubble into the corner of the field nearest the lake.

All hell breaks loose if the motocross club is holding one of its monthly meets on the same day; from modest beginnings, ever since posters started appearing in the village advertising the formation of a new motocross club: the MotoGrifo, this motocross has grown into a monster, even becoming part of a regional circuit that attracts big crowds on race days, with an ambulance in attendance and a powerful PA system blasting out Italian pop songs by Mina or Paolo Conte in between races and sponsorship announcements.

Twenty trail bikes roaring round my backyard all day long is ear splitting loud, and seething, all I can think to do is mercilessly pick them off one by one from the lawn with a telescopic-sighted rifle or better still with a rocket launcher to blow them all to smithereens! I have already invented a noise-zap-ray for the autostrada.

The Motodromo, as it has come to be known, is totally illegal: it should never have been allowed, except none of the locals are complaining nor are the authorities cracking down. The Carabiniere in Lucignano refuse to log my complaints when I telephone, instead demanding I come into the station in person and make a formal complaint, a step I am unwilling to take. In short, the mayhem is welcomed with open arms by locals who argue it's better to have their kids racing round a field in Santa Maria than shooting up in the piazza! Which is a bit rich, even though Italy is in the grip of a heroin epidemic and Lucignano is not unaffected; there is a conspiracy theory doing the rounds according to Gabriele, a young artist friend of mine, that the epidemic is all a cunning Mafia marketing ploy; choking the supply of Hashish (It is true there is a relative scarcity of supply) and flooding the market with cheap heroin instead:

"Something like an introductory offer, suckering the kids in, getting them hooked and then hiking up the prices." Laments Gabriele, as we smoke a joint together, laid back in his caravan 'Madame' parked up on a small block of land with amazing views of Cortona, that his family owns on the outskirts of La Fratta.

Gabriele helped to transport my paintings to the Belle Arti in Siena in the van he drives for work at his father's. Occasionally he comes to stay with us for a few days just to get away from it all and paint without the interruptions. Recently we have been going up to Florence together, with Marina too, for an event, a collective paint-in, he has been organising at the Porta Rossa: a shambling, semi-derelict palazzo just outside the city centre that at one time was a squat until the police forcibly cleared it and now serves mainly as an underground anarchist meeting house. You can't miss the huge gold star emblazoned on the bright red doors at the entrance and there is an edge to the younger crowd that gathers there, many of them punks with all the gear, that makes me slightly nervous if not self-conscious of my age. Political meetings are held upstairs in a small candlelit library, revealing a new generation of Florence's militant youth, albeit for now, sitting tamely on the floor at the feet of their elders, revered, bearded professors, who recline in armchairs and speak in hushed conspiratorial tones.

The only people left objecting to the *Motodromo* are a small group of *stranieri*, mainly the Mosleys, whose villa stands directly above the wooded end of the track by the cemetery. Mosley did some fundraising and offered to buy the field from the farmer at a vastly inflated price but the farmer showed no interest. Another tack taken, if getting the kids off the street is the main concern, was to donate money towards building a new public swimming pool near the tennis courts; a generous offer that equally gained very little traction. The German bibliophile, whose house borders the track, has sold and moved away in desperation and Mosley, a lawyer by profession, started legal proceedings against the club when all else had failed. Unfortunately, there is such a backlog of cases that progress through the courts is negligible, except for the one small glimmer of hope offered up by the magistrate, when he ordered officials from the local USL (the local department of health) to take readings to determine the decibel levels at the track and ascertain if they conformed to environmental standards.

Regrettably the club itself was informed and then requested to provide the bikers for the trial. Sure enough, three bikes turned up on the day, supposedly going through their paces but setting off together at a very leisurely Sunday afternoon pace, totally lacking the usual kappazz: normally the bikes fly off the top of the mounds, their wheels spinning madly through the air, but not on this day: the bikes barely make it to the top before tipping listlessly over the other side. Today, the roar has become a whimper! The lion is a mild-mannered cat. Bloody hell! If that's all the noise they ever made, I wouldn't even be complaining! Now Cosmo wears a crash helmet and rides up and down the banks on his bicycle, ploughing into the piazza with the corresponding sound effects: vrumm vrumm VROOOOM! I can't wait to see what Toto will get up to on his tricycle.

It's actually making life hell; the contrast between this industrial scale noise and the Tuscan idyl. It's like a nagging sore tooth that you can't stop probing with your tongue or an itch that you can't leave alone. So! I've been forced into taking unilateral measures of my own and have entered into a pact with God: in return for closing down the motocross I swear I will no longer kill spiders around the house, at least not intentionally. You might laugh, but I am serious and this is no cushy deal; from zero to total tolerance—having to sweep and dust around them, stay my broom from straying or stop my hand from "accidentally" sideswiping them away or my fist from thudding down on top of these hapless creatures. Instead, I have become a lollipop man shepherding my charges across dangerous highways.

The only relief on competition days is retreating to the other lake on the farm, nestled further away in the woods below Campo Forte, two valleys removed and far enough not to be intruded upon by whining motocross bikes. I secretly roam the farm anyway and can imagine I am the last person on earth, a game of make-believe that scares me because it can feel so real at times.

Approaching the lake through the woods is like stepping onto the shore of another planet. A Fish eye glimpse of a tree circle mirrored in a black shining table of water, diamond suns flickering silently across its glassy ripples, with padded insects scooting the surface and swallows scooping them up: jumping fish are almost subliminal, then the snap-snap of dragonfly wings, or the turquoise-breasted flash of a kingfisher zeroing in. No matter how cautiously I approach the lake, the minute I step out of the trees and reveal myself at the water's edge, the raucous rasping velcro sound of the frogs stops dead, followed by a hundred plip-plopps as they dive for cover under the water lilies and the chorus of cicada's dim like a Mexican wave as I pass by them on the path around the lake. Half-way round, nestled under a strand of pine trees, is a small wooden pavilion and a rickety pole jetty slowly subsiding into the water with a tin rowing boat tethered at the end. The Mozzonis occasionally entertain guests here; Olivero, one of the farm workers, festoons the breezy structure with Chinese lanterns, Maria, the Mozzonis' housekeeper, prepares the meal at La Badia: the Mozzoni's residence and her husband Virgilio or Olivero ferries the food down from the house in an Ape.

Signs posted around the perimeter of the lake declare:

"No bathing and no fishing allowed."

Cassagni, right at the start of our tenure, made it abundantly clear to me that the lake is strictly out of bounds to anyone other than the Mozzonis. As a consequence, I make it my business to know when they are in residence and give it a wide berth when they are here, although I can never be absolutely sure, which makes travelling undercover a pivotal part of the game; on the way over, seeking cover if a tractor is coming along up the trail or sneaking out of home to avoid alerting Lila our dog that I am leaving. Occasionally she gets wind of something in the air and will come in hot pursuit, in which case I have to abort the journey and bring her back home. In summer, Olivero makes the rounds of the farm on his Vespa every evening and isn't hard to evade because you can hear him from a mile off and I can hide behind the *ginestra* bushes near the shore. What would he say if he discovered I was crouching there naked? It is always a relief to hear him coming because he turns off the noisy generator in the pumping station adjacent to the lake and his departure heralds a return to nature's way.

My intelligence network is not always perfect and to this day I don't know if Mozzoni actually caught me *in flagrante* swimming in the lake. He appeared suddenly out of nowhere one evening at the water's edge, a ghostly apparition sitting impassively on his chestnut mare. My head was stranded above water thirty yards away, desperately trying not to bob up and down too much and attract his attention as he leaned forward with his hands folded on the saddle and peered right through the gloaming at me but gave no indication if he had seen me before riding away.

Paying the rent at Campo Forte is always a good opportunity to gather intelligence. Once we have settled up, Cassagni likes to sit back in his chair and chat. He hates the office work and always arrives late for our appointments and finally turning up he reluctantly drags down the Poggio Spinoso file from the bank of folders in the drab gunmetal grey bookshelf lining the wall behind his desk, racking up the figures in the ledger using a ratchet, one-armed bandit calculator as his aid. He grumbles about the farm running at a loss, showing me a bottle of extra vergine olive oil with Mozzoni's boutique label on it as proof: moaning that it isn't for sale but only handed out as gifts to Mozzoni's friends and then I ask him how Mozzoni is and when is he coming next?

Unexpectedly, at our last meeting, Cassagni announced he is retiring. He has been a good ally to me for almost nine years and I will be sad to see him leave. (The rent is still the same!). He came over to Poggio Spinoso after and introduced me to the new fattore Fosco, who seems friendly enough but looks more the office type, although he is reputed to be an expert on cattle breeding. I had noticed how maudlin Cassagni seemed of late: sagging shoulders and stooping more: full of doom and gloom, talking about the Bosnian war and death and how much he hates growing old; so unlike the man of only a year ago, when, unusually, the men were out hand-tilling the fields around us and he joined in just for the hell of it, walking back in with the rest of them after to Poggio Spinoso, stripped to the waist, torso bathed in sweat, and hosing down at the tap with a great big bearish grin of satisfaction plastered all over his face.

Chapter 45.

I am dimly aware of the sound of traffic drifting in from outside the studio window, a volume of noise unusual for Sunday mornings, but pay it no heed since I'm sitting crossed-legged on the floor in a huddle with one of my paintings. I spend more time contemplating them than I do painting them. It is a kind of meditation: either an intense gazing into the future of the work, painting with prescience or it is a dress rehearsal of what is about to be done. There is a logic within each painting, one brush stroke leading to another, this painting leading to the next one, like a series of stepping-stones showing the way forward.

The growing commotion outside finally grabs my attention and curious, I drag myself off the floor and move over to the window. A group of people are congregating in the field on the other side of the *strada bianca*, car doors wide open and engines left idling.

Following their gaze towards the horizon I quickly realise why. It's a fire! And by the look of it on Mozzoni's land, burning right across the ridgeline, great clouds of smoke bent horizontal by the breezes. Rushing downto the garden, I alert Judy and reassure the kids not to worry, we are in no danger being so far away, but I am going to drive up to the farm to see if I can offer my services. Judy takes one look at me and insists I change my T-shirt and shorts. I take her point but smart all the same, being a fire veteran, and change into a long shirt and jeans, grabbing a handkerchief, water bottle, a machete and gloves before heading off to Campo Forte.

Antonella and some of the women are milling in the yard when I arrive, tension in the air, and Shelley shoots through in his car heading in the opposite direction, pausing briefly to say:

"I've been up there but there's nothing much we can do so I am going home."

Antonella seems to agree with him and shrugs but I decide to press on all the same, following the roughening track up the hill to Casa dei Morti (the House of the Dead), one of several *case coloniche* left empty or abandoned on the farm. I park the car closer to the summit well off to one side of the track, leaving the keys in the ignition as a precaution and continue on foot.

Nearing the top, I can see the Maresciallo (chief of police) and the Mayor of Lucignano, talking to Fosco, our new farm manager.

"What a disaster!" I hear Fosco muttering as I approach the group. "Thank God we kept the fire breaks clear after the last fire," he adds, looking up and including me in his remark.

"This looks like a big one." The others nod in solemn agreement. There is a widely held belief on the farm that hunters deliberately lit the last fire, angry with Mozzoni for daring to turn his land into a private hunting reserve. Fosco pats me on the shoulder and points towards the ridge.

"If you're here to help, better get up there, keep walking and you'll run into the rest of the men."

Tornados of smoke are swirling across the ridge-line and heading down in my direction. Flames, orange on grey, are leaping thirty feet into the sky, sucked into the blue vortex. The fire engine has made it all the way up and I can hear men shouting from behind screens of smoke, appearing and disappearing like silhouetted ghosts in fluorescent orange overalls. Not knowing where to put myself and with nobody willing to direct me, I drag my feet hesitating until Virgilio the farm *guardiano* comes hurtling down the track in the old battered Land Rover and, barely stopping, orders me to jump in. Angelino, Beppe and Olivero from the farm are in the back, bouncing around, sweaty and tense, swearing their heads off as we tear down the hill, skirting the woods before plunging back in along one of the old fire tracks, and coming to a halt directly below the left flank of the fire. Fernando is following behind with the tractor, hauling an enormous red cylindrical water tank mounted on a trailer.

Shafts of light captured by the smoke flicker like a movie projector between the trees above us. Above, a pale red sun fleetingly unveils itself. Olivero is feverishly shouting instructions, scrambling up the hill towards the fire as we hook up a hose to the water tank and feed him the line. A chopper is traversing the valley below us, trailing the giant unwieldy water bucket on its swaying length of rope. Suddenly I envisage myself as a superhero: a human rocket niftily zipping through the sky, repeatedly darting in and out with my water laser, zapping the fire from above with pin-point accuracy. Olivero is exhorting us to follow him and madly darts to and fro into the fire as we drag the hose and try to follow him through the smoke. This is how it must feel to be in the heat of a battle, adrenalin pumping, no time for thought, just following orders, welded to the other men instinctively for survival and at the ready for the kill.

Casa dei Morti has become a staging post as the women ferry up equipment and bring provisions of panini, water and beer in wicker baskets for the men, who take it in turns to rest in the shade of the inner courtyard. Someone had the foresight to move my car because the rapidly advancing front of the fire would have shrivelled it up into a molten pyre by now. By late afternoon we have abandoned most of the upper hill and Cassagni is busy supervising the back burning lower down, the lines of containment. I am stationed in a field along the valley floor near the *molino*, stamping out the embers that are falling like red hailstones out of the sky, but by early evening, the work is mainly done and the fire has been brought under our control. Flames sporadically flare up in the darkness, lighting up the underside of the clouds and illuminating the surrounding treetops as one by one the men abandon their posts and melt away into the night. I really am a hero of sorts when I reach home and Judy tells me how the boys spent all afternoon intently watching from the lawn and soon after my departure, they spotted the first helicopters flying towards the fire and started waving and pointing, under the assumption I must be up there piloting the machine!

Mozzoni rushed down from Milan as quickly as he could and a few days later Fosco phones to invite me to a lunch being organised at La Badia for all those involved in the fire-fighting effort. My stock at the farm will have risen a few notches for taking part, especially with the new farm manager, and I would have been happy to leave it at that, but Judy thinks I'm being silly and insists I should go.

We enter La Badia through the garden via Mozzoni's study, where he has conspicuously placed a large sketch of his on an easel by the french doors. He has published a couple of books of his watercolours and line drawings, but I am not a big fan. Where he does become more interesting though are his eccentric architectural ideas: he offered an innovative solution to the problem of the Leaning Tower of Pisa after the tower was closed to the public in 1990 because it is in danger of falling over and Mozzoni suggested it could be anchored to a tree to stabilise it and provided the authorities with detailed architectural drawings of his plan! Currently he is working on his La Città Ideale, a utopian city for 25,000 people that he is proposing to build in Milan; a futuristic design that looks like an Easter egg, a huge oval building,

240 metres in diameter, built out of steel and wood, which he has designed to be completely self-sufficient: a castle in the sky.

Twenty of us are gathered downstairs, seated at a lengthy refectory table placed in the passage way outside to the kitchen. Cassagni, the Mayor and Fosco flank Mozzoni in the centre, with the Maresciallo and the Conte Della Stufa sitting opposite, the rest of us fanning out along benches. I gulp down two glasses of wine in quick succession to help loosen my tongue. None of the women involved in the effort are present except Maria, who has prepared the feast she proceeds to lay out before us, but doesn't sit down, only exchanging a few quips at table with some of the men. The communist mayor Neri, an earnest young man with a bushy black beard picks at his food, head down over his plate, saying nothing and the Maresciallo excuses himself early, apologising to the group:

"L'Architetto, Conte, Sindaco, Signori," nodding, "You will excuse me but duty calls that I must attend to."

I have never seen Mozzoni in such an expansive mood before, smiling and relaxed, leaning back in his seat chatting with his men. Perhaps it is the relief that the fire hasn't destroyed more of the hillside or reach ed Campo Forte; the general with his men reminiscing on an epic battle. The table is merry too, and only brought to a hush when Maria passes Mozzoni the phone and raising his voice, conveys his wife's message of gratitude to the assembled company.

Back home, I'm relieved that that is over; at least I can say i've done my bit, and picking up Cosmo and Toto as promised, we head off once more in the car for our own personal survey of the fire damage. I want to show them what all the fuss has been about. We drive past "Millionaires' Row" or the "Beverly Hills" of Lucignano as Judy and I call it; an enclave of grand houses owned by heiresses, supermarket magnates, diplomats and Belgium brewers, straddling the end of our road in what looks like a glorified housing estate for the super-rich. Ironically the road here is full of potholes and difficult to negotiate unlike where we are, which is always well maintained. (Judy thinks this a deliberate ploy to keep outside traffic away.) Then taking the cheeky short cut across the Count's land to Calcione and turning right onto the Gargonza road, we end up off the road driving through the woods to a place I know that will offer us elevated views.

The scene is a no-man's land as we emerge out of the ring of trees onto the rim of a bowl of scorched earth. A devastating sight of rocky outcrops littered with charred stumps straight out of a World War I painting by Paul Nash.

Pointing this and that out to the boys, a bush suddenly flares up not far from where we are standing and I experience a familiar panic attack, a mental hyper-venting that roots me to the spot similar to that time in Paris when I was caught up in a riot and like a rabbit in the headlights, after everyone else had fled, was the only one left facing a phalanx of riot police, shields up, batons raised, charging down on me, yet stupidly calling out "mercy" (*merci!*) to the flic with the red bulging eyes who started to beat me up; no doubt thinking I was taking the Mickey shouting "thanks" to him. Rousing myself I tell the kids to stay put, and rush over to the flames flaying at them with a broken leafy branch, but my efforts prove ineffectual and the flames begin to strengthen and spread.

"Shit, what if somebody thinks I started this?" flits briefly across my brain.

Scooping Toto up in one arm and pulling Cosmo along by the hand, we stumble-rush back to the car I had parked in the woods and race down to Calcione, the Della Stufa's castle seat, to raise the alarm. I am breathless. A game of tennis is underway on the court off to one side of the castle and I call over for the Conte; the players, pointing their rackets, direct me back to the castle indicating the Conte is taking a nap (after Mozzoni's lunch). Knocking on the main door and getting no answer, I step back into the livery yard and call out his name; I am dressed in a yellow and green striped fluorescent T-shirt, orange day-glow shorts and scuffed leather boots, gravitas is my name. When the Count finally appears at a small upper casement window, he looks down at me (with disdain?) Then thanks me for alerting him and says he will notify the Forestieri before closing the window again. I don't know why I bother, he doesn't seem overly concerned or grateful, but I drive back to the scene out of a sense of responsibility and am relieved to find that the men from the round the clock watch are already on hand and have the situation under their control. At least I am not a suspect but to cap it off the car's fuel line is ruptured driving over roots in the woods and we barely scrape home before the petrol tank runs dry.

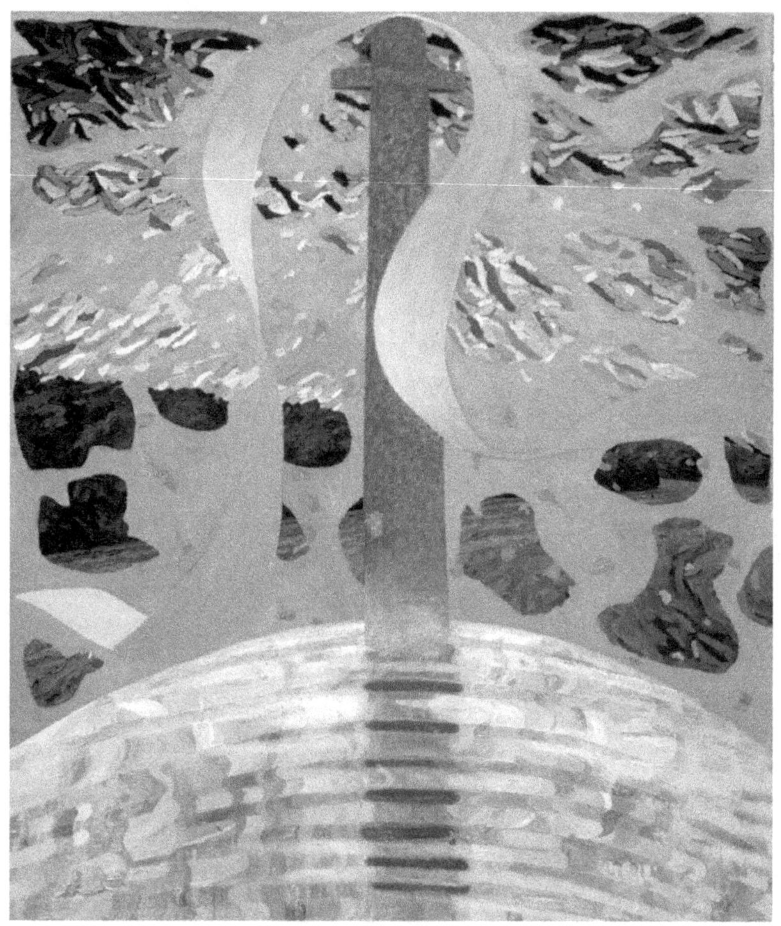

Fire.1993

Chapter 46.

The last time my cousin Antonia stayed at Poggio Spinoso, she came with her boyfriend Carlo. His family is from Napoli and much to the amusement of the boys, he built them a mini-Vesuvius in the garden out of mud and lighting the newspaper stuffed into a hole at the base, smoke poured out of the top of the cone. Carlo's sister-in-law Fabienne has been helping me to arrange an exhibition at the Goethe Institut in Napoli; she is owed favours she says without specifying why and although the Institute's brief is to promote German culture abroad, I qualify because I can claim nationhood! First time ever and not speaking a word of German no obstacle either!

Judy and I both love Napoli and have visited several times. Perhaps it is the third world chaos that makes it so appealing to us, almost a déjà-vu of India: the major thorough-ways leading into the city hemmed in by tenement buildings casting their lines of washing from one side to the other high above the streets; the colour and grime, the love of concrete and iron, the sheer bustle and noise; the nuked empty wastelands and colonial grandeur all mixed in together.

The first time we visited Napoli, before the kids, we checked into a cheap hotel on the Esplanade offering fabulous views across the bay to Vesuvius. The bell boy (sic) led us up to our room, then putting on blue surgical gloves he proceeded to change the sheets in front of us. We hadn't realised the hotel rented rooms by the hour.

Perhaps existing on the knife-edge of Vesuvius is what makes Napoli so acutely alive? Or is it the perception of the Camorra lurking on every street corner, or imagining the *scippatori,* on every passing scooter, ready to yank off your gold chains or snatch up your purse? Napoli is insane, yet still the only city in the world I would ever dream of crossing four lanes of busy traffic on foot and rate my chances of reaching the other side intact. The irony is you are more likely to be run over on a pedestrian crossing. (If you can find one that is)

Carlo's mother Rita, adores the kids and makes us welcome to stay in her apartment near the harbour any time we want to. Her partner Pino, by a strange coincidence, has a summerhouse near San Biagio below Montepulciano that we can spy from our kitchen window on a clear day through the binoculars. I am really pleased to be having an exhibition in Napoli because over the last ten years I have amassed a body of work inspired by several visits to Pompeii and this presents an ideal opportunity to show case them as a group, which I am going to call Sotto Il Volcano (Under the Volcano). The Pompeii casts are what particularly fascinate me; those striking poses of human defiance, or resignation, of pain or fear; perhaps even enlightenment in that final split second before succumbing to death. Artists are voyeurs at heart and here we have the most intimate of sights: the freeze frame of death revealed right before our eyes. How clever was Fiorelli? The archaeologist who first twigged to the idea that the air pockets they were uncovering in the petrified ash were really the vacated forms of the people or animals that once occupied them.

Gianni, who I have now officially appointed cataloguer of my paintings, has been busy again taking photos of the paintings going to Napoli. He has also introduced me to one of his main clients, Mimmo, a Neapolitan who has agreed to sponsor the exhibition and agreed to pay for a full colour catalogue and invitation card. Mimmo runs a successful jewellery business in Arezzo called Diana that specialises in engagement rings and Gianni designs the company's stand at the annual Gold Fair in Vicenza.

The company uses the slogan "Diana per l'arte" in its promotional material and sponsoring an exhibition, fits with their brand. Amazingly, Mimmo has also commissioned a painting from me and is requesting the picture rights, explaining that up until now his company has been using Renaissance paintings to promote the business but he would like to refresh their image with something more contemporary. Mimmo is very reserved for a Neapolitan and he unnerves me slightly; someone you might feel uncomfortable with if left alone together in the same room for too long. He is young with an old man's ponderous manner sitting at his desk. A framed photo of his father hangs on the wall behind him like a Damocles sword, which he brings down to show me, leaning across the desk:

"This is a picture of my late my father; he founded the company in 1984. Do you think you would be able to paint a portrait from the photo? Of course, I will be happy to pay you for it."

Playing the game, I look intently at the photo and respond, tutting

“Please! Of course, I can do that! It would be my pleasure to paint it for you as a gift.”

In Tuscany it is common for artists to seek out sponsors for their exhibitions. Banks and local businesses are always a good place to start, so too are the different Comune. The Comune of Laterina, for example, sponsors an annual artist's exhibition with a very generous subsidy and it is only a small hill town with a population of three thousand people. Shelley had an exhibition there a few years back and Vicky was instrumental in introducing me to Leandro the Comune's *Assessore Culturali* who subsequently offered the 1993 show to me.

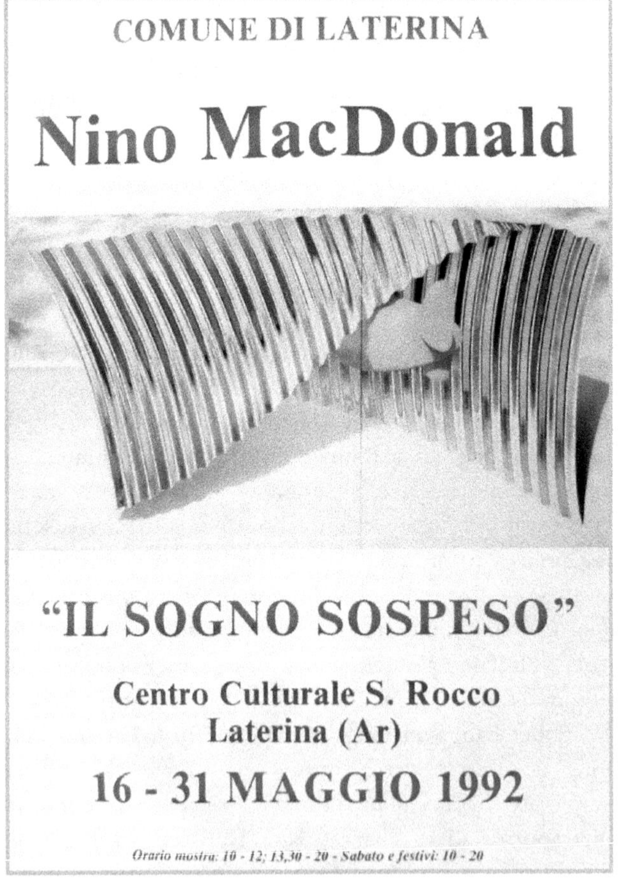

The exhibition, entitled Il Sogno Sospeso (The Dream Postponed), was held in San Rocco, a de-sanctified church now run by the Comune as an exhibition space, and not only did the Comune pay for the full colour catalogue and poster but also paid for a huge banner that was strung across the Corso in Arezzo to publicise the event, and commissioned me to create a limited-edition lithograph commemorating the occasion: sending me to a well-known printer's studio in Florence to execute the work. All they ask for in return is a painting for their collection.

The truck that arrives at Poggio Spinoso to transport my paintings to Napoli is an armoured security van with an armed guard! Cosmo and Toto, standing in the piazza as it arrives, are gobsmacked and so am I when I see the classic Brinks looking truck come up the drive. I had no idea that my work was going to be transported together with a consignment of gold and wonder if I shouldn't have taken out insurance?Arezzo is one of Europe's major gold manufacturing centres and gold heists are frequently in the news. Fabrizio, the security guard notices the kids gawking at him as he helps load the first crate into the truck and calling them over, he obligingly unclips his holster, slides out the handgun, a Glock 22 and laying it in the flat of his palm, invites them to take a look, without touching of course. Judy would have a fit if she saw us so gingerly, I suggest he holsters his gun.

Gabriele, my young artist friend, works in his father, Bernardo's gold chain manufacturing business and I occasionally accompany him on his rounds in the van, dropping off orders to clients at San Zeno, the sprawling industrial park just outside Arezzo where most of the gold businesses are based. Gabriele's father also manufactures murano glass mosaic pendants and brooches with the classic set-piece floral designs and Gabriele and I had been talking about setting up in business together, designing more contemporary looking brooches but employing the same *murano* techniques. Gabriele showed me the bundles of coloured rods of *murano* glass they have in store and how the tiny mosaic pieces are sliced off the ends. Unfortunately, we might have to shelve the idea because the old lady who crafts them, La Signora, is one of the very few artisans left in this area with the prerequisite skills and she is having great difficulty coming to grips with my miniature UFO designs and stylised tulips parachuting out of planes.

The Goethe Institute is close to the harbour housed in a beautiful eighteenth century villa with Doric columns and mosaic floors. It once served as the British Embassy; Emma Hamilton, Nelson's lover, was the daughter of the British ambassador there and Admiral Nelson was a frequent visitor as was Goethe himself.

Whenever I exhibit, my expectations are always high and even though the opening is not as well attended as I had hoped for, I take it as a good omen; the coincidence that right next door is a gallery currently exhibiting an installation piece of multiple miniature replicas of the same Pompeii dog that I have painted and is hanging on the walls of the Institute: Pompeii dog. Perhaps not so auspicious is the Director calling me early in the morning during the first week, apologising profusely because the nylon cord used to hang my work has snapped on several paintings, sending them crashing to the floor! I immediately rush over from Rita's to assess the damage, which fortunately is minimal as far as I can tell. Thank God it did not happen during the opening because I have a recurring fear at openings of seeing my paintings crash to the floor in a series of pops as they are detonated off the walls in front of everyone.

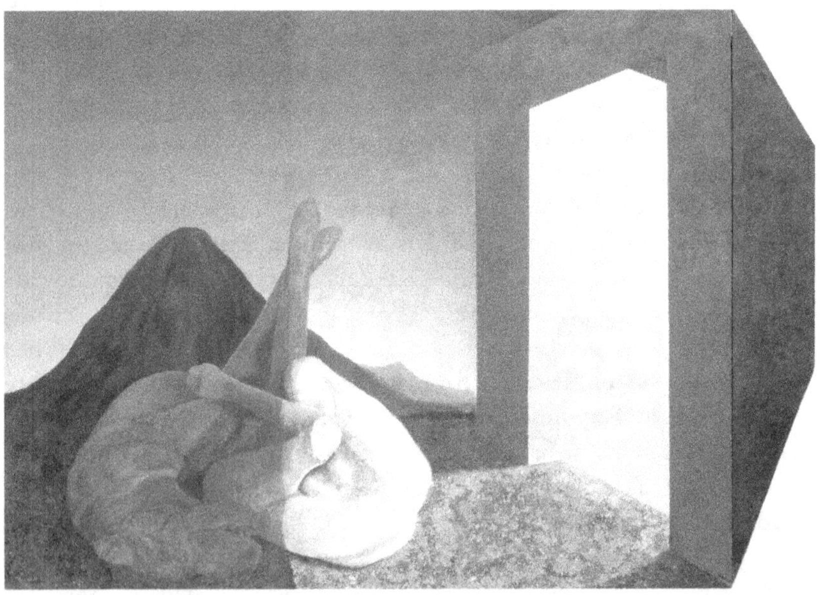

Pompeii, die dog.1988

Chapter 47.

WE did have an electric blanket on our bed until it went up in flames one night. It was only the pungent smell of the toxic fumes that alerted us and Judy and I were lucky to escape unscathed. Instead, we now deploy a traditional Tuscan bed warmer, which so much better anyway. The Prete (the priest), as it is called or alternatively the "nun's belly" is a curved, wooden oval frame that houses a tin bowl, for the hot coals, suspended from a hook in the middle. You slide the sledge sized apparatus under the covers and leave it in until bedtime. The heat radiates to all corners of the bed leaving the sheets sumptuously warm when you climb in, like laundry freshly dried in the sun!

Winter is always a trial of endurance. The house comes under siege when rain pours down the chimney stack and is driven under the kitchen doors, flooding the floor; or insinuates itself round the loose window panes, overflowing onto the sills and streaming down the walls to puddle on the tiles below. Towels and bolsters are shoved up against the windows and the doors but to no avail except to soak up some of the excess. The kids' have a wood stove that heats their room to a comfortable degree but raging storms and howling winds will often see them scramble into our bed; the four poster has acreage to spare, it's enormous. When we first moved in, the kitchen had a classic *cucina economica*; a small wood stove that you cook on, but that has since been replaced by a gas stove and the "warm morning" wood stove: otherwise, the rest of the house is stone cold if not freezing during the bleakest months.

Snow settles on the ground maybe once or twice a year, usually in January when we can be snowed in for a few days with cars unable to make it down the white road. The kids pile up snowmen, sledge into the fields on trays and chuck snowballs at each other, laughing uproariously every time they take a hit: or tumble on top of each other, squashing snow down the neck of the zippered, padded ski suits that Judy buys them at the caritas in Arezzo.

When the leaden skies disperse, slashes of blue appear above the crisp mantle of virgin snow, blushing apricot at the rising sun. Or the thick curtains of mist rumbling across the fields during the day suddenly part to reveal the sun going down and between heaven and earth there are explosions of russet on the oak trees; from the wrinkled autumn leaves stubbornly clinging to them.

After the snow, Gabriele our postman is always the first one to get through in his small four-wheel drive Fiat (in summer he comes on the Vespa). The postal service remains exceptional and personal even after the post office was moved out of the village into a new purpose-built concrete structure beyond the walls, appropriately known to the locals as *il boonker.* Alas though, no more whiffs of the postmistress's perfume, wafting through the room in clouds and greeting you as you entered the old post office. These days conversations are conducted through walls of perforated plexiglass. I can barely hear Eugenio behind the counter anymore: telling me where he is going in summer or what he is planning for the weekend. Still, when I am early enough, Eugenio will call out my name to Gabriele, sorting the mail in the room behind, and if I have some, he will come round and pass it to me through the security bin that straddles the counter.

February is Carnevale when Cosmo and Toto dress up as super-heroes, swashbuckling their way through the streets of Foiano with their friends. The Foianesi like to claim their carnevale rivals that of Viareggio, but that is pure hyperbole, even if they do take carnivale very seriously and prepare for the whole year in advance. Each *contrada* has its own hangar-sized shed where the giant mechanised paper mâché floats, some nearly three storeys high, are painstakingly constructed. The themes will vary from year to year, but caricatures lampooning national politicians, or giant red dragons with bobbing heads and flaring nostrils blowing smoke are always very popular. The floats barely squeeze through the narrow streets of the *centro storico*, with the Foianesi in masquerade dancing in and out between them: with children running amok, shooting stringy psychedelic coloured goo from toy guns at anyone within range and vendors selling big bags of paper confetti, which fall from the sky and turn the streets into drifts of paper snow.

False springs often see me scuttling back to a depleted woodpile just when I thought winter was over with and I have been deliberately piling the logs that are left onto the fire, for the sheer luxury of it and heating the house above seventeen degrees. With a late frost in April, it's not uncommon to heat for up to six months of the year. The village is now connected to mains gas but wood remains the principal source of heating fuel rurally. Woods and coppices are selectively logged every twelve to thirteen years to sustain them; no strand of trees is small enough in fact not to be considered a resource, and consequently one of the main reasons you rarely see a mature tree left standing in the landscape. The canny contadini paint a white line across the top and down the sides of their freshly cut and stacked woodpiles which they leave in the woods to be collected later; that way they know if anyone is pilfering and can take remedial action.

I order our wood in July from Italo, the *boscaiolo* (woodcutter) in Santa Maria just down the road from where the motocross track used to be. Ordering wood is the last thing on my mind in the middle of summer, but important to remember if I want seasoned dry wood in the winter. If I leave it too late, Italo will have run out and only be selling his green wood, which costs less but is harder to burn and throws out less heat. Italo is a big, cheerful, burly man with huge calloused, ham fists. He has a logging concession on a large private estate towards Siena that he works with his dark-eyed rosy-cheeked, muscle-bound son, Andrea. They cut the timber through the winter, hauling it back to the yard in Santa Maria where it is left to season for a year in great piled up stacks before being sawed into the 50-centimetre lengths ready for the stove. It is cheaper again if you buy the metre lengths and cut it down to size yourself, as Bob does at home with his saw and hobby horse, saying he does it for the exercise, but I know Jane budgets carefully. I hardly see Bob these days, although there was a period when he came over regularly while posing for the painting that now hangs in the Renaualt dealership in Arezzo. Leandro, the Assessore Culturali of Laterina is also the manager of the Renault concession and he asked me as a favour if he could hang the painting in the showrooms and subsequently sold it to his boss.

Come the end of September and I am on the phone to Italo's wife, la Signora, to remind her that the wood hasn't been delivered yet and hopefully Italo or Andrea will get a move on before the first tramontana wind arrives and freezes us over. The wood is sold by weight and it has to be transported to the weighing station outside Lucignano before coming here. Italo inevitably writes Poggio Splendore as our address on the official weighing chit, which I much prefer to Poggio Spinoso (prickly knoll) and so never bother correcting him. Once Italo has offloaded the trailer full onto my piazza, I can guarantee that if I offer to pay him right away, he will only laugh and wave me off, embarrassed, as if I'm being unreasonable:

"No, no. Not now, please, another time, what's the rush?" It's the Tuscan way of doing business.

This year Andrea delivers the wood in their flash new tip truck, no more tractor and trailer, things must be looking up but a shadow darkens his cherubic face as he climbs down from the cab and mutters under his breath something about a revolution taking place, genuinely alarming me; it's so out of character for him usually being mild mannered and he sounds deadly serious too. Toto, nervous, has already asked us if the war is coming here after the Balkans war and now NATO led bombing of the Serbs in Bosnia. Low flying jets often zoom in above our roof, shattering the peace, treating the Valdichiana like a playground for their war game exercises; playing cat and mouse, hide and seek, performing cartwheels through the clouds, leaving behind long drifting vapour trails that slowly intertwine like mating snakes.

The very idea of a revolution in Tuscany seems inconceivable; yet these are extraordinary times, ever since Tangentopoli (Bribesville) hit the headlines in '92. The scale of corruption subsequently uncovered by the magistrates' Mani Pulite (Clean Hands) investigations has really shocked the Nation and rocked the political elite to its core; the fall out causing the the First Republic to collapse.

The Christian Democrats, Italy's largest ruling political party since the Second World War, has self-imploded and been dissolved; connections with organised crime and shonky government contracts its undoing, with Andreotti its former prime minister under criminal investigation for colluding with Cosa Nostra. The communist party too, has barely survived the meltdown and has split into two factions as a consequence. Craxi, a former socialist Prime Minister, was recently showered with coins by an angry mob outside his hotel in Rome and has now fled the country for his villa in Tunisia after his conviction on bribery and corruption charges. A popular joke doing the rounds is the one about the Italian Post dropping plans to release a stamp with Craxi's profile on it because they were afraid people would spit on the wrong side! Business has ground to a halt with some of Italy's largest company's mired in the bribery scandal and Industry in general too petrified to make a move in the current climate, waiting to see which way the wind is blowing; whether it's going to be business as usual (corruption) or whether the rules have changed since Berlusconi has taken over the reigns as Italy's newly elected Prime Minister; the man who has filled the political vacuum, declaring during the election campaign that he was climbing into the ring as the Nation's 'reluctant' saviour and addressing delegates to the first congress of his newly formed political party Forza Italia:

"I am a mad man come to meet an equally mad bunch of people..." Berlusconi the media magnate, owner of A.C.Milan football club; *Il Cavaliere,* as he is popularly known: the country's knight in white armour, saddled up and booted, riding through the crisis in a blaze of self-publicity and duly elected on promises to clean up corruption in public life.

Amazingly the public believed him and it's hardly surprising Andrea feels betrayed, now that Berlusconi is himself under investigation for alleged corruption and seeking parliamentary immunity to avoid scrutiny. There was so much optimism in Italy before these elections, the atmosphere was electric with hope right across the political spectrum, with expectations sky high for a new era in political life and sweeping political reforms, except now it has become clear that it's business as usual, only under the guise of a new Republic.

Andrea, seeing my alarm, reassures me he is not about to take up arms: instead, he is about to become a dad himself and breaks into a coy smile when I clap him on the back and congratulate him.

It takes me two or three mornings to shift the pile of logs off the piazza and under cover of the *forno*; the small chapel like building with the oven in the back, that stands at the foot of the outside stairs. It is a convenient staging post for carting wood up to the kitchen. The kids help out when they have a mind to, taking turns to fill up their little toy wheelbarrow, but they soon get bored and wander off or the rows become too high for them to stack.

Angelo, at the Southerns, showed me how to build a proper wood stack using castelli (towers) to prop up the sides like bookends. The real trick, however, he told me, is to successively lean in each row as you build up the successive layers. It is really frustrating watching a half-finished stack fall over and the *castello* provides a good solution. We can burn eighty quintals of wood in a long winter, easy, which roughly translates into eight rows, each about six feet long, stacked six feet high. When I complain to Gianni about the amount of labour this involves, he winks at me conspiratorially and lets me in on his simple trick.

"All you have to do is feed from the back: stack the first row nice and neatly then chuck the rest of the logs in behind, where nobody will see them." A Potemkin wood stack!

Taking Italo at his word, it might be three months before I finally make it down to Santa Maria to settle up the wood bill. I feel marginally guilty about dragging my feet this long, but then again, judging by the wad of chits La signora pulls out of the shoebox kept in the kitchen cabinet, I am by no means the last one to pay my bill.

We will talk about the price of wood for the coming year, with her inevitably complaining about the government's monopoly on pricing, especially if the price of wood has been pegged for another year. She says they hardly make ends meet, but I don't believe her; a new extension on their house has just been completed for Andrea and his wife and their newborn baby girl. If Italo is in the yard he might wander into the kitchen and then bring down a bottle of his vin santo and we will toast heartily to his latest vintage.

Chapter 48.

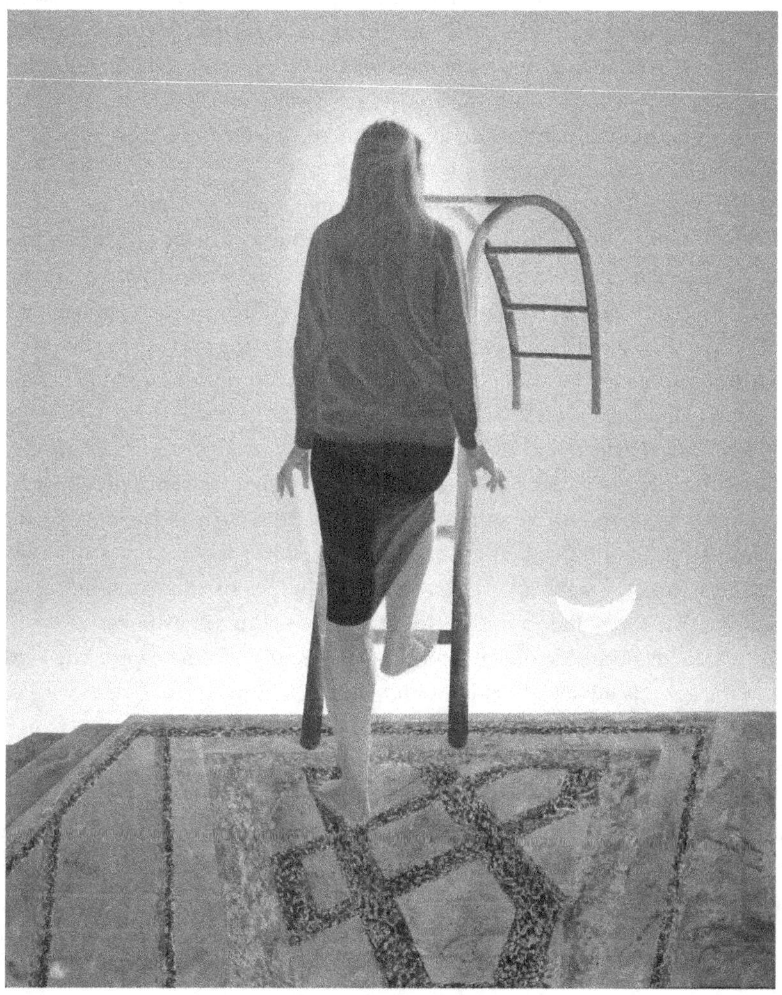

Judy goes to the moon.1989

Ladders are an essential part of my life in Tuscany. Judy suffers vertigo even clambering onto a chair, which means I am responsible for any jobs above head height. My first ladder came with the house; a short, rickety, contadino ladder so riddled with woodworm that Judy won't allow it inside under any circumstance. The rungs are branches secured in the holes by means of wire and rusty bent nails. I retain a certain nostalgia for this one, because in the early days, deployed in two stages I could use it to get up onto the roof of the house; first, onto the ledge of the lean to garage then, pulling it up behind me, onto the roof. Vicky took pity on me when she saw me attempting it one day and gifted us her metal tubular ladder, the one I now use to reach the water tanks housed in the piano room. It sounds like an egg shaker when tipped upside down because of all the loose rust tumbling around inside.

Nowadays I can get onto the roof via the kitchen balcony, propping up the ladder I pilfered from the farm workers after they left it in one of the cantinas during the olive harvest. I hid it for weeks before bringing it out in the open again, then increased the height by two feet, attaching two lengths of wood so that it could reach over the lip of the roof. I venture up there two or three times a year for repairs; part of my charm offensive to maintain the status quo and keep everyone happy at the farm with our tenancy: replacing broken tiles cementing cracks, taking Carlo the TV repairman up to fit the antenna, or when I have to pull the flue pipes of the wood heaters out through the roof and bring them down to scrub out the creosote that steadily builds up inside during the winter. Stepping off the top of the ladder onto the roof is an act of faith: holding onto the top of the ladder with one hand, with one foot on the second to top rung, the other foot momentarily hanging in midair as I step onto the roof. It has a gentle pitch though, and is a serene space to occupy; almost better than lying in a bath, with plenty of time to idle and little chance of being disturbed; the kids are miles down there playing soccer on the piazza, Judy far away over there on the southern side in her *orto*. And the view!

It is amazing how a few feet of increased elevation and 360 degrees comes with such a renewed perspective.

Alerted by a persistent amplified drone coming from inside the chimney and the daily appearance of one or two or three hornets drifting into the kitchen, I am on the roof again seeking out their nest, which I discover is suspended inside the chimney by a thread anchored to the brick near the top of the stack.

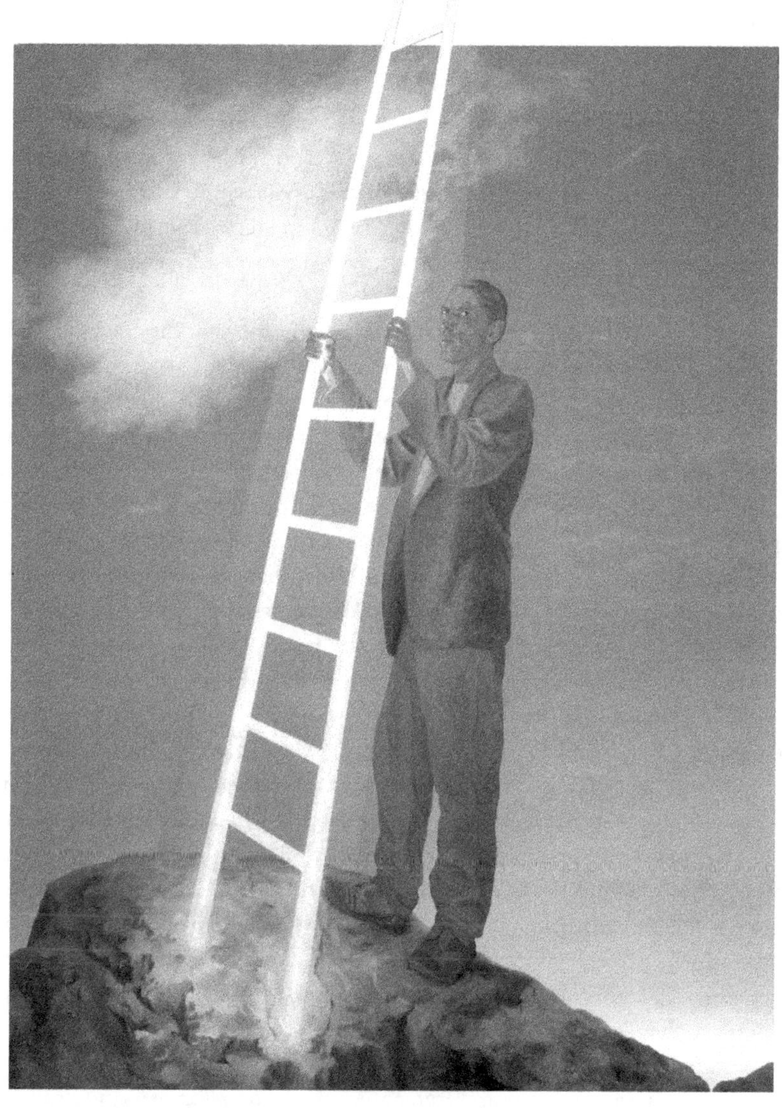

Cosmo next gen.1988

The nest is the size of a large pumpkin with finely interlaced, honey coloured wafers forming a layered conical shape. It would be easy to cut loose and bag it, if I dared to get that close. Cassagni found out the hard way and was hospitalised for several days after being stung by a hornet; his face turning to molten wax and now he is adamant:

"Never go near them. Call the *Pompieri* and let them deal with it." Advises Casagna

The first time I became aware of Tuscan hornets was at a dinner party Tim threw at his place in Montevarchi and nobody was particularly concerned. They were flying in through the open window, attracted by the light above the dining table and dropping down around our plates. We ignored them or casually swatted them away, Tim even asking:

"What are they?"

Now, watching their frenzied attacks at night as they furiously sting the window panes again and again demanding to be let in, they fill me with alarm, especially with children at home. It is a real nuisance keeping the windows closed on hot balmy summer evenings. If a hornet is buzzing around my studio, I put on a wide brimmed straw hat; they can become entangled overhead in the cobwebs of the rafters, then angrily wrenching free they plummet Kamikaze like to the floor and pose a real threat. If i'm quick enough, I can pop a glass tumbler I keep handy, over them and slip a postcard underneath, expelling them out of the window with an angry flick of the glass as a last reminder never to come back.

After due consideration of the risks involved, I have decided not to take Cassagni's advice and devised a plan of my own; I will gas the nest from below using the damper as a shield. Cassagni was puzzled when I requested a damper for the chimney; he couldn't see the point but decided to humour me, sending over my nemesis Silvini, who simply whacked a small steel plate soldered onto a central spike into the neck of the chimney; one end coming through the wall into the kitchen. Silvini, gruff as ever, left the plaster exactly where it fell on the mantelpiece and over the floor. The plate has a chain that hangs down so you can open or close it but you really have to yank at it and sometimes it won't budge if it has become encrusted in creosote, unless I climb up there with the metal ladder inside the chimney, and thwack it resoundingly with a heavy mallet.

"Are you sure you wouldn't prefer me to call the *pompieri*?" Judy calls up tentatively.

I am about to launch the attack with an aerosol from the top of the ladder, my shoulders almost corked in the chimney not leaving much room to manoeuvre as I hack away to open the plate above me. Judy knows how Germanic and stubborn I can be at times… Shsssssssssssssss… shsss, shsss… spraying for as long as I dare leave my hand exposed above the damper, aiming blindly at the nest, before beating a hasty retreat down the ladder, unexpectedly followed by the nest itself, which in the confusion has been dislodged and tumbles down after me through the gap, bursting open in the grate, as I scramble to get out of there and Judy runs for the door; but it's not the cluster bomb I had feared, more like a paper bag full of broken eggs; larvae spilling out of their combs, followed by one or two dizzy drones that are easily dispatched.

It took me five years before I finally plucked up the courage and summoned the energy to tackle painting the house for the first time. The daily showers of old paint flaking off the ceilings and beams, crumbling over bed spreads, smudged across the tiled floors when being swept up, became unbearable and too much of a daily chore. Fortunately, I was no longer bound to shepherd my spiders out of harm's way because miraculously, after three years of hell, my pact with God had finally paid off and the *motodromo* ceased to exist! It was almost an anti-climax, the way it ended, after the farmer's son married and his new bride decided that he was done; she didn't want him risking his neck on a motocross bike anymore. Not that I ever had anything against him personally, he runs the small bar in Santa Maria, a very pleasant guy to deal with but oh! The PEACE. The field has been returned to agriculture. Too late for the Mosleys i'm afraid, they had already sold the Villa and moved away. Apart from the motocross, the final nail in the coffin for them must have been the thieves posing as removal men (sic), brazenly driving up to the villa in broad daylight when the Mosley's were away and taking all of their furniture.

The apex of the ceiling in Poggio Spinoso must be 18 feet, three times my height, and to reach there is a monumental effort of will and stupidity. The only ladder for the job is the one I sequestered from the farm workers and even then I have to position it on top of the kitchen table which has to be jammed into the corners of the room in order to brace the wobbly legs. Judy would have had a fit if she ever saw me doing this but I timed the work to coincide with a holiday she was taking with Sabine and the kids. It was probably the dope, but I was very focused, and thoroughly tested each set up as I moved around the rooms dragging the kitchen table with me, before free-styling my way up the ladder clutching a bucket of whitewash in one hand and the paintbrush in the other, tentatively standing up on the second last rung of the ladder until I am fully erect, with nothing to hang on to except for a shoulder purchased against the wall. Accidents happen: cleaning the ceiling in the kids room I climbed onto their wardrobe, the one with the dodgy foot, and it proceeded to keel over with me on the top.

"Jesus Christ!"

Might conceivably have been my last words on this earth but instead I landed a perfect ten on my feet: on the floor behind the wardrobe, as it pitched forwards; one corner crashing through the window the other skewered above Toto's bed, with the bucket of slops resting on the top, tipped all over the room.

And here I am again a few years later, attempting the feat for a second time. I am older this time and have to admit that I lose my nerve at about the fifth rung from the top of the ladder; when my knees start knocking together uncontrollably and I have to climb down before I fall and bring the ladder with me. Yes, I am older, but also a little bit wiser and have realised I don't need to get to the top of the ladder to reach the ceiling; all I have to do is extend the brush on a pole!

Chapter 49.

"*Sal-tooo*!" Marina keeps urging me: leap! As if I'm permanently frozen mid-step. She calls me lazy to boot.

"How am I lazy?" I bridle.

I work until all hours of the night; weekends hardly exist for me and even then, the painting I am working on is continually playing in my head, to the point that I feel guilty and remonstrate with myself for not paying Judy enough attention or the kids. I like nothing more than her taking off for a day or two to Florence to visit Sabine with the kids, and I am left at home on my own, hungry to feed my obsessions. I suspect they all think I am deluded not just Judy; it wasn't that long ago I was reading Cosmo his bedtime story: The Emperor's New Clothes. On seeing the illustration of a rather pompous looking Emperor wearing a beehive powdered wig, Cosmo turned to me as if something had suddenly twigged in his mind and pointing to the drawing, cried out:

"Nini! Nini!"

Nearly everything I do is sacrificed on the altar of art but in times of trouble I tell myself that the great work must carry on: or I pick up the phone to my mother and have a good moan.

"What you are doing, *Schnipel,* in your paintings is encoding the history of mankind." She encourages me."Be patient. It's only a matter of timing; of meeting the right person, that someone placed on your path purposely to help you along."

"Keep the faith," Bob is fond of saying: as if art is a religion, we its priests and Ma, bless her, is a true believer who has it from a higher authority.

These days she mostly talks about Andromeda and the Council of Twelve; about crystal libraries, or her spirit guides the ascended masters Kathumi and the Lady; the UFO fleet parked in the shadow of the moon; the Greys and the battle for dominance currently raging over planet earth. I am a good listener too and she will tell me about her latest mission planting crystals in far flung places to realign Earth's magnetic fields: all to raise the vibration of world consciousness in preparation for the shift into the fifth dimension. She has her moments of despair too:

"When it's over phlooff!" Ma says, pursing her lips: "I'll be gone so fast out of Earth's orbit heading straight to the outer Pleiades that no one will even see me leave." She swipes her palms together like a rocket launcher.

I was definitely on a mission to meet that person on a trip I made to New York; or was it just another New York high: bulldozing my way into galleries? Following up every lead or phone number scribbled on scraps of paper by strangers at openings; being thorough for a change, cold calling galleries, steeling my nerve to pick up the phone and not allowing myself to be fobbed off after the first few exchanges. Victory is measured by how many times I can get my foot in the door and on that score I did pretty well in New York.

In London too:

"Are you sure you have an appointment with Mathew?" The attractive receptionist at the Flowers East gallery asks sitting on a high chair behind the desk, cupping the phone.

"Yes," I say, "and I confirmed it last week calling from Italy; the girl said I was good to come in."

This is her second attempt to rouse the director, who has gone walkabout somewhere in the old factory building. No matter I can take a peek at the exhibits and feel less conspicuous hanging around the front desk with a portfolio under my arm. Then suddenly everything is a rush after the long wait and Mathew finally appears, towering over me. "What do you want?" He snaps. I begin to explain we have an appointment, but he isn't listening and cuts me short:

"I'm a busy man here, do you think I've got time to drop everything for every artist who walks in through my doors?"

I am momentarily fazed and am unable to respond: a familiar brain freeze takes hold.

"Please don't waste my time then!" Turning on his heels and disappearing. Too late for my riposte when it finally comes:

You bastard don't waste whose time? I've come all the way from Italy just to see you! The receptionist offers me a sympathetic, knowing shrug and I am regurgitated back onto the Kingsland Road feeling distinctly distraught.

Both in New York and in London I was showing my new work, my big breakthrough after a battle of styles that has raged in my paintings for over seventeen years; a never-ending pendulum swinging between the prosaic and the poetic; the proving I can paint realism to degrees of its antithesis: abstraction. The holy grail: searching for technique, some scrap of originality; grasping at hints like dreams on the edge of imagination and gazing in wonderment at the accidental daubs in the margins of my paintings that seem to make more sense than what I see in the middle: signposts in a foreign language, all stepping stones towards the articulation of my imagination.

In 1991 Judy and I went back to Melbourne. (We actually got married in the Melbourne Town Hall, with the kids in attendance, just as I had been as a five-year-old, a pageboy falling on my arse as I strode down the aisle at my mother's wedding in St Columba's Church of Scotland in London). Melbourne became a tipping point of sorts for my progression: I found myself driving endlessly up and down like a slow wave hopper, along the broad avenues that slumber through the suburban landscape, interspersed by the dazzling greys and brilliant creams of peeling gums that spin us through the brittle blue above. The trance like motion of the car undulated in my head for ages after, like the momentum of a train that gives the illusion of forward motion long after it has come to a halt in the station. But how to translate that into paint? Napoli offered a further clue, confirming chaos is order by another name! The Eureka moment finally came in my studio, whilst watching Cosmo and Toto painting all those little masterpieces they so fearlessly produce and with such consummate ease: those busy little hands zipping around all over the place never questioning which way to turn; every direction loaded with equal promise, every colour valid in their eyes or chosen at random, nothing really mattered, results the last thing they are looking for. I call it Fearless Art—the great levelling, the point of no return; no room for hesitation, when the mind and the hand race together, embracing chaos (destruction) to create order (creation) in a single, masterly unified stroke; a place that has no room for doubt, where no such thing as a mistake exists. Intoxicating, like riding a bicycle full tilt downhill then suddenly finding the courage to sit up in the saddle, arms outstretched: confident, and secure in the knowledge that whatever I do, I have the authority to call it art. Now I tiger-pace the studio, prowling, circling my prey, stare intently at the canvas for ages then exploding into action, launching cans of diluted paint from across the room or painting with my eyes closed or with both hands, or spreadeagled on the floor, doing the breast stroke on top of two freshly painted canvases sandwiched together, then suctioning them apart; anything, anything at all to distance conscious purpose from the act of painting, to wrestle intention away from the mind, matter from the sublime.

My relationship with Bob has been cooling of late and we hardly ever see each other now; he is becoming increasingly fractious with age, holding on to grudges over this or that perceived slight and of late I just do not have the energy or time to deal with him. Even so, It was Bob I turned to when I invited him to my studio to come and see my latest works. Even though I have found a new technique and confidence in the actual execution of the work, I still feel insecure about launching my version of abstraction into the public arena. I thought showing Bob would bea way of acquiring a seal of approval, and given he used to be an abstract painter himself, I thought he would be the first one to appreciate the direction my work is taking.

His reaction therefore, was disappointing and far from 'keeping the faith,' I felt he was strangely disturbed and perhaps even looking at me now as an apostate.

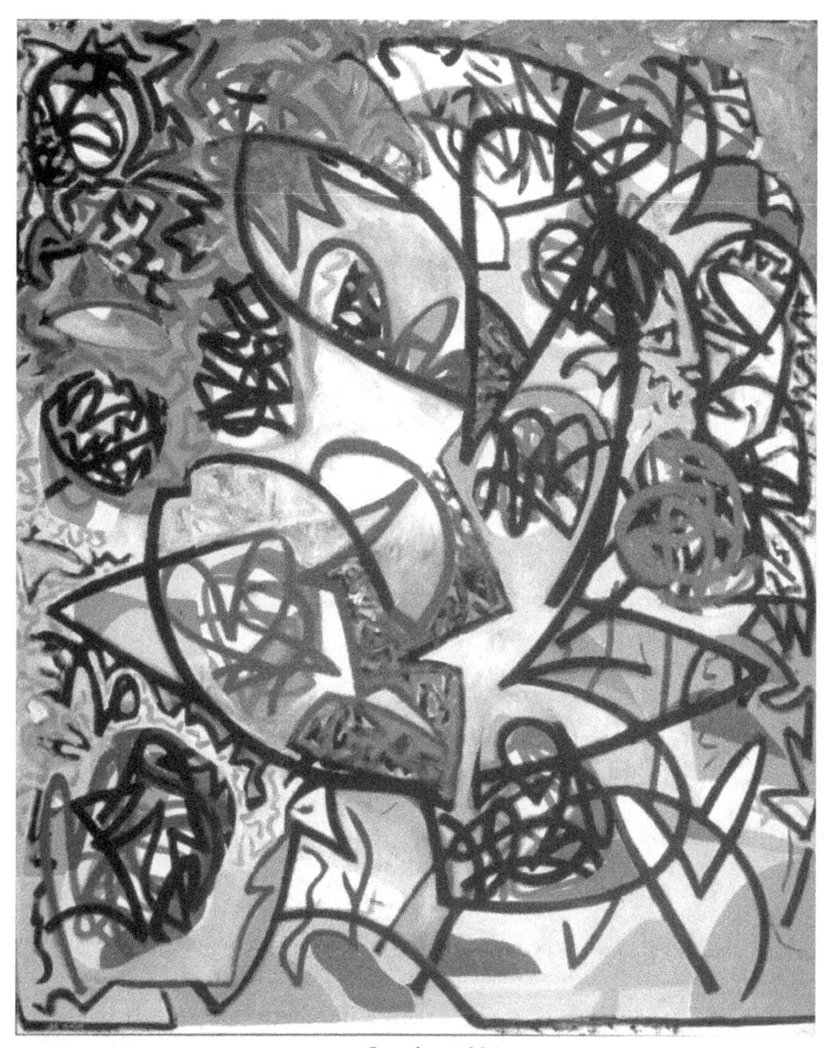

Superhero.1994

Chapter 50.

Each year at the beginning of August, Montisi, a small hill town south west of Lucignano, holds its annual festival: La Giostra del Simone. This year, David an Australian sculptor who has started exhibiting with the Sfinge alongside me, has suggested we set up an artisan stand together for the festival, renting one of the garages along the main street of the village that are vacated specifically for the occasion. We are proposing to sell a range of hand crafted, pageant fridge magnets!

The festival is a jousting tournament and pageant; it has its origins in the 1700's and commemorates the sacking of the village in the 13th century when the then unpopular feudal overlord Simone di Cacciaconti lay siege to Montisi and burnt it to the ground in reprisal for previously having been driven off his lands by the same villagers.

David lives on a property near Montisi belonging to a retired American academic. He receives board and lodging in return for his help, mainly doing odd jobs around the place and looking after the olive trees, the geese and a few sheep that she keeps on her land. The goose that laid the golden egg. When visiting, he sometimes brings us a couple of the large eggs as a gift, which for some reason I can't bring myself to eat even though I do eat eggs.

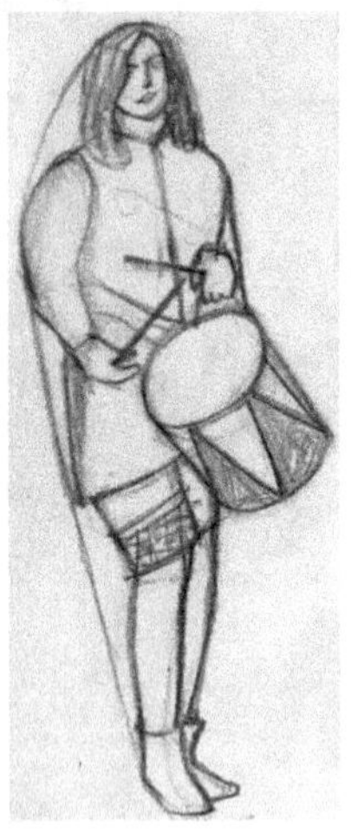

I've been busy for weeks drawing and painting onto hardboard sheets, hundreds of small mediaeval figures that David will cut out with the bandsaw in his workshop/studio: the knights, pages, courtly ladies, flag throwers, musicians and coats of arms of the four *contrade* of Montisi are all represented. David collects handmade toys and in addition to the fridge magnets, he has designed some quirky but simple wooden toy knights that bob up and down on a horse on wheels as they are pulled along by a length of doweling. Much of David's work is quirky, touched by a childlike whimsy; the toy artefacts of ancient civilisations. His sculptures are assemblages taking on the character of people and found objects often within a context of dreamy Tuscan landscapes.

Last year David took part in the festival procession through the village; head and shoulders above everyone else you couldn't miss him, decked out in a renaissance slouch cap, diamond studded pierced ear and wearing a flowing brown velvet tunic edged with gold braid. The mediaeval procession of costumed villagers solemnly parades down the main street then up to the church for the benediction of the horses taking part in the jousting tournament; temples and bells, trumpets and drums, then the four knights of the *contrade* ride out of the village along the road to the tournament ground, a large, good-humoured crowd following behind. The jousting field has a grassy knoll on one side for the spectators to sit on and opposite is a grandstand specially erected for the King and his court. Trumpeters with bannered, long-handled silver trumpets sit along the top tier, frequently springing to their feet to herald the courtly proceedings; the king signals and acrobatic flag throwers perform somersaults in front of the stand and swap missiled flags to drum rolls, then one by one the knights trot to the end of the hollow and gallop back down the centre towards us at full tilt, their extended lances aiming for a metal ring hanging from the outstretched hand of a buratto, an effigy of the much hated Simone di Cacciaconti. The festa, or sagra as it is also known, is an integral part of any Tuscan year, rolling through the hills and valleys like a 'communal wave' of celebration; eating and drinking, song and dance, getting tipsy but never too drunk. They can last for as long as a fortnight, for a few days, or even just one night in places you have never heard of up in the hills behind Cortona or down by the lake.

The biggest and most popular of the *sagras'* is the Festa dell'Unità, held throughout Tuscany principally as a fundraiser for the Communist Party's daily newspaper l'Unità. Tuscany is still a communist stronghold, although the future of the festival in Lucignano was put into some doubt because of factional fighting after the chaos of Tangentopoli. That fortunately has now been resolved and the festa,s future secured with the newly formed Democratic Party of the Left (PDS) taking over the purse strings.

A huge marquee is raised on the gravel area of the public gardens outside Lucignano, above the main road, with seating for over 300 people. A makeshift kitchen and staging area is tacked on behind. A stage is erected in the middle of the gardens, abutting the raised concrete roller skating rink, and market stalls line both sides of the avenue leading up to the top gate of the village and straddle the entrance to the gardens, offering cheap trinkets, Russian dolls and music cassettes, with soft drink vendors and food vans offering candy floss, nuts and glazed fruits and Africans hawking wooden statues and leather belts placed on blankets on the ground.

Franco, who reputedly went mad with remorse after attempting to strangle his fiancée, is feverishly pacing up and down by the public drinking fountains, as he does every day, always dressed in suit pants with an open white shirt and black tie dangling loose at the neck; chain smoking and continually muttering to himself while obsessively kneading the palm of his left hand. He was released from a psychiatric ward into the care of the community in accordance with government policy to close down psychiatric wards and he boards in the old folks home inside the village on the main street. Although he never bothers anyone directly, completely lost in his own world, endlessly admonishing himself, nobody ever approaches him either, as far as I can tell.

The festa lasts for two weeks and every evening easy throngs of people stroll through the gardens and greet each other by the fountain near the memorial to the partisans or form clusters around the park benches or over by the swings; dads on automatic, rocking empty pushers, too busy talking to friends to notice their kids have gone; children scampering the wrong way up the slide is always a popular activity. Dr. Ricciarini loudly hails all comers on his megaphone, raising funds for the sports club and spinning the wheel of fortune for his punters. A lucky straw dip stand guarantees everyone a prize for 1,000 lire and volunteers tout raffle tickets for a new car, displayed prominently by the skating rink, on a slanted platform in front of the makeshift bar. Last year, the organisers closed off the entertainment area around the rink with a bamboo fence, corralling people through a narrow entrance past heavy handed volunteers fluttering books of raffle tickets, in a blatant attempt to boost sales, but the initiative was ridiculed by one and all and has been dropped this year.

Queues form in front of the marquee as people order and pay for their meals before entering, choosing from a handwritten menu nailed to a Linden tree behind the front desk. The menu varies every day but there is always the standard *pasta al ragù, patatini* and *insalata*, along with an excellent local red or white table wine. If the marquee is crowded, nobody minds shoving up on the bench to let you squeeze in at one of the long trestle tables. Teams of busy volunteers, smartly dressed in red waistcoats, collect the order chits, if you can attract their attention, and are constantly ferrying carafes of wine and mineral water and food on platters from the smoky, makeshift kitchen behind the marquee.

Cosmo and Toto will disappear as soon as they have wolfed down their pasta and fries and if we are lucky a bowl of salad, racing off with their school friends, not to be seen again until the end of the evening, unless of course, they pop up for the money to buy an ice cream. A stream of unsupervised children ferry snacks across the road from the bar to the gardens, where they also gather in packs playing football on the grass strips between the chestnut trees, or dart off chasing each other through the crowds, seeking their own entertainments.

In the afternoons, Camilla's partner Francesco puts on popular Pulcinello 'Punch and Judy' shows in the gardens for the mums and their toddlers. Originally from Milan, he hand crafts his own puppets, art works in themselves and is in popular demand around the Valdichiana and beyond; so much so that he has taken on Marina as his assistant and is trying to train her up, although I am not convinced she is going to last for very long. A gust of wind flips up a triangle of the canvas booth revealing Marina wearing stiletto heels. Camilla is English, and like many of the *stranieri*, she has made Italy her permanent home. She lives in Lucignano and also works at the Amity school in Arezzo where she was instrumental in helping Judy to land her job. Her son Oskar, ginger hair and freckle faced, is one of Toto's best friends at the primary school. Like Claire and Gianni, whose kids, Michele and May, are the same age as our boys, we as parents tend to see each other more. The logical procession going through life I suppose, socialising with like, whether single or a couple or as parents.

After our meal, Judy and I will linger in the marquee, drinking wine or moving around the tables chatting with people we know before drifting over to the skate rink to watch the evening's *spettacolo*. The entertainment varies night to night: a local beauty pageant and local bands performing on the stage, or touring troupes of folk dancers from as far away as Brazil or the Ukraine; even horseless Cossacks performing dizzy cartwheels across the rink. The Brazilian dancers, dressed in skimpy carnival outfits, are always very popular and you have to be there early if you want a seat, as is the case with the traditional evening of *ballo liscio,* ballroom dancing; grandmothers putting granddaughters through their paces early on before the swelling throng of dancers needs to jostle for space, foxtrotting and waltzing and even attempting to tango. Dina, the Southerns' housekeeper is always there, tossing her head back laughing, holding on to her new husband Mario, or Lolanda from the hardware store, dressed for the occasion, her string of pearls and make up on, leading her compliant husband crisply across the floor, until finally, slowing, weary couples desert the rink one by one: they kill horses, don't they?

Chapter 51.

Little David and I have decided to take a stall at the monthly Arezzo weekend antique market. Little David, the New Zealand painter as opposed to Big David the sculptor from Australia as we now know him in order to avoid any confusion when talking with the kids. Seen together however there is no mistaking them; a hobbit as opposed to a giraffe, raucous as opposed to self-effacing. Big David has an understated sense of humour and is guarded, more English than Antipodean, whereas Little David, perhaps to make up for his size, is prone to hyperbole and can get into your ear with his exuberance, his high IQ and his lofty impenetrable ideas. I gravitate towards eccentrics, Judy remarks often enough.

Fortunately for us, this year the Arezzo Comune is on one of its periodic drives to promote local arts and crafts and has been offering resident artists an opportunity to apply for a stall holder's licence at greatly reduced rates. When I turn up at the office with my application, I have at the ready a franked envelope with my name and address on it, which I was told, is regarded as sufficient proof of residency!

Normally it is extremely hard to get into the antique market unless you know someone with a stall, like Australian Claire does; conceded one small corner of her friend's table, where she sells her hand printed fabric scarves. I met Claire when we were both taking part in an artists' workshop at the Fortezza in Cortona. The event, lasting all of August, was open to the public, and billed as a performance: "An exhibition not of works but of artists creating works." Exactly the kind of therapy I needed at the time, coming so soon after my father died.

Claire is the one who first introduced Judy and I to Gianni and Claire; They both teach English as a second language at the Academia Britannica in Arezzo and are best friends. Language schools have become all the rage in Tuscany. Michaeli, who is always on the lookout for the next best thing, has bought the rights to a proprietary subliminal language teaching method and hired Rupert to help him set up a language school in his workshop premises on via Coppi. He has a limited attention span and was already losing interest in the Attwoodstove, which Martin and John by then were winding down anyway. Martin told me it was the phenomenal success of the stove that proved its undoing, especially after a feature praising it appeared in The Sunday Times Review sending demand through the roof. He said they were not prepared to take it to the next level and decided to shut the business down. Besides, John is in love and wants to move to Munich and Martin has found an Austrian princess!

I have an assortment of kitchen chairs I want to sell at the market and a collection of cheap tin trays that Judy unearthed for me at the Superal supermarket in Arezzo, all breezily painted in my new "anything goes" painterly abstract style. Little David intends to sell his wife Heidi's vases and pencil holders: hollowed out heads that are modelled in clay with caricature faces painted on that are both comical and cute and he thinks will sell well. Heidi is significantly older than David, a factor she frequently alludes to, although their age differences don't seem to bother him nearly as much, if at all. In fact, they seem very well suited, which I admire, considering my issues with Carolyn before.

They are house sitting a *casa colonica* just outside Trequanda, a situation that has lasted two years and he thinks could become permanent. The owner, an Italian from Rome, has no plans for the house and rarely visits but he pays all their bills including the groceries! Once a week in the evenings, Little David is giving me lessons on his new PC. Judy's father Phil has offered to buy Cosmo and Toto a computer now that they have graduated to the *scuola elementare* in Lucignano and ostensibly I am learning in order to help them later on. I can't wait to get my hands on one. Judy isn't in the least bit interested in computers, she can't even type and has no intentions of starting and neither have Cosmo and Toto shown any great interest; they don't even pester us for a Nintendo like their school friends: instead enjoy more rural pursuits. Along with Antonella's two boys, Marco and Nicola at Campo Forte, they officially make up the farm gang; often disappearing for the entire day on farm adventures, or getting caught at the Southerns' spying on Gunilla swimming in her pool!

Little David can be mercurial if he drinks too much, but installed in front of his computer even with a glass or two or three of wine; he is completely docile. Unfortunately, he tends to hog the screen time, mesmerised like me by the miracle of splashing paint on the desktop with Canvas™; the satisfying thunk of a draw being opened, revealing rows of brushes or paints and lulled by the double clicking knitting-needles sounds made by the mouse. He is as content as a purring cat over a saucer of cream, every now and again throwing out a titbit of information that I might pick up if I'm sufficiently awake.

Judy has suggested buying a Macintosh, which is a turn up for the books knowing how careful she is with money and considering the Mac is the most expensive option. She is the only person I know who scrutinises the docket at the supermarket checkout and surprises me at times, finding discrepancies: or in restaurants, she always double-checks the bill just to be sure we are not paying for something we didn't order. Something I would never do!

"Easier for the kids to learn on a Mac and state of the art computer graphics for artists." Recommends one of her close gardening friends, who owns one. I secretly agree knowing if it was me making the suggestion it would be dismissed out of hand.

"The Rolls Royce of computers" sighs Little David wistfully stroking his beard. "If only I could afford one!" Then sobering: "But you have to ask yourself what kind of roads you're going to be driving on?"

Judy and I have been to lunch at Christian's my old neighbour from Valecchie and he can't stop ringing the praises of his new Macintosh either, especially the new chess app that comes with it. He highly recommends Massimo the Apple distributor in Arezzo, who I will go and visit. Post Carolyn, I hardly ever set foot in the valley; it almost feels like trespassing and makes me feel nervous. Carolyn and I have not spoken for over eleven years although very occasionally I catch glimpse of her sitting outside a bar on the Corso and Judy says she knows who she is although they have never met.

Stone Age man to hi tech guy, Christian is full of surprises. He has cut his hair and shaved his wolf-man beard and almost looks respectable these days; a man of leisure even, his Leica casually strung over his shoulder as he strolls down the Corso taking photos or turns up unexpectedly to my exhibition opening in Napoli. Mary Jane, Christian's wife, is better than I have ever seen her. They have three children now and from what I understand he still takes on most of the parenting but Mary Jane nevertheless is holding down a part time job and says she enjoys getting out. She shows glimpses of what I imagine she used to be like: flashes of humour and a mischievous glint in her dark brown eyes once more come alive. When we are leaving, she promises to be there at the next Sfinge opening as long as I provide the Budweiser beer.

The fall of the Berlin wall and the reunification of Germany has had a beneficial financial result for Christian's family, allowing them to reclaim property they once owned in East Germany, then confiscated by the State. My grandparents haven't fared so well because land they once owned in Silesia, seized by the Russians at the end of the second world war, have been excluded from reparations under the terms of the 1990 German—Poland border treaty.

Hans, Marina's friend the sculptor told me that East German artists received a nasty shock after the celebrations ended because the cost of art materials, previously subsidised by the government, immediately shot up in true capitalist style. In the old days, he said, they could afford to be wasteful, leaving tops off the tubes of oil paint or binning them only half used. I know exactly what he meant, feeling the financial pinch myself and having to utilise a plastic contraption that squeezes out the last drops of paint from the tube; even slicing the tube open after and scraping off what's left on the tin walls!

Little David picks me up in the Landcruiser before dawn on a cold, miserable winter's morning and we head off to Arezzo. We set up our stall in a sunless, designated street on the very fringes of the antique market, miles away from where the real action is and along with the others, spend most of our time trying to keep warm. A maze of stalls radiates out from Piazza Grande down the Corso and up the hill to the Duomo and I can only envy my friend Franco, an artist who is in the thick of it having his studio in one of the converted stables under the loggia in Piazza Grande. All he has to do is throw open his barn style doors and invite the masses inside to browse his art works and the assorted bric-a-brac he sets up on tables for them to buy.

Stallholders come from as far away as Napoli; driving up in over laden trucks full of second-hand furniture, fake antiques and dodgy religious artefacts. They set up camp in the streets behind the Corso and keep warm in winter huddling round improvised braziers, burning off palettes, cardboard and sticks of broken furniture in rusty old oil drums. Africans spread out their wares on the pavement and in doorways along the Corso. They are as jumpy as the pigeons, ready to bundle up their goods and dart off at the first sign of a Vigile and then just as quickly, settle back in place on the all clear. An irate woman making a scene is accusing a protesting stall-holder of selling jewellery that was stolen from her home and the Carabinieri frog-march the unfortunate man away still vehemently protesting his innocence; the crowds that have gathered around to witness the spectacle, chortling long afterwards.

At peak hours in the morning, large crowds jam the streets, jostling for space, making it hard to get near the stall tables, but not where we are! Unfortunately, there is no crush, no rush of marauding bargain hunters keen to lay their hands on one of our bargains. So far, we haven't sold anything and are seriously debating whether it's worth coming back again tomorrow. Probably, we cut unwelcoming figures for prospective buyers although Little David manages to put on a thin smile before it fades again; if someone picks up a ceramic head, turns it over in their hand before putting it down on hearing the price. One thing I haven't anticipated is the awkwardness I feel whenever I recognise someone coming down the street towards us and it's reached the point where I instinctively duck out of sight. Little David hasn't cottoned on yet, why I keep disappearing, but must think my behaviour is a bit peculiar. Say yes I keep urging myself. Front up and stand your ground!

But my problem is that I find demeaning! I feel I am losing face, that people will say: look at him, if he really was an artist, he wouldn't be selling this crap in the street. We are both disconsolate on our way home and have sworn never to come back.

Chapter 52.

I have found shopping in Lucignano to be a pleasanter experience than in Cortona; it is a ritual mutually observed by both sides: shopkeepers giving advice and customers, always with plenty to say, are inevitably connoisseurs with tastes that need to be respectfully considered and catered for. The salami or the mortadella has to be sliced just so thin, the various saddles of prosciutto brought down and inspected, the cheese sampled, its age and provenance revealed and melons are inevitably given the sniff-test for ripeness and then passed round to other customers in the shop for second opinions. More than anything this daily ritual exemplifies the respect they give to food. What was cooked yesterday and what is for lunch today, explaining each course in minute detail is always a topic much expounded at the counter, as is the vexed question of al dente; a real Italian conundrum because taste demands the pasta should be neither hard nor soft, and how long it is cooked for is an open debate, remembering that according to some experts, you need to take into account the extra seventeen seconds it takes on average for the pasta to reach the table from the stove.

This level of sophistication is a far cry from the days I was working in an Italian café in Notting Hill Gate in London, where we pre-cooked the spaghetti in the mornings and reheated it at lunchtime under the steam pipe of the espresso machine as each new order came in.

Back in the shop, the upshot of all this social connectivity is long delays at the counter, but unlike the big supermarkets springing up in new shopping malls outside Lucignano, nobody cares or is in too much of a rush. We had been shopping at Santini's, the Duemila supermarket by the bottom gate, until that is, the day I came home with a loaf of stale bread and a kilo of sprouting potatoes that grandma Santini swore were "an Italian delicacy." Judy thinks I am an idiot and refuses to shop there anymore, which is a pity because old man Santini makes the best 'sold under the counter' vin santo. As a consequence we have transferred our allegiance to the top supermarket, the Crai, another family run business, where the son Massimo gives out boiled sweets instead of small change at the check-out and loves to discuss the merits of Battistuta's ("Battigol") latest goal for Fiorentina: Massimo being a die-hard Viola supporter.

Not long after I first arrived in Cortona, I found myself the sole English soccer fan in a packed Bar Sport watching the England versus Italy match on the TV. Italy scored first and the entire bar rose as one, fisting the air in jubilation; all that is except for me, left stranded on my seat and unsure how I should react should England go on to score a goal of its own, which thankfully they didn't.

As a boy, my dream was to be a footballer and I used to get down on my knees by my bed every night and pray:

"Dear God! Please make me a professional footballer when I grow up."

I dreamt of being a goalie for Manchester United, following in the footsteps of Alex Stepney, even though I was still a Watford fan; but that was mainly because my friends thought it gave us more cred supporting a lowly third division team. Watford did have Tony Currie, a flamboyant future England striker, and Ken Furphy was the manager well before Graham Taylor's time, the future England manager, or before Elton John became the chairman and rocketed the club into being fashionable.

Football is a religion in Italy and it is no coincidence that games are played on Sundays after Mass. The men, dressed in their Sunday suites, walk around with transistor radios glued to their ears listening to live commentaries: everything from Serie A, the top league, to local minor league games. I have seriously intellectual conversations about *calcio* with Gianni or Marina's boyfriend Enzo and of course Massimo up at the Crai checkout in Lucignano.

Sunday evening TV is taken up entirely with the televised highlights, and replays ad nauseam of every single goal scored in Serie A that day, followed by the endless panel discussions and post mortems, dissecting every nuance of the day's play plus in-depth critical analysis of all the referees' decisions.

My favourite program is Il Processo di Biscardi on TeleMontecarlo. Aldo Biscardi, the host, is an earnest, middle-aged man with coiffed tinted auburn hair, who without fail contrives to lose control of his guests as they inevitably start slugging it out between each other, hurling insults and wildly gesticulating, with Biscardi becoming increasingly sullen and tetchy, snapping at his guests to no avail amidst the rising crescendo of noise. It is pure Italian television drama with resolution always delivered at the last moment, everybody suddenly smiling, shaking hands and patting backs. It is so quintessentially Italian to spoil for a fight for instance in a bar or make a great show of fisticuffs on the Senate floor, but only done in the knowledge that there will be someone close by, ready to restrain all parties before things go too far. There is an old joke from the desert war,(originating as German propaganda) about Italian tanks having only one forward gear and three in reverse, that I believe has a ring of truth because it serves as a testament to how Italians never overestimate themselves when it comes to individual survival and how their love of life and living is a priority above all else.

The only time I have ever felt under threat as an "Englishman" in Tuscany was after the Heysel stadium tragedy in 1985, when Liverpool fans, "the hooligans" were blamed for the collapse of the wall inside the stadium that caused the death of thirty-nine Juventus fans during the European Cup final. Even Noemi was wagging his finger at me! The prevailing undercurrent of anger reminded me of the time I was in Sydney with Carolyn and the treatment dished out to Argentinian born Australians during the Falklands war. That was the same year, 1982, Italy won the World Cup, and delirious Italian fans were tearing up Sydney in the middle of the night, blaring car horns and streaming Italian flags out of car windows in wild celebrations.

When Italy hosted the World Cup eight years later in 1990, big screens were erected in the piazzas of every village and town around the Valdichiana and there was a lively, carnival atmosphere across the Nation that lasted right up to the semi-finals when the Italians lost to the Argentinians in Naples and the whole country was plunged into collective grief. The morning after felt like a hangover with an eerie, unfamiliar silence pervading the streets of Lucignano.

We had a repeat two years ago when Italy lost in the final to Brazil. Enzo couldn't bear to watch the penalty shoot-out after extra-time and turned his back on the big screen as Baresi, the Italian captain, stepped up to the spot to take his penalty kick and blazed it past the post, immediately followed by the then Golden Boot boy, Roberto Baggio, lovingly known as *il codino* (the pony-tail), an Italian legend, who famously ballooned the decisive kick high over the bar: a sight so rare it wasn't worth missing, I told Enzo after.

The Lucignano football team is in a minor league but it is always well supported at home games. The *stadio* is just past the cemetery at the corner of our road; a small floodlit ground with tiered concrete bleachers running down one side and changing rooms slightly down the hill behind the dug outs on the opposite side. Cosmo and Toto both made their debuts on this ground and playing youth tournaments they still give me goosebumps as the teams line up in the centre circle before the start, all holding hands and their names are called out over the loud speakers.

Juvenile football is taken very seriously: training is twice a week and the licensed coach is respectfully called "Mister" (Meester) by the kids, just like the big league coaches. Kit bags with logoes have to be regularly replenished with new gear—a tracksuit for match days, a different one for training: quilted anoraks with zippered sleeves for winter and Autumn, the latest soccer boots, and always the ubiquitous hairdryer. Changing rooms equipped with multiple wall sockets, are bedlam after training or matches, with parents busy blow-drying children's hair or towelling them down, shaking out clothes and getting them dressed; new kids, at least initially, hoping to slink off home without having to take a shower.

A serious business but parents aren't screaming from the touchline at their sporting prodigies; we manage to hide our disappointments and want the kids to enjoy themselves, reinforcing the idea that the game is an important stepping-stone in the children's socialisation.

Cosmo and Toto are now playing for Sinalunga where the club boasts a covered stand and Plexiglas dugouts for the mister and subs. Other Dads (Giovanni and Giacomo's, for instance) agree that Cosmo is a gifted player and although I have no ambitions regarding his sporting future, I see him in the David Beckham mould and can get genuinely excited watching him play; those dreamy midfield runs with his long blond hair flowing, dribbling past the older boys, his yellow boots covering every blade of grass as he never stops running, floating in those lovely crosses that seem to hang forever then clip the bar.

Chapter 53.

Christian gloats when I visit him at home, going out of his way to show me the precious Persian carpet he has hanging on his newly whitewashed wall, trilling in his pleasant faltering baritone:

" Where your painting should've been!" (*The year of dying quietly*).

At least we are friends again; for a while he thought I was trying to rip him off, claiming I had originally quoted him a much lower price for the painting then accusing me of being greedy because I knew he had come into some money! As if! Never mind, I missed out on a sale because of the misunderstanding but I was ambivalent anyway about selling that particular work, painted in memory of my father.

We duly bought the computer from Massimo in Arezzo: a power Macintosh, the very latest model, thanks to Phil, Judy's father. Massimo is very personable and a consummate salesman, projecting himself more in the mould of a trusted personal adviser. He runs the Apple dealership with his brother Paolo, out of a cramped office space under a modern residential block on the outskirts of Arezzo. Paolo is more circumspect, the nerdy technician, his head stuck in the guts of a computer on his cluttered desk, or fielding urgent telephone calls from distressed clients in need of instant assistance and rushing out of the building. You can feel the tension as soon as you walk in, dealing as the brothers do with the high levels of angst and the low thresholds of their customers. Apple itself is in danger of going into liquidation. I think they appreciate how calm I appear in comparison and if there is a lull in business, Massimo and I will head off to the bar for an espresso.

Massimo completely understands my need for discretion as far as Judy goes and how much she knows about what I am spending to turbo charge the new computer. The beauty of computers is that they keep their secrets well hidden inside: nothing to show where the money is going. Judy is worried about our finances at the moment because she has been out of work since the collapse of the Amity school and is thinking about setting up her own gardening business; mulling over an offer from our new neighbour Ita, to redesign her garden at Belvedere Antico up on Millionaires' Row.

The Amity school was brought down after it was rocked by a series of sexual abuse scandals involving members of staff and the Director and founder of the school. The students went on strike as a result: refusing to attend the obligatory daily counselling sessions known as "raps" and "propheets": the one-on-one, the peer group or group therapy sessions that were a core part of the school's mission.

Group sessions, sometimes lasting all night, could be gruelling and extremely confrontational in nature; young souls often subjected to torrents of emotional abuse, pressured into laying bare their darkest secrets and innermost feelings. Judy sometimes complained her students could hardly stay awake in the mornings after those sessions. The final nail in the coffin came when the parents started pulling their children out of school in a vote of no confidence, causing the school to collapse.

My mother thinks Judy could grow a garden in the middle of the desert if she had to and Ita was equally impressed with Judy's efforts at Poggio Spinoso. Ita has big plans for Belvedere Antico, a grand villa her father bought her as a wedding gift. She is young (in her twenties), attractive, wealthy and already onto her second husband, a former tennis pro, now employed in her father's menswear empire.

Judy enjoys new challenges; she likes reinventing herself and even before Amity folded, she had been toying with the idea of starting up her own garden design business. The only thing that has been holding her back, she says, is her lack of confidence in speaking Italian. I disagree, she underestimates her Italian, especially since the kids started school, and I encourage her to take the next step. We have even been down to Sinalunga to the do-it-yourself printing kiosk, to print out a new business card for her: the "Green Thumb" adding her green thumbprint on after.

Last year our garden was included in the itinerary of a guided tour of Tuscan gardens when we hosted a lively group of Australian retirees over lunch. The pullman tour bus bringing the group couldn't make it all the way down *la strada bianca* to our house, forcing them to walk the last kilometre and afterwards I had to ferry them all in twos and threes in the car, back to the bus.

Judy is passionate about gardening and has even devised her own philosophy; believing a garden should gently meld itself into the surrounding landscape and not just stand apart from it. Her favourite bedtime reading is the seed catalogues she subscribes to and ever since arriving in Tuscany she has been pouring over plant and gardening books, acclimatising herself with the flora and the prevailing growing conditions. Early on she joined the Mediterranean Garden Society and has written articles for their quarterly magazine; with her coterie of gardening friends, she regularly goes on jaunts visiting private gardens and she likes nothing better than to ferret out specialist nurseries, travelling the length and breadth of Tuscany to do so.

By now, I'm used to stopping the car for her at a moment's notice as she jjumps out to pick curb-side Easter daisies or larkspurs or lilacs, or anything with promise for her vase arrays and gift bouquets. (She jokes I'm so doggedly German when driving down the autostrada, refusing to stop for anyone, and this is her revenge.) Then she thinks nothing of hopping over someone's garden fence to take a cutting (even in India) justifying it as being an acceptable part of gardening culture! Local train stations are happy hunting grounds for her too, as she attentively scans the neatly arranged flower gardens laid out alongside the platforms; lovingly tended by stationmasters' wives, and a point of stationmasters' pride as well as fierce rivalry between stations.

Trained as a historian, Judy's thirst for botanical knowledge is equalled by a fondness for research; once inveigling Gabriele to invite us to lunch at his grandparents, specifically wanting to question them about the herbs and plants that were popular with the contadini in by-gone days.

The collection of succulents and small plants in old rubbish tip vessels that line our stairs are a part of a contadino tradition she points out, and there are similar displays around their houses, as well as around the Maesta along the roadsides; the shrines to the Madonna that are lovingly tended by old ladies and are such a common feature of the Tuscan landscape.

Working through the winter at Belvedere has been hard on Judy: looking as delicate as a rag doll, hacking at the frozen solid earth, toiling through hail or shine, laying out her garden plans from architectural drawings in preparation for the plantings in spring. She is hands on and a meticulous planter: holes need be just so deep, this wide and that far apart and they must be dressed and mulched correctly afterwards. How many times have I been told to carry on digging when I thought the hole was big enough!

The *contadini* assigned to assist her are resistant at first: they have never heard of mulching and anyway find it hard to take orders from a woman.

Far too often she ends up doing the work herself but by so doing she is slowly winning them over, or shaming them, with her enormous propensity for manual work; enough to gain their respect and now be addressed as l'architetta. Judy has also impressed Di Banella, the architect supervising the renovations at Belvedere Antico, a local man, who has started introducing her to some of his other clients and in turn bringing her prospects of even more work.

Chapter 54.

I had not seen Marco since he was teenager, when he unexpectedly resurfaced again a couple of years back at a party Judy and I were attending outside Cortona. He used to visit the tower with his sister Mira to see Jef and then dropped out of sight whilst doing his military service in a parachute regiment somewhere over Italy.

Marco swaggered into the party that night like a conquistador with his dark beard and potbelly, only missing the comb morion and a sheathed rapier, claiming he had been living in a Jesuit mission in South America during the intervening years. Marco has always been a great story teller and you never know if what he says is actually the truth: that is his art, like the work he does in the theatre as a director; a life lived full of imagination, inevitably pulling you into his theatre of dreams and equally spitting you out but with just enough charm to insure you will be back again. Was he really calling me from the Balkans in the middle of the war? Claiming he was there on an assignment for an Italian newspaper!

Tiziano, Marco's best friend from school is another case; they did have a reputation in Cortona as wild boys, now only tempered slightly by the fact that they are both married. I was wary of Tiziano initially because he was always drunk and, in my face, whenever I saw him, usually at Imola's wine bar. He liked to flaunt his credentials as a *muratore,* one of the proletariats, viewing me with suspicion being an artist and middle-class, even though he wrote poetry and his mother is a well respected school teacher.

Imola's bar the Enotria in Via Nazionale, is the place people meet these days, especially the drinkers, and it's the place to go if you are ever looking for someone and can't find them. Bar Signorelli's attraction has waned since Benito took an early retirement to go fishing and the regular Saturday morning crowd of *stranieri* has long since dispersed or else the well healed crowd you find in there these days isn't one I am familiar with.

The confined space of the Enotria is usually thick with stale tobacco smoke and intoxicating wine fumes. Imola holds court perched high on a stool behind her small polished bar, laughing, cigarette in hand, sparing no one with her wicked wit, as she doles out glasses of wine and a constant supply of toasted *ciaccia* bread appetisers to help keep us sober and in line. Meanwhile her husband Italo, a former mayor of Cortona, his coat elegantly draped over his shoulders, his brown leather briefcase tucked under the chair, sits in the back playing cards with his cronies.

The only people you won't find in there are Bob, who after a few blips on his road, is now the picture of sobriety, or Rupert who I rarely see these days and steers well clear of Cortona anyway. His growing family of three kids kept him at home at first as a home Dad, writing articles for a business magazine to make ends meet while his wife Donatella went out to work and supported him studying for the *libero professionista* exam in Arezzo, which has now paid off as they both run an agency letting holiday villas. Frances Mayes mentions him in her book *Under The Tuscan Sun* as the "puzzled" British Estate Agent who helps her find Villa Bramasole; although when I asked him why he told me he has no clue why she referred to him as such.

Her book is turning Cortona upside down with all the attention it has garnered and the busloads of American tourists on pilgrimages to her villa must drive her insane with all the intrusions on her privacy. Bramasole, Jef reminded me, means "longing for the sun"; an appropriate name and ironical given the title of her book. I can remember looking down on the villa years ago, when I was perched high up above it in my secret garden behind the fortezza and always thinking how sad and forlorn the house seemed, all alone and stuck in the shadow of the city wall.

I have come to appreciate Tiziano the more I get to know him. Surprisingly for all his bluster, he is actually a sensitive soul and surprisingly articulate, especially when it comes to his comprehensive knowledge of the cinema. This year, he and Marco have successfully organised a festival of Independent film to be held in Teatro Signorelli; Cortona's very own mini La Scala opera house built in the nineteenth century, replete with a decorated oval ceiling, imposing semicircular tiers of private boxes stacked high above the auditorium and plenty of gilt and red plush to dazzle the eye. The festival (Cinemautografo) will screen every Thursday night during December and February and is offering a full program of films including new works by Kiarostami, Loach, Kassovitz and Italian directors like Martelli who is presenting his film Pole Pole in person. Marco and Tiziano have asked me to design the festival poster in return for a season ticket.

They are financing the festival entirely out of their own pockets, hoping just to break even by selling season tickets and vending books in the foyer during intermissions. They take it in turns to man the ticket booth and play host afterwards, strolling down the aisle together to the front of the auditorium with their guests and presenting each film to the audience. Tiziano goes out of his way to look scruffy and shuffles with his hands in his pocket, feeling uncomfortable in front of a crowd but when called upon he usually has something interesting to add. Marco on the other hand, ever the showman, loves the attention and regales the audience with his stories; as long as, that is, he has not had one too many to drink when his mood can shift to petulance.

After the evening screenings a small group of us, Marina and Gabriele included, sometimes with the director in tow, will head for a bar and buy bottles of good wine out of the festival takings! Marco is generous that way, or we will go to Route 66 for a pizza, usually ending up late into the night at Marco's place just outside Cortona, talking about films and how we could be making a film of our own.

Chapter 55.

Almost as an afterthought Judy yells up from the bottom of the stairs:

" See you later!"

She is always in a rush these days as I watch her leave from the boys' bedroom window, sprinting down the drive in the car. The number of her clients is increasing as word spreads of the beautiful gardens she is creating throughout the shire.

The month of May is her busiest time of the year, when she juggles the trillion things she has to do in her head, forever coming and going through the day, loading and unloading the car with row upon row of potted shrubs and mountains of discarded flowerpots lining the shady side of the house by the piazza; transferred during winter into a makeshift greenhouse that I have cobbled together in the pigsty under my studio on the other side of the house.

Ten minutes later the phone rings.

"Pronto?"

"It's me." Judy says in a low, apologetic voice.

"I've had an accident...

"In the car…

"I'm calling from Le Cadute (The Fallen sic) ...

"Yes really!...

"I'm not joking...

"No, I'm okay…

"Yes, I'm fine, but I think I've written off the car! …

"Yes, a write off…

"I don't know how it happened…

"By the cemetery…

"No. Nobody else was involved…

"I must have hit something, it's all a big blur …

"I was going slowly! The car must have flipped over...

"Todisco came by, he said he'd call Romano…

"They let me use the phone here but I better go. Get up here as soon as you can...

"OK, bye. But hurry, please." And she hangs up.

I chase off up the hill to the cemetery on foot; the kids are at school, and when I arrive Judy is calmly snapping photographs of our sad, defeated looking car. Romano is already on the scene tut-tutting in amazement, sweeping broken glass off to the side of the road; Romano our friendly car mechanic whose garage is close by. The Renault 5 looks like it has been ignominiously dumped in front of the cemetery gates like a half-squashed, brightly coloured bug; the Renault 5 that I drove all the way across Europe from Edinburgh after my father's funeral, a gift from him to Sue who then decided to give it to me and for sentimental reasons keep his beloved silver Merc. Our Fiat Panorama was in desperate need of repairs and has been left abandoned in the stables under the house for the last few years; Cassagni even made room for it, taking away some of the farm machinery that was stored there.

Judging by the state of the Renault, it's a miracle Judy has survived, and with hardly a scratch on her as far as I can see.

"Shouldn't you sit down?"

She must be in shock I'm thinking.

"I'm okay. It happened so fast" She replies calmly.

I give her a hug.

Judging by the caved in roof, it looks like the car somehow did a somersault and the landed back on its feet. Unbelievable! At some point Judy must have sailed through the air upside down.

"Lucky I was wearing my seat belt."

"What happened?" I ask.

"I think I must have clipped the curbstone there and flipped over."

I walk back twenty yards to inspect the black stone on the corner, set into the side of the road.

"Yes it appears to be scratched." I call over my shoulder. "But solid enough because it's hardly budged."

"I've taken a look at the car" Romano announces with an air of commiseration,

yanking back the front fender, peeling it away from the wheel.

"You should be able to drive it home but in my opinion the damage isn't worth the expense of repairing it."

Antonia, my cousin, once crashed the Renault when she was staying; it's all downhill driving back from the village to our house and she misjudged her speed approaching the tricky left-hand corner just before the Mosleys' old place. The car slewed off into a small olive grove as she was braking, taking a few olive saplings with her and buckling the chassis under the passenger door. It could happen to anyone, considering the *strada bianca* is a badly cambered roller-coaster ride; one I have driven a thousand times and still can't get the hang of: sheets of black ice cover it in winter and the steeper gradients are bedrock with the rain.The Comune rarely repairs it and in summer, on the flat stretches, the steering wheel handles like a machine gun over the ruts and the coating of finely powdered white dust makes it slipperier than an ice rink.

I was sideswiped once in the Fiat Panorama by someone coming round a bend not looking, then braking and skidding into me and had the nerve to claim it was my fault. Roby managed a head on once almost in front of Poggio Spinoso, having just departed with great fanfare after a weekend stay. Soon after we heard a great smack from the road and he was back again on foot this time. Fortunately, nobody was hurt but I had to drive him to the station and Romano came down and towed his car away.

I felt bad about the damage done to the olive trees after Antonia's accident and decided to look for the owner, suspecting anyway that he probably already knew who I was. I have often noticed a contadino working up above the road on the opposite bank and it was more than likely that he would have told the owner, who it transpired is the shepherdess's husband. He was grateful that I had bothered to track him down and not wanting reparations was happy to leave it at that. Some months later however I received a payback of sorts when I encountered the shepherdess with her flock on the same stretch of road and moving my car over to the side and onto the verge to let them squeeze by, a couple of the sheep panicked as they were passing and started clambering up onto the bonnet of the Renault, badly scratching the red paintwork, but I didn't point it out to the shepherdess and nor did she mention it.

Judy is amazing; she shows no sign of delayed shock and I've been watching her closely over the last couple of days. We managed to limp home with the car and have parked it out of sight behind the forno. With family commitments and of course with Judy's work, it's essential we have a car and as luck would have it, Romano has a Fiat Uno for sale at his garage. He doesn't normally sell cars but this belongs to an old client who recently passed away so he is happy to vouch for it, having looked after it for a number of years and happy to get it out of his garage.

Romano is my mechanic, the mechanic I swear by and who I will always recommend to anyone who asks. Besides being a mechanic, he is an armchair philosopher who likes nothing better than lighting up a cigarette in his office, tipping back in his swivel chair and putting his feet up on his empty desk (except for a telephone book) before launching forth into the meaning of the Global economy and the rise of the Chinese. Age, tinged by some personal tragedy has marked him; his wife died at an early age of leukaemia, leaving him to bring up their two sons. He has a furrowed forehead, jowl cheeks and often wears a hangdog expression; nevertheless when you win his attention a light switches on and his brows ruck up as he betrays a real schoolboy's delight. He is not above gossip either as we discuss the implications of his friends' latest adulteries.

Romano chain-smokes, puffing away on his tortoise shell cigarette holder, which, he tries to convince me, is good for his health; never tiring of flipping open the cylinder housing the disposable filter to show me just how much tar it collects. I know better: the holder is only a ruse to enable him to smoke with greasy hands, or when he is flat on his back under a car; the cigarette holder permanently stuck in his mouth.

About the only thing he isn't philosophical about is the *superstrada*, which he can't wait to see built because he can't sleep, having to put up with the traffic and the hydraulic breaking of the lorries trundling up and down the hill right past his front door. Locals have greeted Mozzoni's latest attempt at appeasement with howls of derision, after he offered to turn the farm into a "*Parco Lucignanese*" with the one condition that the proposed route of la *superstrada* is moved away from his land.

The widow of the Fiat Uno's previous owner lives in Santa Maria where I bring her the change of ownership papers to sign. She is a pensioner and invites me in, offering a cup of tea and once seated she starts reminiscing fondly about her late husband; telling me how he used to chauffeur her around everywhere because she doesn't drive, tears starting to well up in her eyes. I feel guilty as I pull out of her drive, watching her in the rear-view mirror standing on her doorstep waving goodbye, perhaps stranded there for all time now she doesn't have a car or her chauffeur.

This is a first! Driving a car with Italian plates; even then I am still not legal on the road because of my UK driving licence, which I should have exchanged for the Italian one a long time ago like Judy did. I feel uneasy enough anyway, driving around the Valdichiana these days. When I first arrived in Cortona it used to amuse me seeing the carabinieri by the side of the road suddenly sticking out a hand, their red and white lollipop wand waving you in. Or racing around Piazza Navona sirens blaring, waving the lollipop stick out of the back window of their Alfa like it is some kind of Papal benediction. Those were the days! Now it's a game of Russian roulette, running the gauntlet of the endless road blocks, confronted by raw recruits in kevlar vests, armed to the teeth, nervously toting their *berretta* sub-machine guns: especially knowing that accidental shootings do happen.

Chapter 56.

It is one thing to be talking up making a film, late at night at Marco's, submerged under clouds of hashish smoke, entirely another rousing the lads out of their beds early on a Sunday morning, in order to get them up to Arezzo to shoot the opening scene of our first short film.

There is no script, just an idea taken from an article I read about the white Fiat Uno (my car) being the preferred car of bank robbers because they are so common on the road that nobody takes any notice of them. Tiziano, Gabriele and Roberto the musician I first met at Rupert's, play the part of a trio of bank robbers on their way to a heist. Marco is operating the camera and lending his expertise to me as the director; he runs an experimental theatre company with his sister Mira and his wife Galatea, an up-and-coming young actress from Rome.

Roberto is a very discreet guy who normally shuns the spotlight and is cagey about taking part in any video, making it clear he doesn't want his real name to appear in the titles.

"Bob Freeman will do." He insists.

"But it's not Italian."

"No, but it's a literal translation of my name so it's good enough."

"People will still recognise you in the film, you know."

"Not with a stocking over my head!" He grins.

Roberto has experienced a short spell under the spotlight, mentoring and producing an album for Jovanotti: the young Cortonese rapper Lorenzo Cherubini, who has gone on to become an Italian pop idol; these days performing in TV specials with the likes of Pavarotti. Cortona is probably the only place in Italy where Lorenzo isn't mobbed, as he strolls across the piazza to the gift shop his mother runs in piazza della Repubblica, pushing his baby daughter in a stroller, completely undisturbed.

Tiziano plays the get away driver and the thumb he recently smashed at work is heavily bandaged, looking like a huge turban peering over the top of the steering wheel as he executes a smart one-handed bootleg turn, tyres screeching to a halt through the gravel.

"But that's our car!"

Judy exclaims, when I show her the take. Except what she doesn't know (and it doesn't hurt) is that we filmed it in three separate takes.

Marco would have been much better suited to my role as the director because I am really struggling to extract any kind of performance from my actors; being amateurs does not help. Marco has the presence and the authority born of confidence and experience, as well as an innate ability to animate pictures with words and then populate people amongst them.

Not having a script is a huge problem for this bunch and driving around Arezzo in the car filming in the interior I exhort:

"We need some actions!"

"Everything clear?" Rouses Roberto in the front seat, taking out his phone and pressing the keys after a long-drawn-out silence.

"Clear as oil!" Gabriele responds banging the roof with his fist then falling silent once more.

More disappointingly, Tiziano, usually so loquacious, is strangely mute in the car. In an effort to loosen his tongue I introduced a friend of mine into a scene without Tiziano knowing; we were halted at traffic lights when my friend approached the car with a bucket and sponge in hand, offering to wash the windscreen. I knew Tiziano would refuse but instructed my friend to insist. We had a camera taped to the dashboard in order to capture what I was sure would be a strong reaction from Tiziano, who besides be loquacious is well known for his colourful language. Lamely at first, Tiziano tells the guy to "go away" because "we are filming!" Then inexplicably, he switches off the camera and we lose the very powerful dialogue that ensues as my friend starts washing the car windows.

Another scene could easily have ended up in disaster and shows just how ill prepared and cavalier we really were. The story changes as we go along and is now about the kidnapping of a girl driving a van. This particular scene entailed filming a van speeding through a railway underpass from a car drawn up alongside it, thereby taking up both sides of the road. We stationed a man on the further side of the underpass who would give us the traffic all clear on his mobile, with both vehicles then taking off side by side, racing into the tunnel, driving blind round the curve and out the other side. Everything seemed to go to plan, and only later was I told that after the all clear had been given, a cinquecento suddenly appeared along the road and refused to stop on our man's signal; instead, heading straight for us on a collision course, only averted at the last moment because miraculously the car turned off into a lane just before the tunnel's entrance.

Roberto has introduced me to his friend Massimo at Extravideo in Arezzo who has agreed to edit the film at not too exorbitant a price. Made on a shoe string, this represents the only real production cost but I don't mind paying because sitting in with Massimo I will be able to learn some of the techniques of video editing on a computer and understand better what hardware and software I will need to do it myself. I commute every morning to Arezzo on the *pendolare* train from Monte San Savino, a journey of about thirty minutes. Recently, this single-track branch line was the scene of a fatal accident, when two trains collided head-on, killing three people, including a guard only weeks away from retiring, and injuring 70 others. For weeks after, people could be seen trudging around Lucignano in plasters and wearing neck braces; and everybody knew somebody who had been on one of the two trains. Judy herself should have been! She was supposed to be putting up posters for me in Arezzo, for an exhibition I was having at the Caffè dei Costanti with Franco Fedeli, only we had an argument the night before and she subsequently refused to go!

Caffè dei Costanti is the bar in Piazza San Francesca made famous by Roberto Benigni filming scenes for "Life is beautiful." Benigni was born in the Valdichiana, in Marciano, although the family moved to Prato when he was a boy, and during the filming he was much feted by the Chianesi, claiming him as their own. Hundreds of us turned out under the hot sun, to see him in Castiglion Fiorentina; seated beneath a grand panoply in the middle of the piazza with other town dignitaries, he played the court jester, giving us a comedic masterclass lasting over an hour.

Massimo is pale and twitchy by the end of a day's editing, sitting in his darkened studio in front of his computer and TV screens, but we are making headway, even trawling through the out-takes in search of dialogue that can be over dubbed: there was aplenty when everyone thought the camera had been turned off! I am learning to be creative to plug the silences using sound effects and the car radio has unexpectedly taken on a starring role too. Roberto has generously donated one of his compositions for the opening credits: a haunting guitar solo with a deeply satisfying jungle beat that gives me goose pimples every time I hear it and makes the opening titles my favourite part of the film.

Massimo doesn’t come across as being overtly political, but in the course of our many conversations during the last week, he has revealed that he knows Licio Gelli, a controversial figure in Italy, who currently is under house arrest at his residence Villa Wanda, just outside Arezzo, waiting to be sentenced for his part in the Bank of Ambrosiano affair: the Vatican money-laundering scandal. Massimo has been hinting that he runs the occasional errand for Gelli up at the villa, which is worrying because Gelli is also reputed to be the head of a covert Masonic lodge known as P2 (Propaganda Due), a powerful group of high ranking politicians, industrialists and military brass, who according to the left wing press, are dedicated to a right-wing takeover of the country. A list of names revealing all of the P2 members has been discovered by the Carabinieri in a safe at the villa, which even more worryingly has Berlusconi's name on it! At least he is no longer the Prime minister. Claims are often made in the Italian press about an ongoing civil war between the Left and the Right, particularly after the assassination of Aldo Moro, the Italian Prime Minister in 1978 and allegedly in retaliation the Bologna bombings in 1980, when eighty-five people died.

I feel totally elated leaving Massimo's studio clutching my very own copy (a VHS cassette) of the final cut of "AR(Driver)". Hovering inches above the pavement on this brisk afternoon, the sun, is low over the rim of the city and shining straight down viale Cristoforo Colombo directly into my face; everything around me is bursting into gold as if I am walking through the golden sunset of a Claude Lorrain painting.

AR(driver)

AR(driver)
con
andriolo
chiuchiurlotto
chiovoloni
freeman
schippa
di
nino macDonald
musica....roberto manfreda

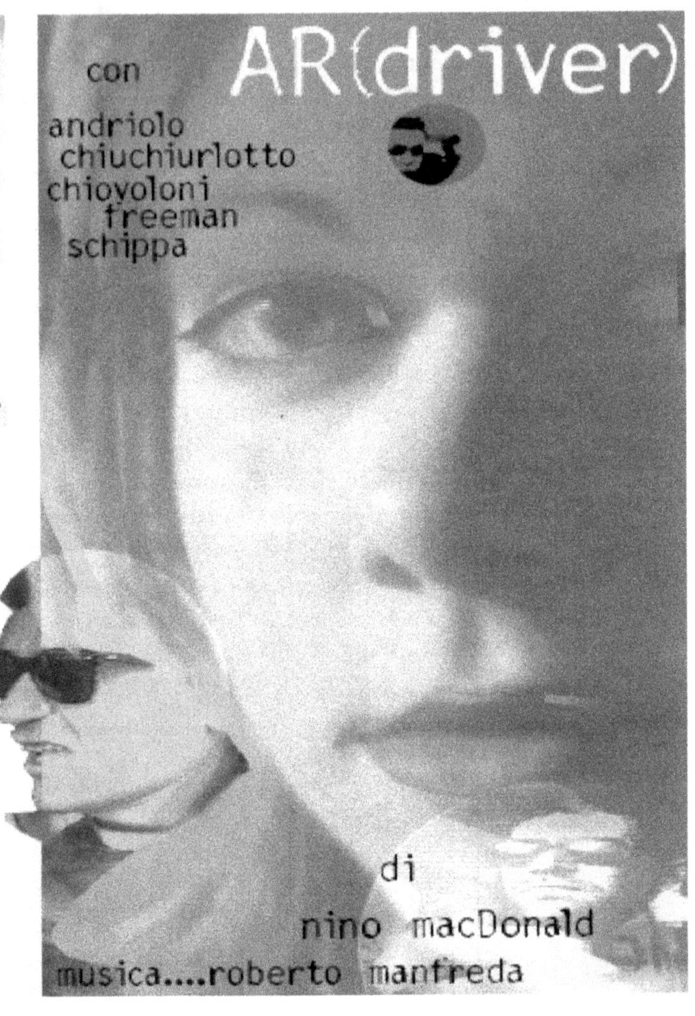

Chapter 57.

Winter is waking up blissfully warm under a mountain of blankets and never wanting to climb out of bed.

"Good morning, Jude!" Condenses into a vapour cloud above our heads. I must ask Martin, keeper of the weather records, the last time he saw snow on the ground in November it seems so unusual. A day off from school, Cosmo and Toto are using each other for stationary target practice in the piazza, taking it in turns to drag a dirty old shirt through the slush, ball it up and chuck it at one another, laughing uproariously together whenever they get a direct hit. They traipse back through the kitchen into their bedroom chattering brightly, leaving muddy trails across the floor! But for once who cares, I'll mop the floor gladly! In one more month we will be winging our way to Bangkok and then on to Melbourne for Christmas; a truncated winter with a double dose of summer is definitely something to look forward to. I have nothing to fear either, having already been initiated into the beleaguered parents' long-haul flight club; Cosmo puking all over me in the Jumbo and Toto refusing to settle in the basinet hooked onto the wall directly below the movie screen and feeling the dagger looks of fellow passengers behind me.

After the fiasco with the electric blanket, we threw out the foam rubber mattress and Vicky gave us a thin *paillasse.* Sleeping on a hardboard base, I'm used to waking up in the mornings with sundry aches and pains, but with only two weeks left before our departure, I have been experiencing an unusual pain that refuses to go away; it's akin to someone having winded me with a base ball bat. I am staggering up the kitchen stairs, struggling with the wood basket and pausing every three or four steps to catch my breath; a fact that i'm reluctant to mention to Judy because I know she will pack me straight off to see the doctor. But with so little time left…?

Frowning, Dr. Ricciarini detaches the stethoscope from my chest and immediately picks up the phone. "I am going to arrange for you to have a chest X-ray at Foiano this morning."

Then dialling the number, he speaks with some urgency.

"Make sure you bring it back to the surgery straight away after."

The young technician sporting a pony tail, nods knowingly as he comes out of his cubicle with the results, slipping the X-rays into a yellow manila envelope for the doctor and then informing me:

"*Haemopneumothorax*."

"*Scusi*?"

"A collapsed lung, but don't worry!" Breezily, "All they do is stick a tube inside your chest to drain the fluid on your lung and you'll be fixed in no time."

Dr. Ricciarini takes one look at the X-ray and immediately orders me to the new hospital in Arezzo, offering to call an ambulance if I need one. Judy thinks I'm kidding when I arrive home and start packing my overnight bag. I gasp one last cigarette in the fireplace before she drives me to the hospital. It is mid-morning and the kids are back at school.

"Are you sure you wouldn't prefer me to come in with you?" Judy asks, concerned, depositing me outside Emergency, slush piled up on the sidewalk.

"No, I'll be okay, you'd better get home for the kids." I lie, desperately wanting her to come in with me but incapable of articulating the desire and hoping instead that she insists.

I hesitate outside on the pavement for a moment watching the car disappear down the street, before taking that step into the bowels of the Leviathan. Gaggles of doctors with nurses in tow, zig-zag the hangar sized triage area, still under construction, and disappear behind curtains pulled closed, orderlies bring up the rear trolleying medical equipment and medicines or shunting patients around on gurneys to all points of the field.

It is a relief of sorts to be told I am being transferred by minivan across town to the old sanatorium. Cosmo and Toto have both had operations there so I am familiar with the environs; a classic Leopoldino Villa set in a small park that used to serve as a sanatorium for tuberculosis patients. Driving in through the gates I fantasise we could easily be guests arriving at a stately home for a weekend house party, except, quickly disabused, we are led down to the servants' entrance, along a dingy basement corridor with boxy metal conduits bracketed onto the low ceiling, then ushered into the pit of a broad stairwell leading up and up to the wards, women to the left, men to the right, puffing and panting all the way, accompanied by others: some looking pale, in shabby terry towel dressing gowns; cancer patients just back from their radiation sessions.

Toddler Cosmo and baby Toto both had hernia operations here; Toto, such an impossibly small bundle curled up in one corner of the gurney as they wheeled him into the theatre and Cosmo desperately struggling not to be released from my arms when it was his turn.

Matron, a friendly, petite blonde of indistinct age, leads me to a room with six beds in it, four of them are empty and she tells me to choose. I immediately take the bed next to the window, my escape, yet I can't help but be reminded of dreaded boarding school: that sinking feeling on first going through the wrought iron gates at the beginning of term, overcome by the sheer helplessness of it all. Matron instructs me to report to the day surgery at the end of the hall as soon as I have changed into my pyjamas and not knowing what to expect I knock on the door with the frosted glass panel and step in A well-groomed bored looking doctor is reclining behind a desk, repeatedly stubbing the stiffened corners of a stack of X-rays with his thumb. Two male nurses are hovering near a cupboard over by the window, one indicating for me to take my top off and tearing a strip of double-ply paper from the roll and smoothing it down on the examining table, motions me to hop on and lie down.

I am mentally detached and bodily numb as the nurse uses a bic razor blade to shave a rectangular patch of hair on my chest below the left collarbone. The Doctor rouses himself when the nurse has completed the task and leaning over me administers a local anesthetic, repeatedly pin-pricking the shaved area, waiting, then making a quick short incision with the scalpel passed to him by the other nurse. Out of the bottom of my eye I can see the blood welling up and bubble over, the nurse swabbing then liberally dabbing on the Mercurochrome. Tearing open a vacuum-packed length of black tube, the Doctor proceeds to push one end through the incision and deep down inside my chest. He has my full attention now and it comes as a shock to realise I can't feel anything there, as if my chest is a cave. A rubber washer is stitched onto the skin over the hole to secure the tube in place and a glass bottle is attached to the other end and placed on the floor beside me.

I feel relieved to have that over with but after a while the Doctor is shaking his head, puzzled as to why the fluid is not draining into the bottle as it normally should and in conference with the nurses, comes to the conclusion that something is wrong.

"We better take an X-ray and find out what the problem is."

I am ushered off the table into a wheelchair and taken down to the X-ray department via the service lift. It is dark outside by now and cold air presses against my exposed shins. Surprising myself, I find it quite relaxing, not to have to be in charge: to be moved from point A to point B at someone else's whim.

The X-ray confirms the doctor's suspicions and clearly shows the tube has kinked. "The tube must be the wrong size." He realises. "It's too big."

And grabbing another packet out of the cupboard, I am submitted to the whole process over again this time in reverse before replacing the old tube with the new one and stitching me up again. Again, they all gather around watching the bottle intently and before long a dribble of pinkish fluid begins to slowly trundle in. Satisfied with the result, the good doctor concludes:

"Now all you have to do is wait for your lung to spontaneously re-inflate and we can send you home."

Thankfully the windows in my room are huge folding glass doors that open onto a balcony enclosed by black mosquito netting running the full length of the building. Plenty of fresh air was the cure for TB patients in the old sanatorium regime, and I am grateful that prone on my bed I can spy a generous wedge of sky above the tops of the mature fir trees. On my side of the room over in the corner is a thin, wiry, tired looking old man; a contadino who refuses to touch the food his family brings in. For most of the day he lies stock still, staring blankly up at the ceiling then at night he turns over onto his knees and griping the raised bars of his cot he starts rocking crazily from side to side. On my third night he dies. I am woken near midnight by a bustle of activity around his bed before he is trolleyed away, thankfully not in a body bag. The young man in the opposite bed is a Tunisian who was involved in a serious road accident. He reflects:

"I was riding home on my motorino, you know, after work; not thinking about anything in particular except perhaps what my wife was cooking for dinner that night when wham! A car came out of nowhere and smashed right into my bike! Now look at me!"

Hamdi is lying in traction, plastered from head to toe and tells me he will need several operations and months to recover before finally making it back home.

I lie quietly, uncomplaining, wedded to my bottle and pinned to my bed with a drip in one arm and an oxygen tube pulled out of the wall and plumbed round my head and into my nose. The kids freak out on their first visit when they see haggard old Dad clutching his bottle like a handbag, with a tube poking out of his chest; consequently, Judy and I agree it's better to keep them at home.

The contadino with emphysema in the bed diagonally across from me, proudly displays his stump, amputated above the knee, on top of his bed covers, and undeterred, regularly wheels himself down to the bathroom for a smoke. He went ballistic the time Matron tried to confiscate his cigarette stash; the one his wife smuggles in to him and he keeps hidden in his bedside table.

My doctor, a classic smoothie in his early forties, is always impeccably dressed: neatly laundered white overcoat, gingham shirts and pleated pants, wearing tartan socks with tan brogues; he sweeps into the ward every morning doing the rounds, followed by an entourage of internees and nurses, Matron and the medicine trolley wait patiently at the door. They settle like crows by each bed, picking at patients as if we are road kill. My overriding concern is getting on the plane; Judy has managed to change our departure date for a couple of weeks hence and explaining my dilemma to the Doctor I ask what my chances are of leaving the hospital in by then? "If you must go better make sure a Doctor accompanies you on the plane." He responds sarcastically. "And just pray your lung inflates soon, otherwise…" and turning his back on me to address his adoring audience; the young internees hanging onto his every word. "...this patient will need to undergo surgery. The procedure can be performed with the new laser technology, but normally the surgeon will cut open the chest sawing through the rib cage, then glue the lung membrane back to the cavity wall."

What?!! That's the first time I've heard that! I am stunned but the doctor just moves on to the next patient without further explanations. There is something I don't like about this doctor, something too casual or indifferent in the way he conducts himself. Perhaps it's an attitude he harbours towards foreigners? Because I have noted that he treats Hamdi in a similar way.

Left to ruminate on my bed alone, my brain is working overtime cranking up the paranoia. I should have asked whether the hospital has this new laser technology or am I going to be cracked open like a cadaver in a sixteenth-century anatomy class? Judy always says I need to be more forthright and ask lots of questions but I easily lose heart; or perhaps it is because I feel safer not knowing the answers.

Friends visit breaking the tedium: Marco and the boys bringing a bottle of good wine; Jef is back in town for a surprise visit, coughing and wheezing, the chronic smoker that he is. I don't think he is going to be staying too long; not with the reminders of the havoc smoking wreaks so evident all around us. He and Marina and their son Martin moved back to Rome, after his current affairs program was axed; a victim of the recession and he is now working in the British Embassy's press office.

"Given the economic downturn it was a bloody miracle to find any kind of job."He sighs, worried about his mortgage and the responsibilities of being a family man.

Notwithstanding ongoing back issues, Jef has always been a serious biker; now days he rides a Beamer, a lingering goodbye to his Easy Rider counter culture days as he commutes daily down the Aurelia into Rome wearing a suite under his leathers.

Ironically, I seem to be the only one complaining about hospital food and Judy supplements my diet, cooking corn fritters and bringing me pasta salads and carrot cake. The hospital meals are catered from the outside and bused in meaning the pasta and rice stew in their big metal cauldrons; plus, they seem to douse sunflower oil over everything, which I hate, having become a cold pressed extra virgine snob. The orderlies don't understand 'vegetarian' either and think a pear or an apple or a muesli bar is a good enough substitute for not eating meat.

In my second week, the renovations next door we were warned about, begin in earnest: the very loud drrr krrr drrr krrr of a jackhammer sounds the alarm at eight one morning; not that time has much relevance here, we are woken by the medicine round twice nightly and day and night begin to blur together like a muddy smear across once bright uplands. By the second day, chips of plaster are falling on the man napping serenely unaware on his bed opposite, followed unbelievably by a drill bit screeching through the brick and grinding to a halt not three feet above his head!

I feel more desperate than ever, given my lung shows no inclination of spontaneously re-combusting into life and imagine myself under the threat of the knife. On top of everything Judy informs me she is preparing to go with the kids as arranged, fearing she will lose the tickets altogether if she doesn't use them now. I am furious when she tells me! Dismayed! I was expecting her to cancel altogether and start shouting at her over the phone:

"Go to Australia then and while you're at it don't bother visiting me again!" Slamming down the payphone in the hall, not caring if I am making a spectacle of myself!

Finally, the reprieve only a couple of days before her departure and my lung spontaneously begins to inflate and suddenly all is well with the world again; yes even with Judy and the kids who are leaving me here all on my own. Going to Australia is so family orientated anyway, I rationalise: my mother-in-law Vivienne and I are polite with each other but circumspect; we tolerate each other for family unity's sake and never get into contentious conversations like why aren't you in a proper job. Judy doesn't have much time for my mother either; she can't stomach the New Age stuff and thinks my mum gives herself too many airs and graces:

"I don't have much to do with ordinary people these days…" says my mum; reinforcing Judy's opinion of her as an elitist. She knows how to wind me up too, whenever she refers to my mum as: "The Queen of Sheba."

I get on better with Judy's dad Phil, who is less judgmental and just an all-round good bloke. All he really cares about is his daughter's happiness. The first time we met was in Melbourne when I was invited to their house for dinner; the very same night Judy announced that she was coming to Italy with me. There I was, a complete stranger in their house, whisking his daughter off to the other side of the world, yet Phil, as we were leaving, took me aside and firmly clasping both my hands, earnestly recommended his daughter into my care. I was touched by the gesture not that I am Judy's first: Tony her ex-husband was at our wedding and giving a speech at the reception I clumsily referred to him as passing on the baton (how embarrassing) then made even more of a fool of myself in front of her parents, saying Judy wasn't exactly "vaginal" coming into this marriage when what I meant to say was "virginal".

I can hardly believe I'm actually getting dressed and about to leave the hospital. Goodbye Hamdi, anchored to your bed like a flying nun. Good luck Rossi down the hall with terminal lung cancer and swollen feet. Goodbye Doctor and thanks a lot. Calling me into the day surgery for a final word, my recent Cat scans are up on the light box.

"Good news and bad news MacDonald."

I look at him blankly.

"The good news is that you do not have lung cancer. The bad news is you have Emphysema, see that little spot there?"

Judy and the boys are now in Australia and Marina has come to fetch me. Stepping outside, I gingerly gulp down the crisp air. A pale Arezzo sun is hanging misty yellow over the old town and my three week ordeal is over!

Chapter 58.

On the way back to Lucignano, Marina breaks the sad news that the hot spring at San Giovanni, our not so secret winter spa, has been bulldozed to the ground after a man had a heart attack and an ambulance was called. I can't blame the owner of the land: the location has been an open secret for years and it has been getting out of hand with people lighting fires and having parties, litter strewn on the ground, even syringes left lying around. Hans says they have moved the outlet pipe from the top of the gully into the stream below, making it impossible to start anew and he is very disappointed.

Hans has been offered a new place in exchange for his cottage in the hamlet that developers want to turn into a holiday village à la Club Med,. He was the only one to hold out after his neighbours all sold and as a result the developers, after a couple of years, have finally caved in to his demands. His new house is a large *casa colonica* perched on a hill with stunning 360-degree views and enough pasture for him to bring his horses down from Germany, which is what I suspect he was holding out for all along. It is near the tyre dump that went up in flames last year; a narrow gorge below the road, piled waist-deep in discarded tyre treads of all sizes. We could see the black pall in the sky from Poggio Spinoso, miles away, and it was months before the smoldering toxic blaze was brought under control.

Judy and the boys are away for five weeks and I have moved into Cosmo and Toto's room to be near the stove. Before departing, they thoughtfully stockpiled wood on the balcony outside the kitchen door, saving me the journey up and down the stairs and friends who drop by are helping to replenish it. Not that I am an invalid, both lungs are working normally but I'm taking it slowly all the same, being cautious. The good doctor warned me I had a congenital condition and that it could happen again at any time, adding I shouldn't be getting on a plane any time soon. I won't easily forget the grim look of that young man in the corridor wedded to his bottle, staring blankly out the hospital window; in for the third time in as many years, he told me resignedly.

Giuseppe and his wife Zvonka regularly turn up unannounced bearing treats from the Pasticceria in Lucignano, that Giuseppe, beady-eyed, proceeds to wolf down at the kitchen table: he claims to be a connoisseur of pastries and needs to sample them all, smacking his lips with relish and wiping crumbs off his greying beard. Giuseppe is a writer and he has offered to help me write a script for a new short film I would like to make. Taking pity on me being on my own, they often invite me around to their place for a supper. Zvonka comes from Slovenia and cooks pork especially for me, insisting on feeding me up. I love the taste of pork and feel guilty, being a vegetarian, although just for now consider it a reasonable excuse. Or Zvonka cooks *bryndzove halusky*, a Slovenian speciality, slyly telling me to eat only the potato gnocchi and scrape off the bacon topping if I really insist! When I tell Judy, she laughs over the phone:

"It must be those German genes of yours."

After dinner, Giuseppe and I will retreat to his study at the top of the stairs, taking with him his beloved Alsatian dogs: Ulysees and Joyce. He is an apassionato of James Joyce and has published several novels including: James Joyce, Rome and Other Stories. It is a rare privilege to be invited into his book-lined study; his usual collaborations are done by fax, and like my studio, this is his inner sanctum and sipping brandy we will bounce ideas around for a new script.

Doctor Ricciarini is keeping an eye on my progress and viewing my CAT scans he commiserates with me for missing out on Australia.

"Must be hot this time of year, do you see many kangaroos?"

He is around my age, loves jogging, is slightly balding and has the beginnings of a paunch but fresh-faced and content with his lot in life. His surgery used to be next to the petrol station in front of Lucignano, jammed in between a florist and a funeral parlour and carpenter's. More recently he has moved into modern premises in the new development below Lucignano, with shop front plate glass windows.

"Air pressure! You need to careful in the future." Dr Ricciarini reminds me, leaning over his desk to polish his spectacles.

"To be mindful of flying yes and but also avoid deep sea diving. Have you been to the great barrier reef?" The last time I was at his surgery I bumped into Silvio, Alfredo's brother, and took the opportunity of congratulating him on being his pharmaceutical company's "sales rep of the year" for the second year running. Emilia proudly gave me the news when I last saw her in

Cortona. Noemi passed away after a brief illness when Judy and I were in Australia and I rarely see her at all, but when I do, I try to persuade her to come and stay with us for a few days holiday to get away from it all, but she will not be tempted to step outside the city gates. I can still envisage Noemi at the head of the table, winking at me conspiratorially, simultaneously teasing Emilia about her phobia of the countryside, hardly daring to leave Cortona, not even to visit him in his orto. Her only exception is accompanying her niece Maria to Arezzo for dialysis every week. Everyone thought Maria was the one in delicate health so it came as a real shock when her son Giuseppe, in his early twenties, died at work of a heart attack. I remember him fondly too: first as a toddler playing with Voss on the mat under the dining room table as we ate, then as a teenager; how with endless patience and good humour, he would entertain toddler Cosmo sitting under the table, playing together with his old collection of kinder egg figurines.

At least Silvio doesn't queue-barge like most of his colleagues do; flouting the strict queuing etiquette at the surgery, trying to muscle in ahead of everyone because they always have something more pressing to do after; often leading to frayed tempers and occasionally unseemly pushing and shoving at Doctor Ricciarini's door as it opens with his last patient exiting and him calling out from behind his green desk:

"Who's next?"

Etiquette dictates that as you enter the surgery you should inquire who was the last one in before you, thereby knowing your place in the queue.

I should have known I wouldn't last that long not smoking; not once I was out of hospital and the initial shock had subsided; slowly at first: one or two a day, then three or four, seamlessly sliding into smoking as many as before I went in. I sometimes think I wouldn't be able to create at all without a cigarette. I blame my addiction on my mother who smoked with me inside her.

My grandmother, Momo, a non-smoker, had an interesting philosophy regarding smoking because she believed it was her duty to smoke at the dinner table, if she was hosting a dinner, just to make the smokers at the table feel at ease!

Whenever I enter the Tabaccheria in Lucignano on an overcast day Gianfranco will trill: "*Tempo Scozzese!*"

Or else "the London fog" when a heavy wet blanket that car headlights can only slap off, squats over the Valdichiana; the same fog that looks like powdered snow from above in Cortona.

It has become a standing joke between us and I will remind him that what he is actually referring to is the Italian weather.

At least Gianfranco understands the difference between the English and the Scots.

"*Dio buono*!"

He reminds me often enough:

"The Genovese are as tight fisted with their money as you Scots!"

Gianfranco enjoys the banter: a tall, balding man who holds court from behind the counter with his *simpatica* wife Marcellina. He is in the wrong business for a reforming smoker, yet remains solidly upbeat with the stub of his unlit Toscanello permanently glued to a corner of his mouth. I suspect Marcellina is forced to "hot-box" in the backroom while she does the accounts.

Last year, the Lucignanesi were up in arms over a regional lorry strike cutting tobacco supplies to the village for over two weeks. Gabriele our postman was rationing out the odd cigarette on his postal rounds and circulated rumours of impending deliveries, when crowds would rush to Gianfranco's tobacco shop. By the second week of the strike, Gianfranco was forced to ration his dwindling stocks to one pack per person; queues formed outside the Tabaccheria every morning, Russian style, stretching down the street, and I even saw Vasco, the town clerk, come out of the shop with his ration and immediately rejoin the back of the line for another go, as did Romano my mechanic and many others too. Gianfranco, always scrupulously fair, and his diminutive wife, certainly didn't deserve the kind of abuse they were subjected to by their ill-tempered customers, and everyone was ragged but visibly relieved by the time the strike ended.

This summer I am visiting my mother in England with the boys for three weeks and with the trip in mind, Giuseppe has come up with a genial script: *La Bicicletta Rossa* (The Red Bike), based on a suggestion I made that we use the trip as a basis for the film with Cosmo and Toto in the main roles. I thought it would be fun for them, filming as we hopped on and off trains and buses and planes; a way to keep them amused even during long boring journeys, as well as contributing to the look of the video, as well as giving the film more appeal by the its rich back drop. The boys agreed to do it and to help them to learn their lines we are in rehearsals at Giuseppe's place; only the truth is they are more interested in his swimming pool and he is just as keen to show off his water polo moves; he demonstrates a surprising athleticism in the water for a man who has to live with chronic back pain.

Chapter 59.

I have seriously miscalculated in thinking the video would be fun for the boys to make. We have hardly set off on the first leg of the journey on the train to Rome airport and Toto is already asking if we are nearly at *Nonna's*, becoming agitated and grumpy when I say no and not wanting to take any part in the filming; me muttering darkly under my breath from behind the camera:

"I'll strangle you if you don't!"

I did have a moment as the plane took off, remembering the Doctor's warning and that news story about a passenger on a 747 who suffered a collapsed lung mid-flight and was only saved by the quick thinking of a doctor using brandy and a wire coat hanger; no doubt jacking the poor fellow's chest open like a thief would crack a car door! As the days pass, I realise too, just how much I have underestimated the task confronting the boys, especially filming in public. In England they are embarrassed to be seen reciting their lines in Italian; one scene took several takes with Cosmo reciting in a crowded lift at the Victoria & Albert Museum. Then it's the huffing and puffing just to get them to wear the same clothes every day we are shooting; a critical component of the film.

We are staying at my mother's place in Wiltshire, being good tourists: visiting Bath and Longleat safari park, checking out Stonehenge and the White Horse on the Downs, when on the radio comes the shocking news of Princess Diana's accident followed soon after with the confirmation of her death. In the next few days, we hear little else on the radio and almost instantaneously, masses of flowers start appearing in village squares and at crossroad obelisks and monuments throughout the Wiltshire downs.

Tim has invited us to stay with him in London; having abandoned his toe hold in Tuscany, he is still pursuing a career in writing film scripts; mirroring my own perseverance and lack of success. He helps out in the florist shop underneath his flat in Pimlico and almost as soon as we arrive, we are whisked off to Kensington Palace in the back of the florist van.

“A witness to history,” he suggests, walking us through Kensington Gardens in the closing light, solemn and respectful; everyone around us in the grip of a collective trance: endless lines somnambulating towards the Princess's palace, clutching bunches of flowers to be laid at her gate. Kensington Gardens, the lake, the geese, the dying Dutch Elms; this used to be my rural refuge when I lived just down the road in Queensgate terrace.

The sea of flowers in front of the palace gates is staggering when we come upon them: wave upon wave, knee-deep and stretching 50 feet back from the black and gold palace railings; each bouquet bowed to her in homage and grief. They dazzle with a thousand flash bulbs ricocheting off their cellophane wrappers. Above the milling crowds, the mums and dads and kids in strollers, or hoisted up on dads' shoulders like Toto to get a clearer view: the pensioners and the teenagers, the office crowd and shop assistants, the soldiers from Kensington barracks and the police: above the makeshift shrines of teddy bears and candles and ribbons, cards and scribbled notes and photographs attached to the trunks of the trees lining the broad avenue to the Palace, the sky is a dripping livid pink on blue, shot through with golden streaks.

“Ooooh!” Sighs the crowd in unison: “A sign from Diana.”

We venture north, somber as the Nation's mood, because no breach would be tolerated lightly; away from the auld enemy back onto Scottish territory and even there, nonconformity feels like a dangerous act of defiance especially during the minute's silence held after her funeral.

We are in Edinburgh to visit Sue and my step sister Kelly who is two months younger than Cosmo yet still his aunt! The last time I saw her she was a baby and my father was still alive and now when I see her I find the similarities between them uncanny: those familiar eyes and the set of her cheeks; a mischievous smile and she has his attitude too.

Sue has found a new partner, Stuart, who lost his wife tin similar circumstances around the same time as my father. Adding to the symmetry is his son Ali, who is the same age as Kelly, and also the reason they met in the first place: Kelly and Ali attending the same nursery school. Again, it amazes me how much patterns play a part in our lives: Kelly will never know her real father just as I never knew mine and just as her father became a father to me, Stuart has become a father for her. We have become the brothers who aren't really brothers, the sisters who aren't really sisters and the fathers who aren't really fathers, but only in name.

I hope I haven't completely ruined the boys' holiday acting as such a hard task master with regard to filming; only once started there was no turning back. At least they can relax now we are back in Tuscany and I have enough raw material to pull it all together editing our short film titled *La Bicicletta Rossa.*

Without a doubt, Mozzoni is the main reasons we have survived in Tuscany for this long; we couldn't have afforded to live here otherwise and nowadays, where in the world would you find a landlord prepared not to raise your rent for nearly 14 years? Fosco, our fattore, periodically threatens to increase the rent but has turned out to be just as accommodating as Cassagni ever was. Fosco is a hero in the classic mould, coming out of retirement, as he frequently reminds me, to take on the job of saving the farm in times of economic down turn. A sign of the times: up the road at Belvedere Antico, Ita's husband is crowing about globalisation and what an opportunity it is for the company to move jobs offshore to China. Sabine is worried about her work prospects, as textile companies go bust in Prato. Prato, historically, a major European textile manufacturing centre is also being forced to come to grips with the new reality of production moving off shore. Prato has a lively contemporary art scene built on textile wealth unlike her rival Florence just down the road. All she has to offer is the annual Modern Art Expo, held in an office block and crammed full of mostly uninspiring local and "international" artists. I receive letters from the organisers congratulating me on being selected, then flipping the page I discover they expect me to pay for the privilege.

Roby was only half joking when he likened Italy to a sinking ship far out at sea:

"With ten captains on board, all too busy squabbling about what to do next to notice that the crew has already abandoned ship!" Adding: "Italy is probably one of the few nations on earth where a government could collapse and nobody would notice the difference." Fosco doesn't think the farm will be too affected in the current crisis, even though Mozzoni has been forced to rationalise. Unemployment stands at over 11% and most of the farmworkers have taken an early retirement leaving only a skeleton work crew.

Under Fosco's stewardship the farm has refocused on cattle breeding with most of the arable land being turned over to pasture or for winter-feed. We no longer see the gangs of men and machines descending on the fields like locusts, or in winter, burning off the banks in a blaze of activity, hungrily moving on to the next job. Even the willow trees along the *strada bianca* have been abandoned, once so assiduously pruned each year, the young supple branches providing the *contadini* with stays for the vines or used to fashion punnets for the seedlings sold at the markets.

Fosco seems more concerned with Vicky's position at Rocchetto, now that Shelley has run off with a younger woman and left her to fend for herself. For once I can return a favour and do my best to reassure Fosco that she is managing on her own and quite capable, which is far from the truth: she is barely coping and very anxious about what the future might hold. All Shelley left behind were a few paintings that she thinks she might be able to sell, if that is, he doesn't come back and try to reclaim them, as she suspects he will: the paintings and Billy, the cantankerous blue tongued chow with bad eczema in need of constant medical attention. At least he makes a good guard dog for her because she hears noises at night and calls us up worried burglars are on her roof and I have to reassure her that they are only the barn owls.

Chapter 60.

La Bicicletta Rossa has been selected as one of the twelve finalists in Meno Cinque, a short video film festival held in Sansepolcro annually. Short film festivals have become all the rage in

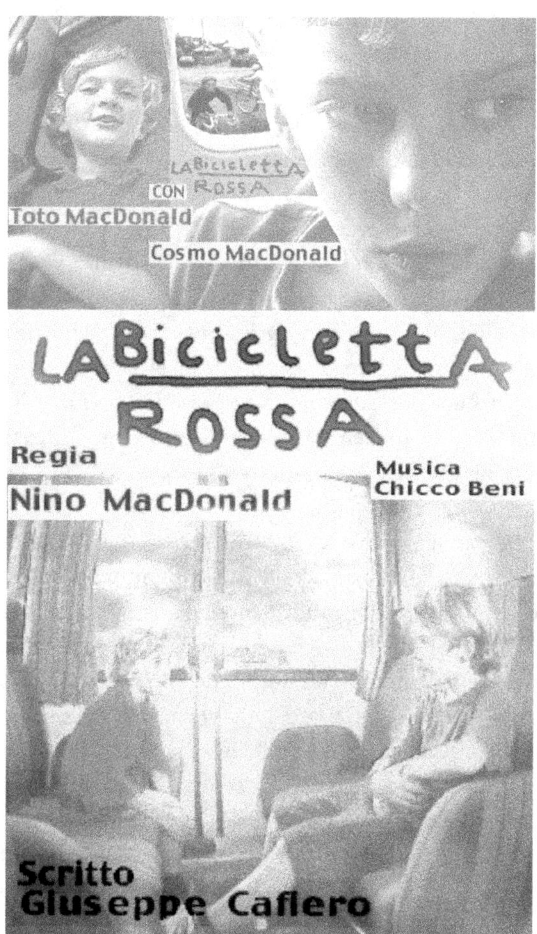

Tuscany, with an outpouring of popular video-making exploding onto the big screen and attended by large festival audiences.

As finalists for Meno Cinque, we are put up for two nights by the organisers, in a local monastery and bussed around town in the VIP minivan. We sleep in tiny cells: claustrophobic whitewashed rooms with sticks of furniture and eat with the monks in the refectory; not that we mingle because we are tucked away in a corner on separate tables out of harms way. Meal talk is mainly about films; I keep tight-lipped about my aspirations, not wanting to make any claims or really having any to speak of, unlike one or two of the company who are busy emphasising the distinctions between "filmmakers" and "enthusiasts": the us and the them, and who for all their self-hyping are made to look foolish on the big night judging by their bland offerings.

La Bicicletta Rossa has not won any prizes but I did feel strangely naked sitting in the audience under the stars: electrified even, totally lit up in the dark, as if everybody could see who I really was and knew that it was my film playing up there on the big screen.

Marco wants to include "AR(Driver)" in this year's season of Cinemautografo, an idea I have been strenuously resisting, except now he is insisting on screening it alongside "*La Bicicletta Rossa*". He won't take no for an answer and my name is already on the festival poster. I stipulate only on the condition that I am not called upon to present the videos in person. Judy, Cosmo and Toto are all present at Teatro Signorelli for my double bill and the main feature of the evening is another Director's debut: "The Brave" by Johnny Depp.

Sure enough, can I believe it? There is Marco calling me out of the audience and down to the front of the auditorium, where I burble on for a minute or two about a revolution in the making for popular culture with the advent of the camcorder and affordable desktop video editing, creating armchair film makers out of us all. Or some such like. I was only aware of the boys gazing in my direction and Judy giving me encouraging looks as I spoke. I find it slightly absurd to be showing my films in a cinema because as much as I enjoy making them and feel a sense of achievement, they certainly have no commercial merit and I don't consider them art.

One absurdity leads to another because Santi, the owner of the Foto Ottica (camera shop) in Sinalunga, was in the audience and he has asked me to trial for him as his assistant videographer on one of his wedding assignments. I have agreed, thinking that maybe I can impress Judy, even though Santi has not offered to pay, he says it could lead to a weekend job in the future. We have been on friendly terms ever since I started taking him Gianni's transparencies to be developed; the format was unusual enough to arouse his interest and now whenever I go in we start chatting and he delights in taking me into his studio at the back of the shop to show me his portrait stage or his video editing suite and his latest wedding videos. Santi is in his late fifties; a short man who dyes his hair black; he is fastidious but has a pleasant demeanour and dresses sartorially, favouring the Dean Martin fifties look with white polo necks and navy blue blazers with gold buttons.

I feel like a total idiot standing right at the altar, shoulder to shoulder with the priest and the bridal couple, treading gingerly behind the priest for a full frontal of the couple as they exchange their vows; filming close-ups of the rings panning up to their faces, then moving cautiously to the front of the dais, fearful of tripping over, for a shot of the congregation. It really is embarrassing but Santi was adamant beforehand: this is how we do it, pushing me into the apse from the wings, so to speak.

The wedding is being held at the Abbazia di Monte Oliveto Maggiore near Asciano, a stunning mediaeval monastery complex run by the white-habited Benedictine monks. Judy and I make a point of taking our visitors there, particularly to see the impressive Sodoma frescoes in the cloister. The Abbey is also situated in the stunning Crete Senesi; a blaze of flowering clover in spring, which by autumn is nothing but scorched earth: black stripes branding the lunar landscape of impossibly steep eroded clay precipices. I feel more at home in the middle of the crowd after the service, with the newly-weds exiting the church under a hail of dry pasta, or with the bride and groom strolling hand in hand through the gardens as I walk backwards at a crouch, taking fancy shots from the hip. At the reception I have to keep reminding myself I am here to work and being conscientious, leave Santi at the table eating wedding cake.

Santi calls me the next day unimpressed with the results; he says in fact he can't use the footage and hints that I have spoiled the couples' big day as we can hardly go back and do a second take. I am deeply offended, given the effort I put in and swear never to go back to his shop, which is a pity in a way, because without seeing the tape I will never know exactly what he meant.

Chapter 61.

"*Pallone*!." Shouts Cosmo, startling me out of my reveries, the lingering smell of Olivero's two-stroke still cloying the air long after he has disappeared over the crest of the hill on his vespa.

"*Eh! Babbo* (Dad)."

The football is rolling down the drive and I pick it up and punt it back towards the piazza. Toto considers heading the return then thinks better of it and lets the ball bounce. Lila our dog moves off to one side as a precaution and settles back down on the grass verge keeping a distrustful eye out for anything coming her way. Patting her for reassurance and urging Toto "head it next time!" I can see Judy in the *orto* as I disappear up the stairs into the house; everything feels so normal yet my world is about to be turned upside down, almost literally if I ever make it to Australia!

What choice do I have after Judy delivered her bombshell; to stay here by myself? This is all down to Judy's epiphany, which she has tried to explain even though she doesn't understand it herself:

"I was sitting at the kitchen table that morning and I swear I wasn't thinking of anything in particular. When boom! I was suddenly filled with this knowing, literally dropping out of the sky into my mind."

She makes curly-cue finger gestures with both hands raised high and slowly moving down.

"Like an absolute knowing that now is the right time for us to move back to Australia."

She traces the flow of the invisible lines that were anointing her head.

I've rarely seen Judy so resolute; she comes across to the outside world as being such a confident person but I know how much she hides her self-doubt and insecurities; often she will be talking to someone but looking at me for assurance, is a good example.

I know I shouldn't have been so shocked by her revelation; Ma told me years ago this would happen while she was channelling Master Kathumi:

"Judy will be the one to know "absolutely" when the time is right to move the family."

Ma has been urging me to trust in Judy's intuition and give her my support because she needs to feel loved right now but I just can't do it: I'm devastated at the thought of leaving, at war with myself and everyone else. Yet we have always known that one day it would come down to this; Mozzoni isn't going to live forever and we both knew it would be better to leave under our own steam rather than wait to be pushed; only in the past we have always agreed to disagree: when one of us thought it was time to move and the other didn't, we left it at that. Today Judy is not going to be budged, that is becoming abundantly clear to me and she has even suggested I stay if that was what I really wanted.

After a month of bad-tempered sulking, I face the inevitable and walk up to the farm to announce our departure at the end of the year. Fosco, like everyone else, can hardly believe it, but there is no turning back now; bridges are burning and cogs are beginning to turn. Cosmo and Toto are both completely unfazed by the news, much to our surprise. Perhaps they don't really understand what is about to happen to their world, nevertheless Judy and I are concerned by their attitude and we worry something must be wrong with them, when in fact we are the ones with the problems. Even though it is Judy's decision she is not immune to sellers' remorse and the enormity of the change confronting us.

My mother is not surprised by the kids' frame of mind, reassuring us:

"They are Indigo children after all."

Judy revs up the troops with her" bold new start" and we tell friends we are moving "for the new millennium". Tuscans are harder to convince: for them, moving away is tantamount to betrayal, or an admission that there might be somewhere else in the world better than Tuscany? Instead, Judy intimates she wants to be nearer her ageing parents, which is something Tuscans can understand.

For the first time, this year of all years, our *contrada* Porta Giovanni has contacted Judy and asked her to take charge of the flower arrangements for the base of their float in the Lucignano *Maggiolata*. This is a great indicator of her new standing in the community; locals have grown to respect her not only for her creative endeavours and incredible work ethic but also for her willingness to share her knowledge with them.

The Lucignano *Maggiolata* is held every year on the last two Sundays of May; it is famous throughout Tuscany for the magnificence of the floats of the four *contradas* that are made up entirely of carnations, each one using up to 20,000 flowers. At the *contadino's* yard where the float is being assembled, a crane is brought in to lift the heavy steel armature; a giant replica of a *brocca* wine jug about 12 feet high by 8 feet across, onto the flatbed trailer that will be pulled around the village by a tractor. The carnations are trucked down from the North and stored in a cantina: kept fresh in cattle troughs filled with water and wheeled across the yard to the hay barn as needed. Teams of volunteers cut each of the stems down to a standard size before individually poking them through the wire mesh covering the frame, using a specially designed T-shaped brass tool.

In the weeks before the festival the two giant fir trees standing at the entrance to the village receive their annual trim and are artistically pruned into a petticoat of hula-hoops. The village is closed off on the day and I always look forward to seeing "the showman"; a regular fixture, appearing as the compere: a TV personality from a bygone age that no-one has ever heard of, with stringy long hair the colour of a nicotine stain, who always wears Saturday Night Fever cream suits and delivers a running commentary on the progress of the parade from the VIP podium below the Collegiata. He loves cracking unfunny jokes and making fashion statements that are broadcast around the village on the PA system.

The floats are pulled around the village two times; in amongst a procession of costumed folkloric dancers, whip-crackers, flag-throwers, town bands with high-stepping majorettes, two white Maremma oxen pulling a decorated cart. My friend Luca from the *Estemporaneo* is on horseback, decked out as the town "Marshal" riding at the head of a mediaeval procession of town's folk.

After all that hard work, on the final Sunday on the last lap of the village, the floats are ignominiously torn apart, stripped bare by festival goers and gangs of children clambering up onto the frames, throwing the flowers into the crowds and up to the overhanging balconies crammed with spectators. This year our *contrada* has won the prize for the best float and everyone is over the moon; dancing in the street and hugging each other and congratulating Judy. Later in the afternoon we will all go back to the farmer's yard for a celebration.

We are now on the slow countdown to blast off in December. I'll need a rocket to launch me out of this bubble, to shoot me beyond the stars and out of Tuscany's reach! At least the question of where we land is still open to debate and I have put my foot down when Judy suggests Melbourne as the obvious place; I can't imagine living in a city again and I know she's nervous about being too near to her parents so she is not championing the idea too strenuously. Maybe it's her way of appeasing me or should I say pleasing? As a compromise, we have been considering Myrtleford in rural North East Victoria (a small town with a large Italian community), but then thank God for Sean! (One of the posse of Judy's ex-boyfriends who originally saw her off at the airport when she first came to Italy.) He has been here visiting and talking some sense into us as we sit round the kitchen table drinking wine.

"Myrtleford!" He splutters! "You really must be off your heads. Why go there when you can go anywhere in Australia? Make it count, go somewhere special, somewhere tropical even. The far north coast of New South Wales for example, around Byron Bay or Mullumbimby. It's beautiful country up there, you'd love it, I know it."

Neither of us has been to the Rainbow Region as it is commonly known, although Carolyn and I nearly took a trip there from Sydney; Byron Bay sounded intriguing in the early eighties: the new Shambala, full of hippies with dope growing wild by the roadside! Ma is all in favour too and can't praise Byron Bay enough, having held a series of alignment therapy workshops there after travelling to Uluru to plant her crystals. She calls Byron a centre of the New Age and one of those very special places on earth that people feel drawn to; but i'm keeping that particular nugget close to my chest.

Chapter 62.

The subtropics sounds appealing to me as in no more winters! I try to conjure up palm trees and sand and glittering surf; imagine fishing villages with bluewash houses and dazzling whitewashed streets as if I am on a Greek island or otherwise verdant mountains shredded by low lying rain clouds à la Jamaica. Judy doesn't mind the heat, in fact she prefers it and she loves the idea of bougainvilleas flowering all year long, of rainforests and bush tucker and growing tropical fruit; so I think it is decided; we will stay with Judy's sister Sue in Melbourne and spend Christmas with her parents, before buying a car and heading north.

When I first arrived in Italy, I could fit all my worldly goods into the back of my car but now we need a container to get us out of here and taking the punt we are directing it to Brisbane, the nearest port for Byron Bay. I try not to think about Australia or what our future might bring. Instead, I am focused on taking Cosmo and Toto north again, heading in the opposite direction, for an extensive "goodbye to Europe tour": first to my mother's in Wiltshire, then on to Edinburgh where I am putting on an exhibition at Sue's place during the Edinburgh fringe. After, we are travelling to Hamburg to see my Uncle Adrian, my mother's younger brother, who is proposing to drive us to Silesia in Poland, on a tour of the old family estates.

Uncle Adrian went to boarding school in England and like the rest of my mother's family the Tschirschkys, he speaks fluent English. We are planning to visit my grandmother's family home Eisersdorf and then on to Költschen where Adrian grew up with my mother and Eliette and their elder brother Puschko. The old house with its clock tower, familiar to me from sepia photographs with serrated edges of my mother as a child, no longer exists, but the Tschirschky chapel and graveyard have survived. Adrian, a devout Christian, is raising money for the restoration fund and visits the site regularly to supervise the work. Eisersdorf has been turned into a state-run holiday home for retired workers now known as Zelaznoa. It looks more like a French chateau with peach-coloured walls and turrets: with a steeply pitched, pressed metal roof, a grand colonnaded marble entrance and a huge wrought iron conservatory built onto one end.

According to family lore, one of my ancestors, a charcoal burner in Bohemia, was ennobled in the fourteenth century, after he was attacked by a buffalo that he managed to kill with his bare hands. He presented the carcass as a gift to his sovereign who in turn granted him lands as a fief and a title. Adrian has inherited the title Baron from my grandfather who died in 1980, but he has chosen not to use it.

My grandfather was a diplomat working on the staff of Vice Chancellor von Papen at the time Adolf Hitler became Chancellor of Germany. He wrote a memoir published in Germany titled Memoirs of a Traitor (Erinnerungen eines Hochverraters), which describes this turbulent period in the early nineteen-thirties and his involvement in a plot to push Hitler aside and restore the German monarchy. The first phase of their plan involved enlisting the disgruntled German regular army, the Wehrmacht, to disarm their hated rivals the Sturmabteilung, better known as Hitler's storm troopers: the dreaded SA. The second part would then see the Reichspräsident von Hindenburg, the President of Germany, declare a national state of emergency and install a new executive. Von Papen hesitated for too long in initiating the plan, while Hindenburg in his dotage was indecisive with no clear understanding of what was at stake, and History then overtook them with the events of 1934 known as the Night of the Long Knives when Hitler ruthlessly purged the SA command structure, thereby mollifying the unrest in the Wehrmacht. He also seized this opportunity to neutralise anyone who opposed him, heralding his unprecedented rise to absolute power; the point at which the rule of law became the rule of lawful extra-judicial killing.

My grandfather was lucky to escape with his life, others in the group were summarily executed in front of him and although he was arrested by the Gestapo and sent to a concentration camp, he was released soon after through the intersession of powerful friends. He eventually found refuge in London where he was interned at his own insistence for the duration of the war; otherwise fearing retribution against his family still living in Silesia (German territory), if it was perceived by the Nazis that he was walking around free. Only towards the end of the second world war, after rumours started circulating that he had slipped back into the country, did the Gestapo come to arrest the family, forcing my grandmother, mother and her siblings to flee with only a few hours advance warning. My grandmother was friendly with one of the telephone operators at the local exchange who overheard a conversation about their imminent arrest and was able to forewarn her.

Their home, Költschen, was already filled with refugees fleeing west from the advancing Russian army and the yards were crowded with horses and carts; when in the middle of the night on January the twenty-second 1945, the snow piled high and the temperature minus twenty-three degrees Celsius; my grandmother gave the order for two wagons to be prepared for their flight: a double horse heavy farm wagon and single horse four-wheel cart, piled with carpets against the cold and taking with them the cook, a maid and another refugee family, they hastily departed on a dangerous trek across Europe to safety in Holland: bribing their way through German and British lines with jewellery they had sown into the linings of their clothes. Adrian was seven years old; his only worry, could he take his Christmas presents with him, particularly the Meccano set he had always so coveted.

It was a traumatic journey through a war-torn landscape in the dead of winter and especially so for my mother, who as an attractive young girl of sixteen years was raped by a British army officer. Given the context of the war this was not an unusual event, perhaps even normalised by society at that time; yet obviously on a personal level it has had a huge impact on my mother's life and goes some way to explaining her tendency to shrink from physical contact and shy away from company; quite the opposite to my father who was such a warm, gregarious man by nature. The family made it to safety in Holland and eventually were able to rejoin my grandfather in London, who post war took up a post in the diplomatic corp at the German embassy.

Chapter 63.

Sue is convinced she has the buyers in Edinburgh for my work so I'm crating over a couple of the larger canvases and preparing a series of smaller paintings for the exhibition. My style has evolved again; the pendulum swinging back towards figuration, only this time using stencil motifs: parachutes, tulips, angels, planes and combining them with abstract backgrounds. "Limp figures" is how a curator from the Trevi Flash Art Museum derogatorily put it after I'd finally managed to drag him into my studio all the way from Umbria.

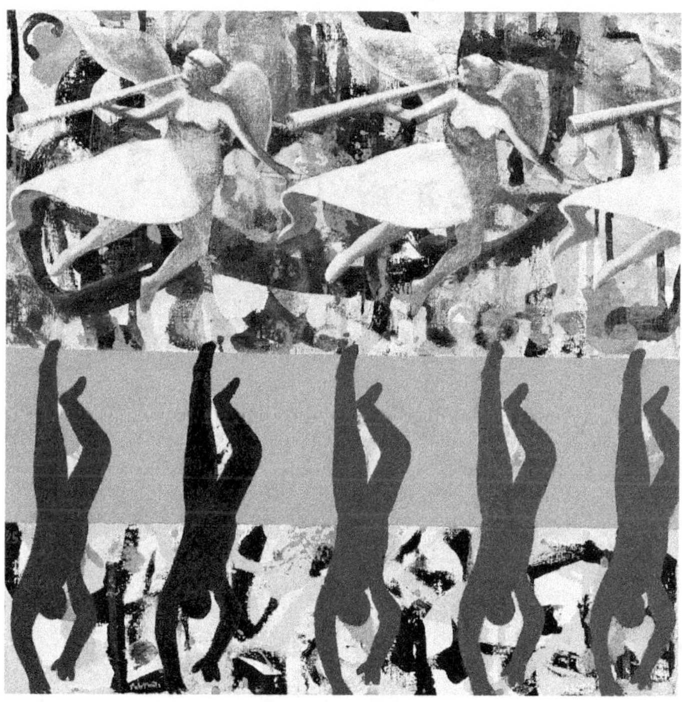

Downfall.1997

Sue has become one of my most trusted collectors, her house already filled with my works including that gigantic three-metre-high Indian drawing

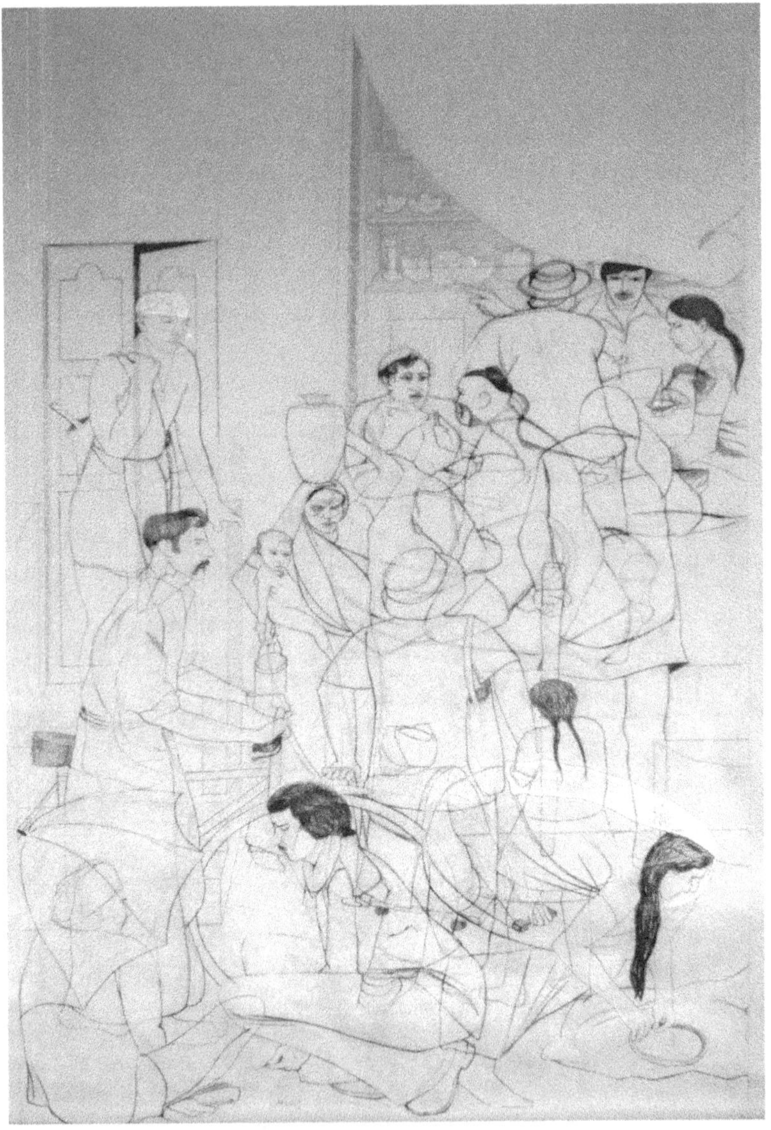

Sadhu's progress.1982

on paper that is hanging in the stairwell of her flat; the same drawing I gave to my father as his get-well card during his illness because it was one of his favourites: the first in a series of four pastel drawings that I exhibited privately for my parents in the drawing room at Belton, on our last Christmas there together. It was a homage to my parents for their support and encouragement for me to become an artist.

Looking back, I realise how him seeing the drawing might have affected him because it was not long after, that he and my mother separated: a young saddhu (Prabhu Pada) is leaving home, clutching a shoulder bag containing all his worldly possessions; the road ahead is as yet unknown but combined with a sense of the chaos and confusion of the world he is about to enter there is a promise of an unprecedented freedom. Sue had trouble finding a framer for the drawing owing to the size and the glass that would be needed, which became a story in the local press: "Son sends dad a giant get-well card." Alongside the article is a photo of my very sick looking father, gamely smiling at the camera, sitting next to Sue on the couch with the framed artwork leaning against the wall behind them. I met Prabhu Pada in Goa, when I was on my way back to Cortona having just met Judy for the first time in Kovalam. He would pass by me every morning walking down the beach and in my mind, I would will him to stop and talk to me, which one day he did! He had just left his home in Bangalore, a young man from a middle class family, setting off on his life's journey as a pilgrim, as a sadhu. He wouldn't allow me to draw him when I asked, so each time we met I memorised an area of his face and sketched it later in the hotel room in my notebook.

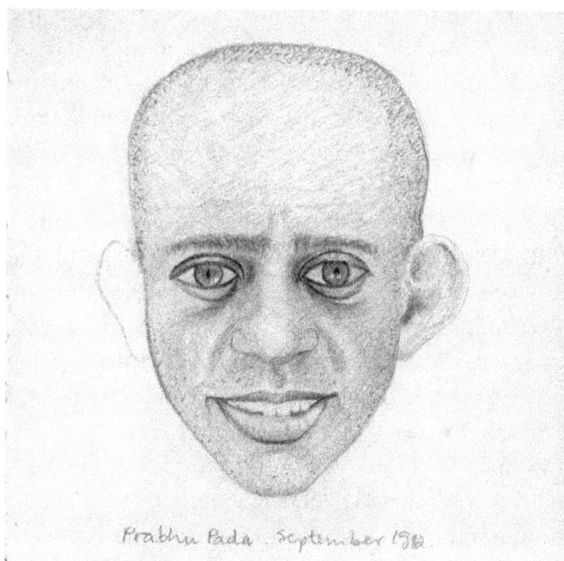

Chapter 64.

Judy has been winding down her work commitments, taking on her last client in March. Word of her garden exploits had finally reached Mozzoni's wife's ears: Maria Giulia, the Contessa and Judy has been planting out a small flower and herb garden for her at their residence La Badia. How ironic that it's taken fourteen years for them to meet and now after all that time, the Contessa who is the President of the FAI (Fondo Ambience Italiano): the Italian equivalent to the National Trust, has been trying to persuade Judy not to leave, offering her a plum job managing trust properties in Lombardia. Judy is flattered and has given it some serious thought but remains on course. Even I was tempted to argue the case to stay but then the thought of living near Milan put me off and we both agreed it wouldn't work.

We have already been down to the Australian embassy in Rome several times to see about my visa. She is infuriated every time we go: first it was the Australian newspapers in the Consular offices being three months out of date, then it was the consular official, an Italian, lecturing me on how to become an Australian and finally, on the very day we lodge my application we discover the cost of my residence visa has gone up by over 700 Australian dollars!

I suspect the only reason Judy comes with me to Rome is to make sure I actually go through with it! My attitude of late has been cavalier, tempting fate with a nonchalant "how can they possibly refuse entry to the father of Australian children" approach. The visa section is always crowded: mainly East Europeans and Russians desperate to get into Australia, soliciting any Australian prepared to listen to them, to be their sponsor in Australia and making me feel ashamed of my sense of self-entitlement.

I have also been in Rome to secure British passports for the boys presuming it would be a mere formality, and was upset to find my "Britishness" brought into question, requiring me to furnish extra proof of who I am: Hermann Pöhling the German or Nino MacDonald the Scot?

I will drop in on Jef when I am at the British embassy although security is tight and I am always escorted down to his office; he is now head of the press office, which sounds like a promotion but he grumbles is as far as they will allow him to go within the service. He is convinced that being hired "locally" as opposed to someone parachuted in from the UK, is an impediment as to how far he and others in a similar predicament can rise in the service. Instead, he is quietly counting down the years to an early retirement and a pension; anathema to me, being an artist without a pension plan, or any plan at all for the future. Still, I tell him, maybe he will take up writing again to which he only laughs.

The shipping container is due to arrive a week before our departure. According to the shipping clerk it can take up to three months to reach Australia, depending on the volume of traffic, which suits us fine as it will give us time to gather ourselves once we are there.

I have been alternatively catatonic heading for a black hole or cruising on autopilot steadying for the mother of descents. Judy goes at it hammer and tongs and then crash lands and then starts over again. Make it all about timing, I exhort myself and focus on harmony; on reaching the end at precisely the right moment.

The gutting of Poggio Spinoso gathers pace; I establish a beach head in the art deco guest room at the back of the house next to the bathroom: this was our deep-sleep dreaming room when needed or alternatively a temporary refuge in times of estrangement; advancing quickly through to the piano room and onto the middle room: distilling our lives into neatly stacked rows of professionally sealed cardboard boxes. I bought a metal hand tool specially adapted for cutting and tensioning the polypropylene strapping and sealing the straps with the heavy duty galvanised open seals. Judy insisted on buying packing boxes all the same size for their ease of stacking in the container, something that had not occurred to me, and as I go about my business, she meticulously lists the contents of each box with a sharpie written on the outside, something else I probably wouldn't have done. Judy has been working in the kitchen, carefully wrapping the Waterford crystal and our immense collection of Tuscan pottery and ceramic plates, while Cosmo and Toto are doing what they can in their room. They remain unbelievably up beat, whilst their parents are permanently on edge.

Both my Fiat station wagon and the Renault have to be moved off the property. The problem is, having foreign licence plates, they do not officially exist and therefore can't officially be disposed of! The wrecker says I have to pay him to tow them away and has the nerve to claim he's the one doing me the favour. Lila, our softheaded mutt, will need to be found a new home, and who better to turn to (besides Vicky who has offered as a last resort) but one of Judy's English gardening friend Carol, who's dachshund Simon is already a friend.

With less than a month to go before our scheduled departure I still haven't received my Australian visa and Judy goes into overdrive haranguing the Vice Consul in Rome over the phone; par for the course for Australians who can be so brutally direct and I feel confident her outbursts will have no lasting effects on the poor Vice Consul. The telltale baby white scar under my collar bone has been the reason for the delay after my first medical checkup in Rome led the Doctor to sending me to a specialist in Florence for further exploration; just to be certain I will present no undue financial burden on the Australian people in the future.

Over the years Judy has brightened the house considerably with her spectacular arrays of cut flowers from the garden and the sprays of wild flowers she gathers in the fields and woods: a bouquet with every gift she gave and for every friend we ever visited. When we are gone nobody will be here to look after the garden, so Judy has made the painful decision to give it all away; a sorry sight considering its former glory, after we hold a succession of weekend garage sales, mainly as an excuse for friends and acquaintances to gather and say farewells but also to pick up stuff we no longer need and to dig up the garden and cart away her plants and pots.

Lila surprises me when Carol arrives to fetch her because all I have to do is pop open the hatchback of Carol's car and Lila hops right in. Not a nod goodbye or even a wink. Normally she cowers if I try to put her in the car and we leave her home. This time she must have sniffed something good in the air: prime dog-food perhaps, not just our leftovers; a bit of shampooing and grooming judging by Simon, no more matted and dirt caked long hair; or her very own basket by the fireside next to her friend's, instead of being relegated to the cantina on a threadbare upholstered armchair. Yes! Lila must be thinking, wagging her tale, not even glancing back as Carol disappears down our drive: I have come a long way for a stray mutt!

Marina is throwing us a farewell party at her place with all our friends and the kids have a full agenda of events that need to be catered for as we give them unfettered access to their friends with more than generous offers of chauffeuring.

I had to take one last nostalgic trip to Valecchie. Margherita closed the shop after her husband Nello died a long time ago, and lives with her daughter towards Cortona, where Jef, who knows Margherita's daughter, told me she is "happy doing nothing for a change." I found Dante the carpenter in his shop and Amelio too; he was on the baby tractor up behind his house, his lanky legs sticking out, the same old Cossack hat and hunting jerkin on. We haven't been in touch and he was surprised to see me. Dominique too, looking as waif-like as ever, appeared with a handful of carrots from Amelio's *orto*; someone I hadn't seen for more than a decade but she gave me a warm hug and wished me well, said she still had my drawing hanging up in the new house they built after the log cabin. We were standing just below Carolyn's place and I did look up, but I couldn't bring myself to ask Amelio if she was at home. He told me the sad news about Voss; stepping out into the road, no doubt without a trouble in the world, and was run over by a truck in Camucia: the wanderer to the end.

Chapter 65.

The container is now perched four feet off the ground on a trailer in the piazza: like a sphinx or a Trojan horse! I hadn't considered the elevation and have had to improvise a long ramp with planks, in order to reach the container's doors. Gabriele and his friend Oberdan are helping me to load it. Gabriele, ever exuberant, flashing his full set of pearly teeth, his waist length crinkly black hair usually coiled tightly around his shaved temples now set free; merrily trolleys the first stack of boxes down the stone steps from the kitchen without a care in the world and as if they have nothing in them, and has to be immediately reined in. Olivero was over earlier from the farm with the fork tractor, and after we teased the heavy upright piano out of the house sliding it on rags to avoid marking the terracotta floors, he confidently speared it off the top stair of the kitchen balcony with his two sticked shining metal prongs and forked it smoothly into the container in only a few deft maneuvers. When my father's piano originally arrived from Scotland, there was no way the lorry driver from Liverpool and I were going to get it up the stairs and we left it in the cantina, where it lingered for a year in the damp before I finally managed to rescue it with the help of five male friends, hauling it up the stairs like a gang of pyramid builders using long straps.

Yes! Rainmaker, miracle man I am! I have spent months imagining exactly how to fit everything into the container, which is now perfectly packed and I am literally latching closed the heavy metal doors when the truck hauling it away, races up our drive and hitches up. The ground is muddy from recent rain falls and the driver nearly doesn't make it back up the steep S bend near the Southerns' place. He has to gun the rig hard three times before he successfully drags it over the brow, with his young off-sider halting any oncoming traffic from coming down.

I have one last duty to perform before I can finally cut myself loose and give this all away: Australian quarantine laws; how they love their aerosols the Australians! Unrepentant officials, in blue shorts and long cream socks, welcome you to country, walking up and down the cabin aisles continuously spraying before eventually allowing you to disembark the plane. The container needs fumigating too before it can be shipped into Australia and is waiting in the Arezzo rail yard. I want to be there because I have some concerns about the chemical reactions that might occur when spraying my paintings with methyl bromide and phosphine; concerns that are heightened when I catch sight of the masked man suited up head-to-toe, as if we are in a nuclear zone and in danger of radiation, heading in my direction. But this is Italy after all and I needn't have worried. He totally understands my concern for the paintings inside and instead of blasting the container as he usually does, he agrees to give it only a couple of formal squirts!

A pile of rubbish off to the side of our piazza progressively jettisoned from the house over the preceding months is destined for a bonfire on our final night: tonight, December the eighth 1999, another damp evening. I have always prided myself as being a one match to light a fire person and tonight of all nights I can't get the fire going without dousing it in petrol. This is a sombre affair, with friends like Marina, Sabine and Roby, Gianni and Claire, with parents and kids from the neighbourhood and the farm, forming a long chain in front of the bonfire, bottles of wine being passed up and down the line. Long shadows from the flames shoot across the piazza, dancing along the crumbling stucco wall of the house; the house soon to be drained of us. Carol's partner John is driving us to the airport early in the morning, playing the executioner's role.

Cosmo, Toto and I, hand in hand, rush through the house one last time, bowing to each room in turn. Respect. Poggio Spinoso, dearly beloved and nearly departed. As a parting gift I had hung a large picture frame on the wall in the piano room, with stalks of dried corn artfully arranged on the floor beneath as if they have just tumbled out of a painting. Then Gabriele comes along and asks me if he can have the frame, so now only the stalks are left on the floor. In a cantina downstairs I have propped the old rickety bora-infested ladder up against the wall under the half-opened casement window and left an empty Antler suitcase standing there.

Fosco and Olivero make up the official departing delegation, lining up at the bottom of the stairs, ready to receive the keys and lock up the house after us. Olivero is emotional and has had a discreet dab with his handkerchief, tearing up just like Giulio from the *cartoleria* in Cortona and Emilia did when I announced our departure. Spontaneously I take off my favourite greatcoat and hand it to Olivero before getting into the car:

"Where I'm going, I wont be needing it!" I say glumly.

"*Certo*, and don't forget the postcard if you ever get there," he replies regaining his composure.

The coat positively enfolds me but hardly girdles his waist, and the last thing I see as we slip down the driveway is Olivero struggling to get his arms through the coat sleeves, a gesture to please me I'm sure, because I know he'll dump it as soon as we are round the corner.

Lucignano glides by in a smear of dreary dishwater grey, just like my first day on arriving in Cortona. Marina is standing on the street corner by the post office waving us by as one by one the familiar markers of everyday life slip into shadow, now destined to live on only as memories.

We are all exhausted, slumped in the airport departure lounge, hardly able to speak or grasp what is happening and so I quietly detach myself from my family in search of a private space to savour the ritual of my last cigarette before quitting forever. Yes, I have chosen this moment to give up and have been chain-smoking for months in preparation. Jef has already indicated I won't be seeing him any time soon because he wouldn't be able to last that long on the plane without one.

Sitting down, I press my forehead into the coldness of the plate-glass window and gaze out vacantly at the sheets of rain raking the tarmac. Ground crews in yellow snub-nosed vehicles are pulling long lines of trolleys, chasing cover from plane underbelly to plane underbelly and for once I wish I could be out there with them …

… I wake up with a jolt (my mother says this a sure sign of an out-of-body experience). Everything is a deathly hush around me and then it floods back. It is too quiet, and they don't announce departures any more do they! Hurrying back to where I left Judy and the boys (how long has it been) they are nowhere to be found! I glance at the departure screens finding the little red light urgently blinking next to our flight. Why on earth had nobody looked for me? Panic sets in and confusion, did Judy think I... A dismembered voice pipes up across the hallway:

"This is the final call for passenger Nino MacDonald on flight QF365 to Melbourne. Please proceed immediately to boarding gate 16, the flight is now fully boarded and ready for take-off. Final call for…"

You can view a selection of my short films:

http://www.youtube.com/user/ninomac

AR(Driver)
La Bicicletta Rossa
1799

Like on Facebook:
https://www.facebook.com/LaStradaBiancaTuscany/
Follow On TikTok:
tiktok.com/@ninomacdonald

Contact the author:
ninomac@aapt.net.au

A final word.

A quiet thanks to my good friends Geoffrey Watson, who patiently sat me through the numerous drafts involved in the writing of this memoir and Gianni Vasca, for always taking the time to photograph my work; I will miss you both. Lastly, a very special thanks to my father for supporting me.

www.ingramcontent.com/pod-product-compliance
Lightning Source LLC
La Vergne TN
LVHW020534100826
845148LV00010B/1457

* 9 7 8 0 6 4 6 8 7 7 9 3 8 *